AF471010

JUST LOOKING

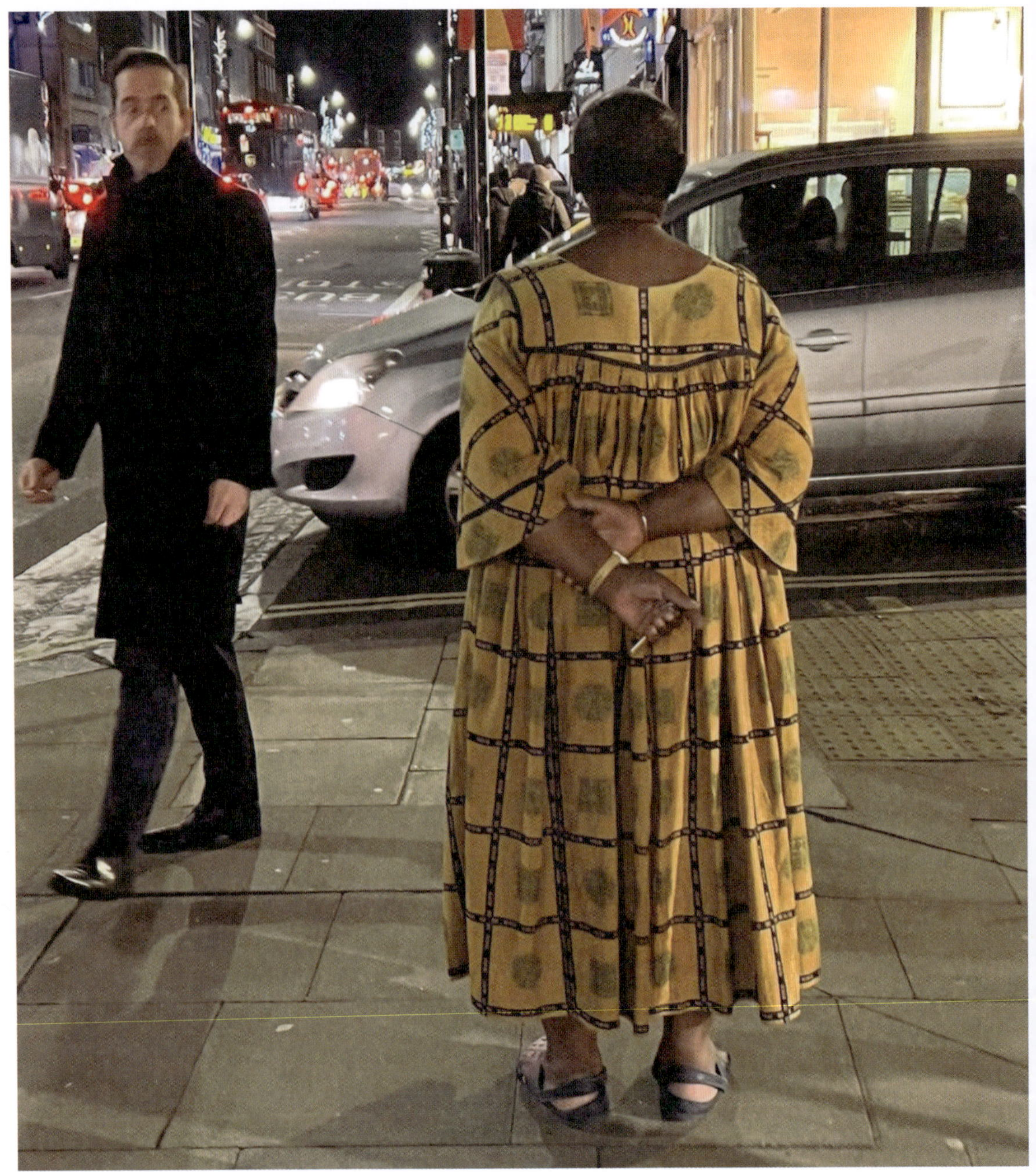

Cornelia Parker: Yellow dress.

JUST LOOKING

snapshots, close-ups and portraits of the everyday

edited by julian rothenstein

introduction by jarvis cocker / observations chosen by ian sansom

REDSTONE PRESS, LONDON

First published in 2026
Redstone Press, 7a St Lawrence Terrace, London W10 5SU
redstone.press@gmail.com www.theredstoneshop.com

ISBN 978-1-7395976-4-1

Design: Julian Rothenstein
Artwork: Clare Skeats
Production: Geoff Barlow
Manufacture: 1010 Printing International Ltd China

Compilation © Redstone Press 2026
Introduction © Jarvis Cocker 2026

Picture credits:
156: Jimmie Durham: poster for *It's Urgent!* a project by Hans Ulrich Obrist. Luma Westbau, 2019/Luma Arles, Parc des Ateliers, 2020. © Courtesy the artist. 161: FKA twigs: post-it note from *Remember to Dream* by Hans Ulrich Obrist, Heni Publishing 2024. 162: Jimmie Durham: poster for *It's Urgent!* a project by Hans Ulrich Obrist. Luma Westbau, 2019. Luma/Arles, Parc des Ateliers, 2020. © Courtesy the artist.

Images from Aveek Sen's Instagram reproduced with the permission of Sarmistha Das.

Thanks to:
Salwa Beloubaine, Tiffany Chang, Rose Dempsey, Leo Hollis, Natalie Hume, Hiang Kee, Ella Rothenstein, Lucien Rothenstein, Jennifer Higgie and Harriet Walter.

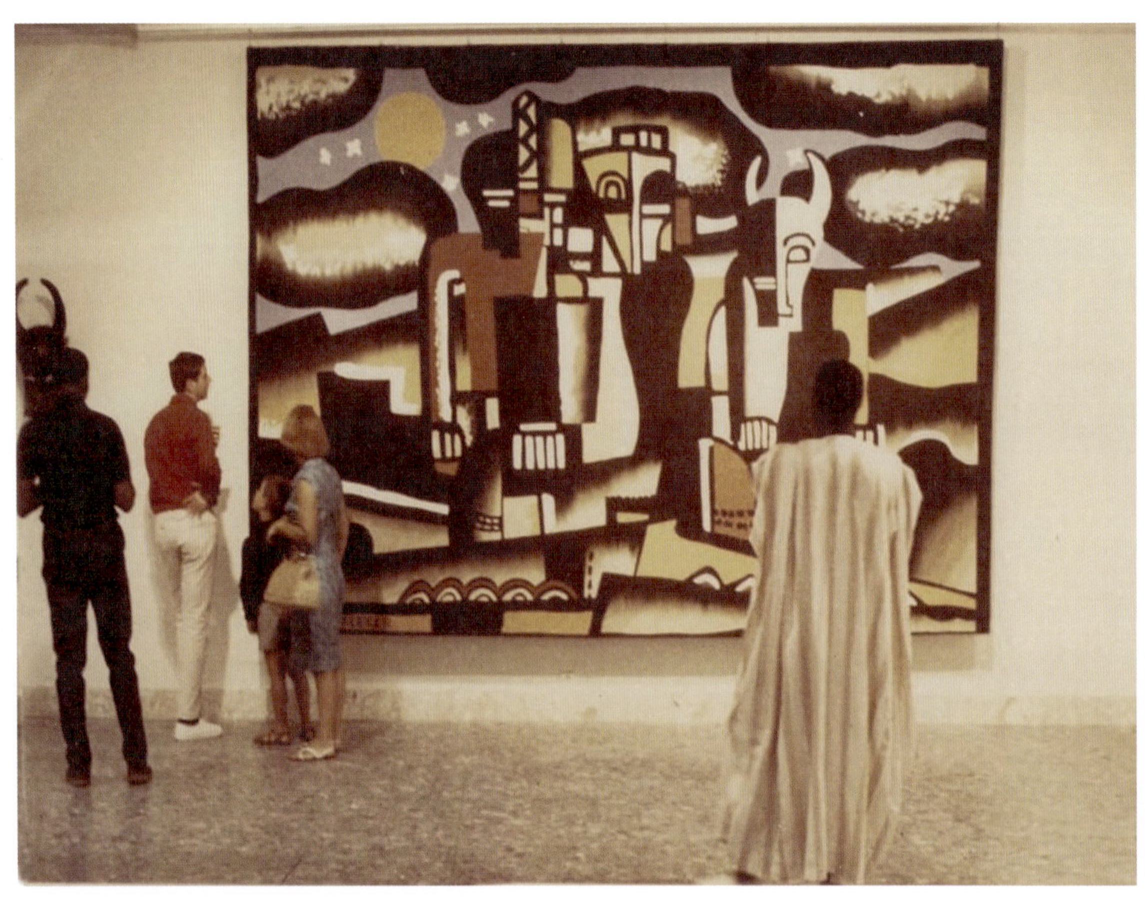

Kofi Iddrisu: People looking at *The Creation of the World*, a tapestry by Fernand Léger in Dakar, Senegal, 1966.

CONTENTS

INTRODUCTION BY JARVIS COCKER

My wife and I have "lively discussions" (definitely NOT arguments) about looking. She will say, "Stop staring at me" and I will reply, "I'm not staring – I'm gazing."

You will find both of these modes of looking included in this book – along with "Observing", "Surveying", "Watching", "Contemplating" and "Noticing". "Gazing" feels to me, like the most romantic of these ways of seeing. You might not agree – perhaps "watching" is what does it for you.

But this book is not called "Looking", it is called "Just Looking" – and there's a good reason for that.

"Just Looking" is usually perceived as an apologetic phrase: you might hear it uttered in a shop when a prospective customer is being pressured by the shopkeeper to make a purchase. It's an excuse: it means "I'm not buying, I'm just seeing what you've got". And it could very well be the beginning of an argument. Or a lively discussion.

This book attempts to rehabilitate the phrase. Within these pages, "Just Looking" means something different. Through photographs by people such as David Byrne, Olivia Laing and Kamila Shamsie, this book will try to make you look at the world anew. To actually really see it.

We tend to think of the human eye as being something like a camera – we turn our heads in the direction of something and we see it – but do we see it as it actually is?

What if I told you that the human eye can also be a projector? That it sees the world according to the obsessions and sensibilities of the brain behind the eyes? And that every one of us is doing this every single day of our lives.

Scary.

The only way to attempt to move beyond this skewed mode of perception is to become aware of it – and the easiest way to begin that process is to start taking photographs. A photograph is always a choice. You choose when to snap the shutter. You choose the subject and the way to frame it. A photograph tells the story of what you like to look at and how you like to look at it. It tells other people about your opinion of the world you are looking at. Each photograph is not only a picture of the outside world but also a snapshot of the interior life of the person who took it. A self-portrait.

There is a trend within modern music that concerns itself with the idea of "just intonation". Practitioners deride the Western harmonic scale that divides the entirety of musical expression into a 13-note scale. Just intonation uses the notes between the notes of the Western scale. The quarter-tones of Eastern music and beyond. The idea is that this connects modern man (or woman) with the original magic of musical expression – the way it was in the beginning before we tried to make it conform to man-made conventions. The way it really is. Music in the raw.

I'd like to think that this book is called "Just Looking" in the same spirit: that the photographs in this collection are simple, unaffected representations of the way certain people alive at this point in history perceive the world around us. There are no right or wrong ways to see the world: there's just your own way. And once you combine many different people's views of this one world that we all inhabit, you might just start to get an inkling of the brilliant complexity of life on Earth. The beauty of it. The majesty of it.

And how very funny it can be.

Just look.

1: NOTICING

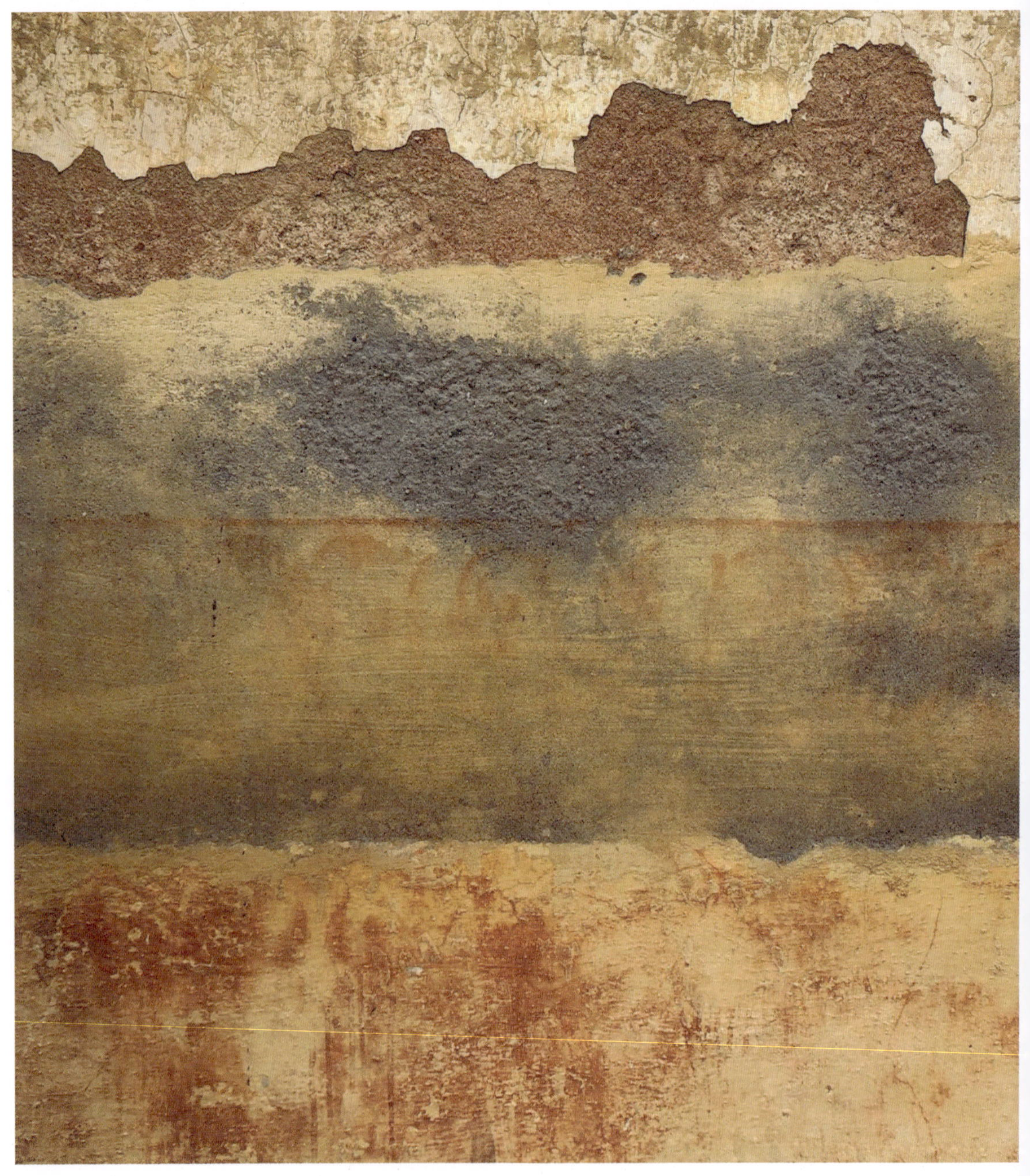

Aradhana Seth.

One way to open your eyes to unnoticed beauty is
to ask yourself, "What if I had never seen this before?
What if I knew I would never see it again?"

Rachel Carson, *The Sense of Wonder*, 1956.

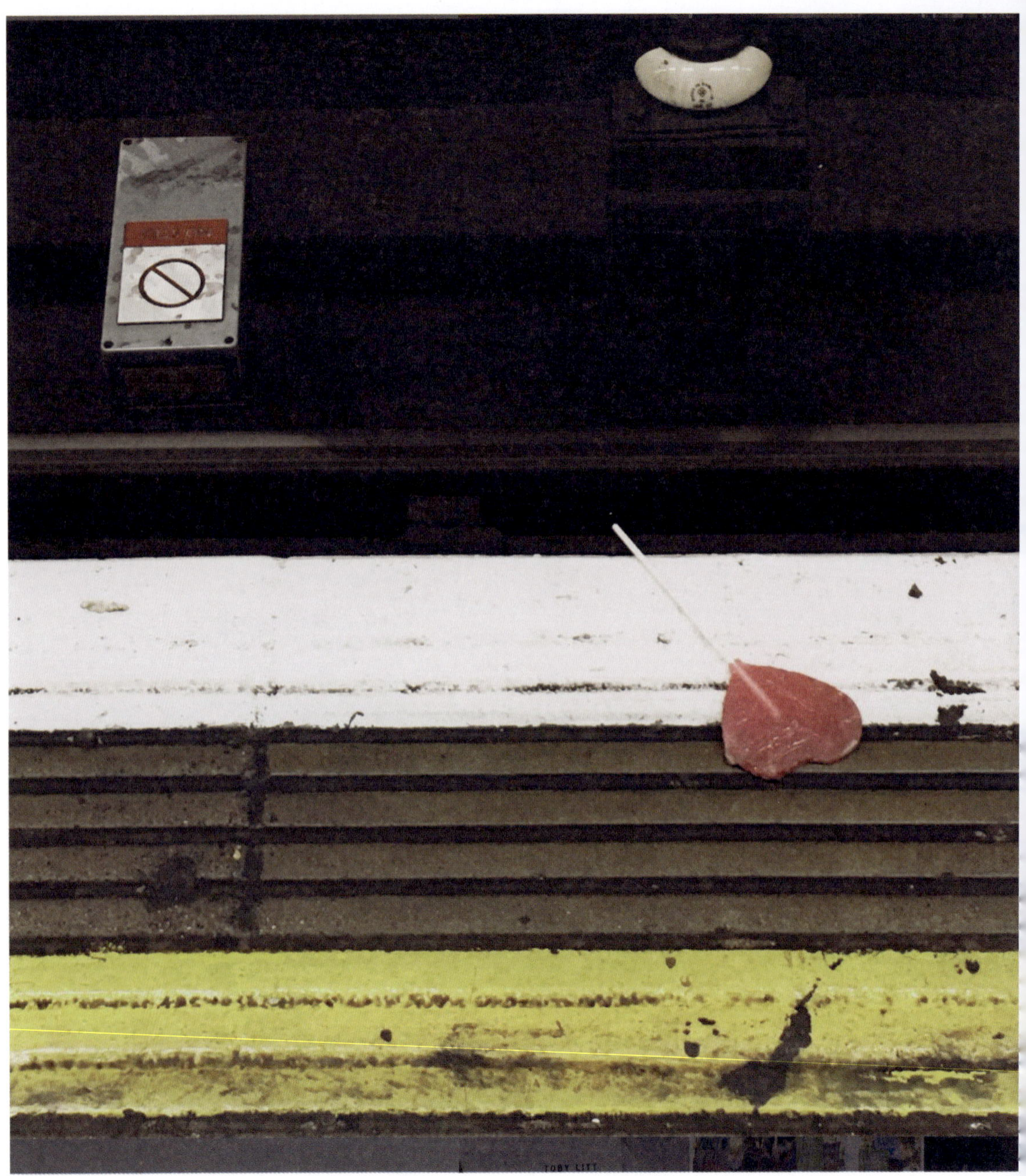

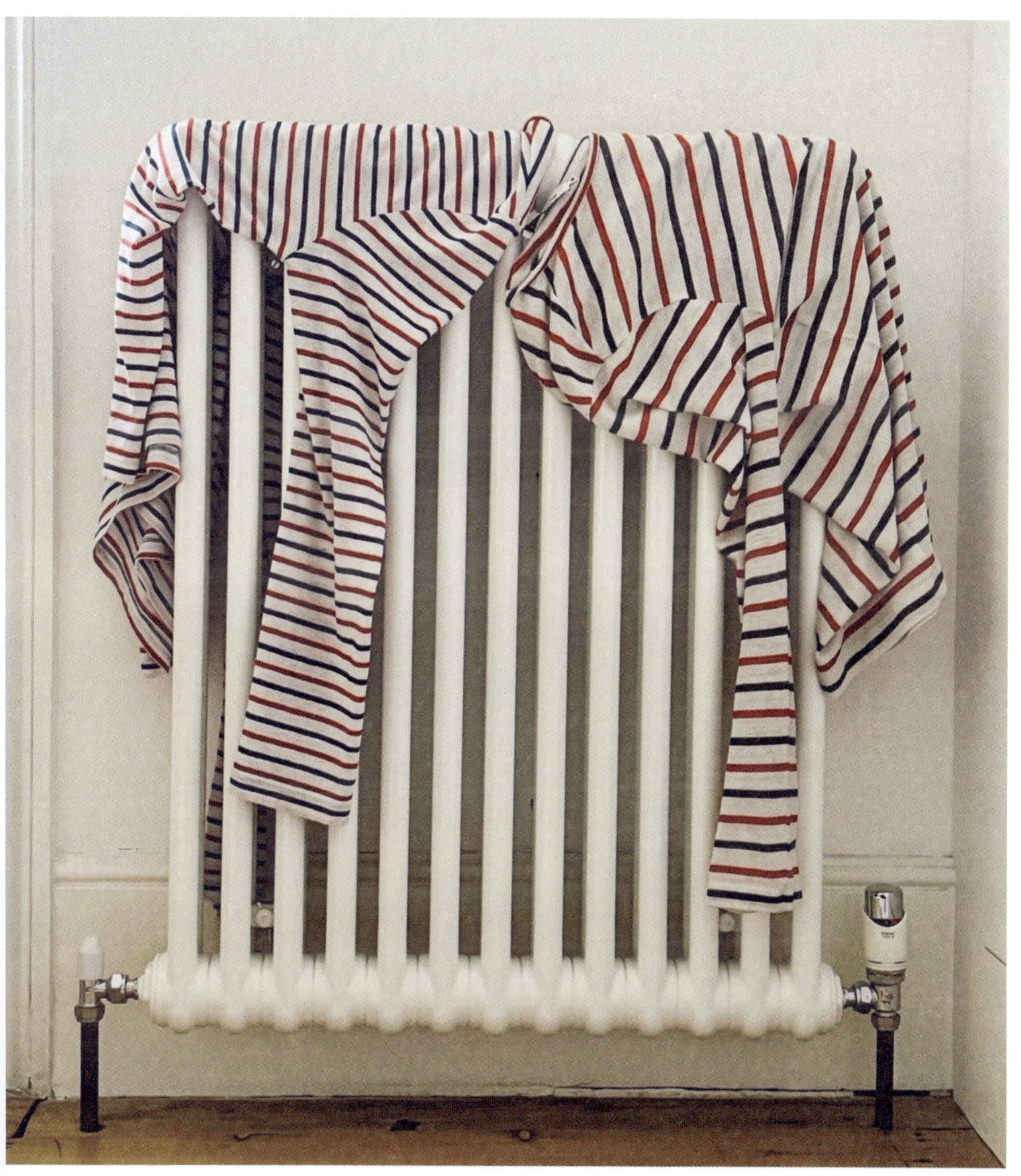

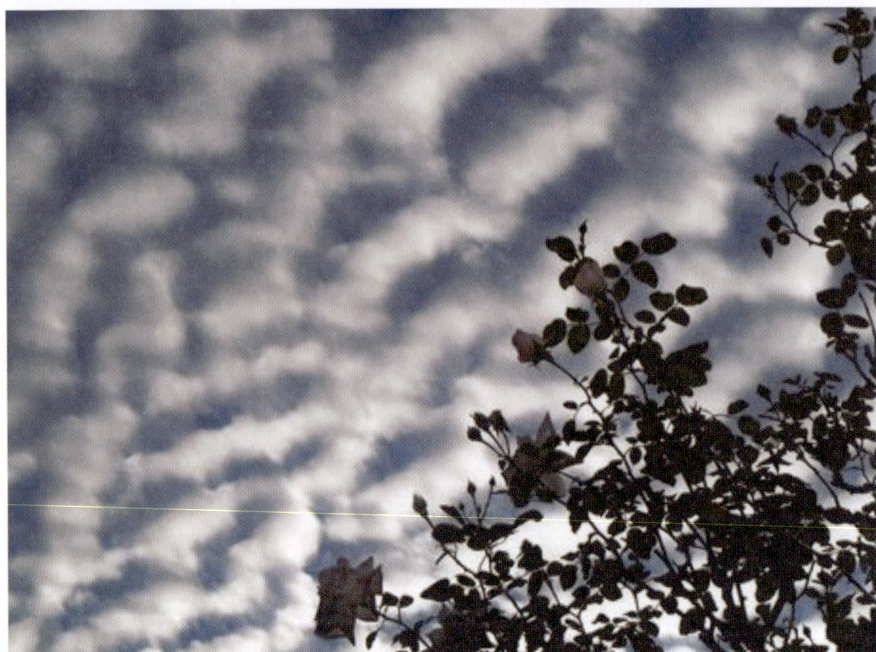

Polly Samson: TOP: Catnip cherub. ABOVE: Clouds and roses.

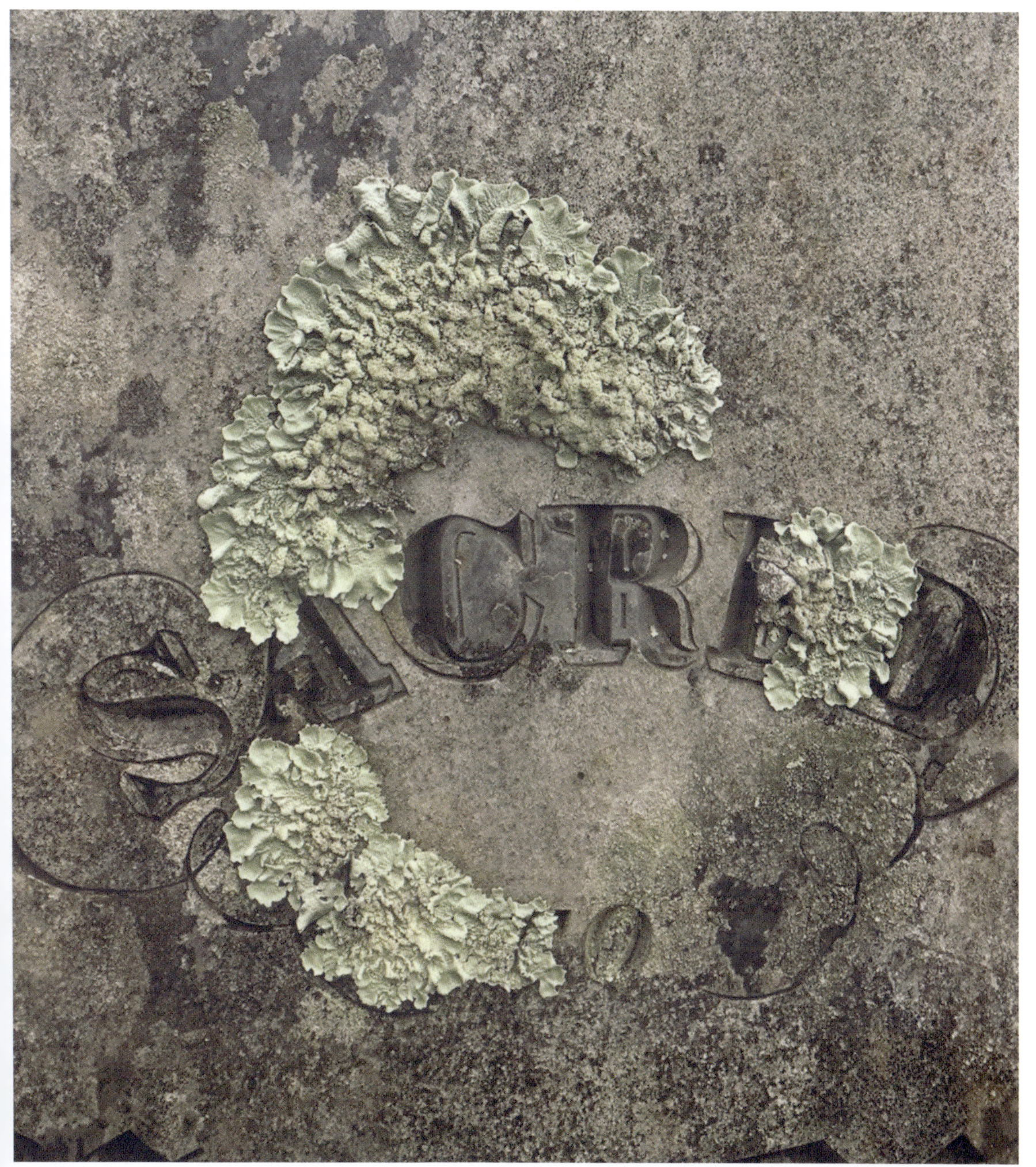

The things with which we concern ourselves in science appear in myriad forms, and with a multitude of attributes. For example, if we stand on the shore and look at the sea, we see the water, the waves breaking, the foam, the sloshing motion of the water, the sound, the air, the winds and the clouds, the sun and the blue sky, and light; there is sand and there are rocks of various hardness and permanence, colour and texture. There are animals and seaweed, hunger and disease, and the observer on the beach; there may be even happiness and thought. Any other spot in nature has a similar variety of things and influences.

Richard Feynman, *The Feynman Lectures on Physics, vol. 1*, 1963.

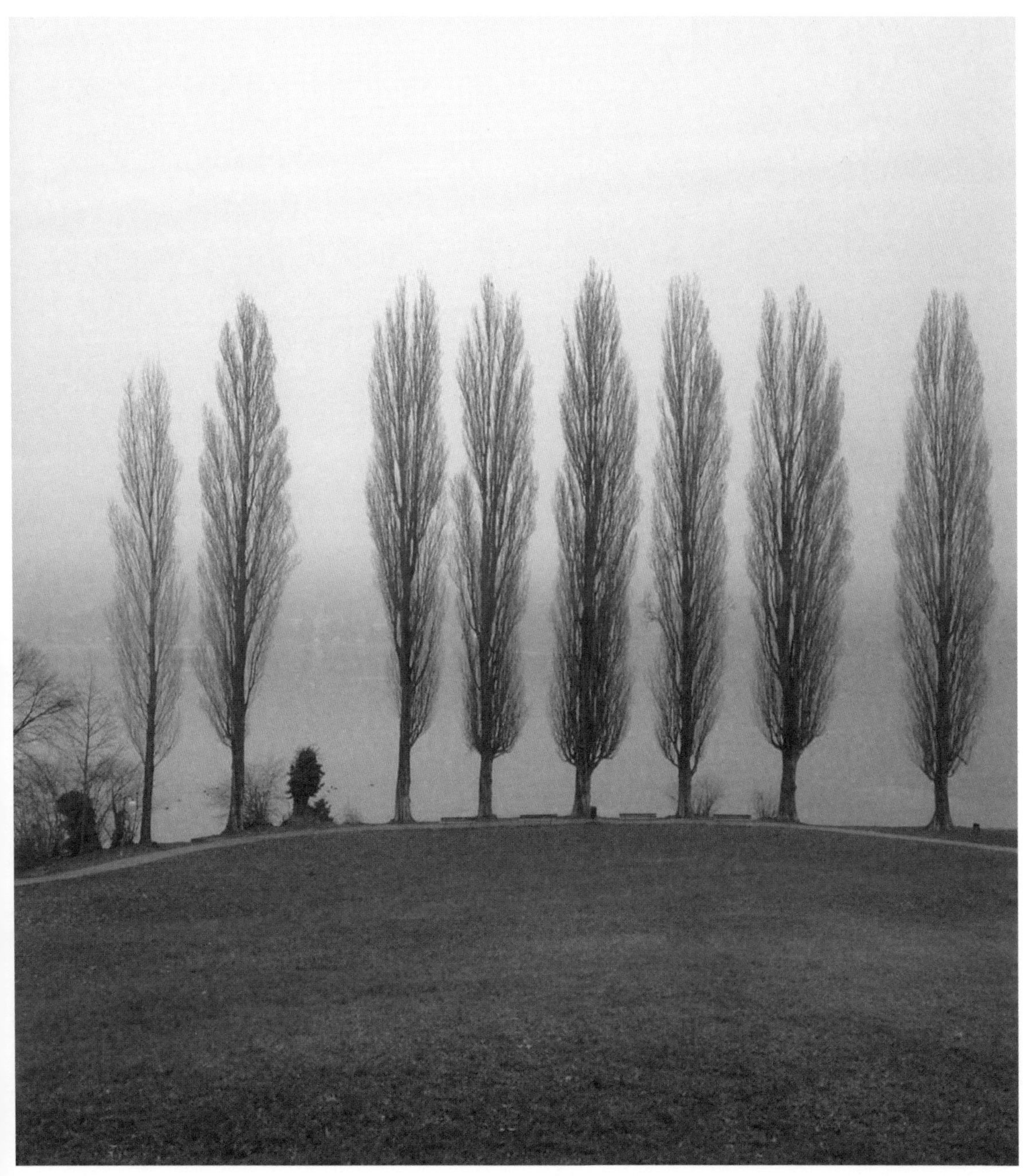

Thomas Adès: The lake where Wagner went to sulk.   23

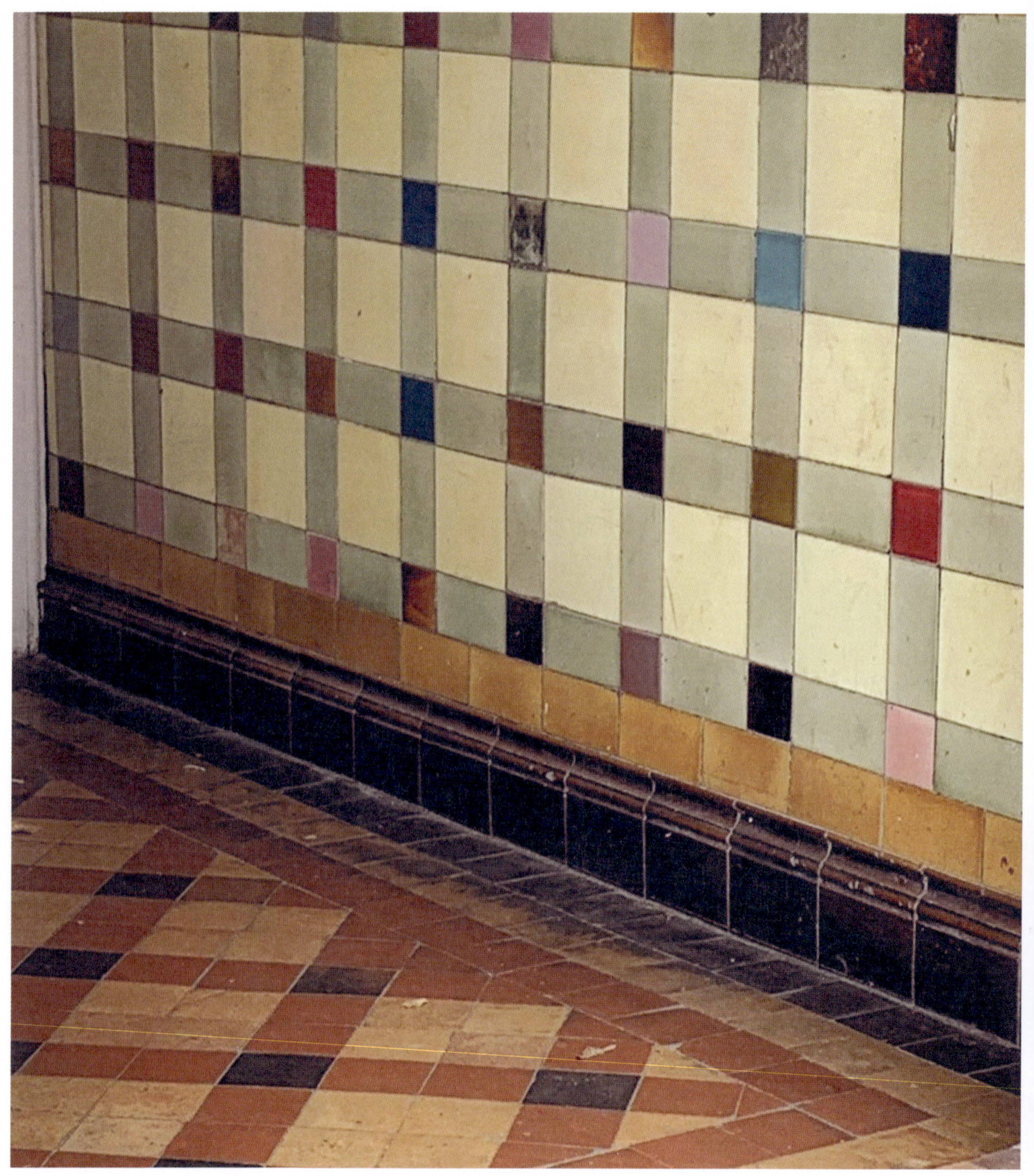

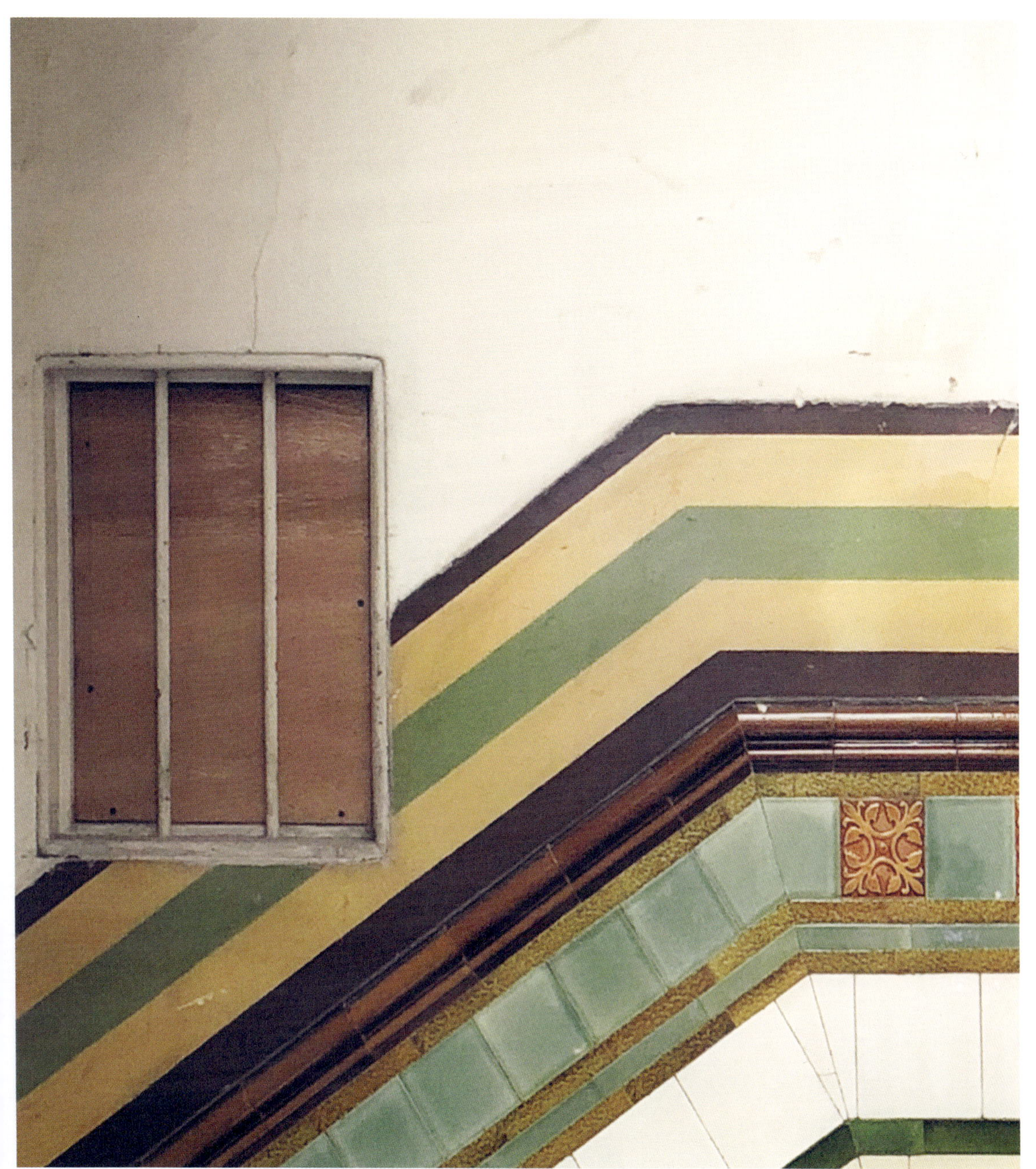

Calum Storrie: Glasgow wall.

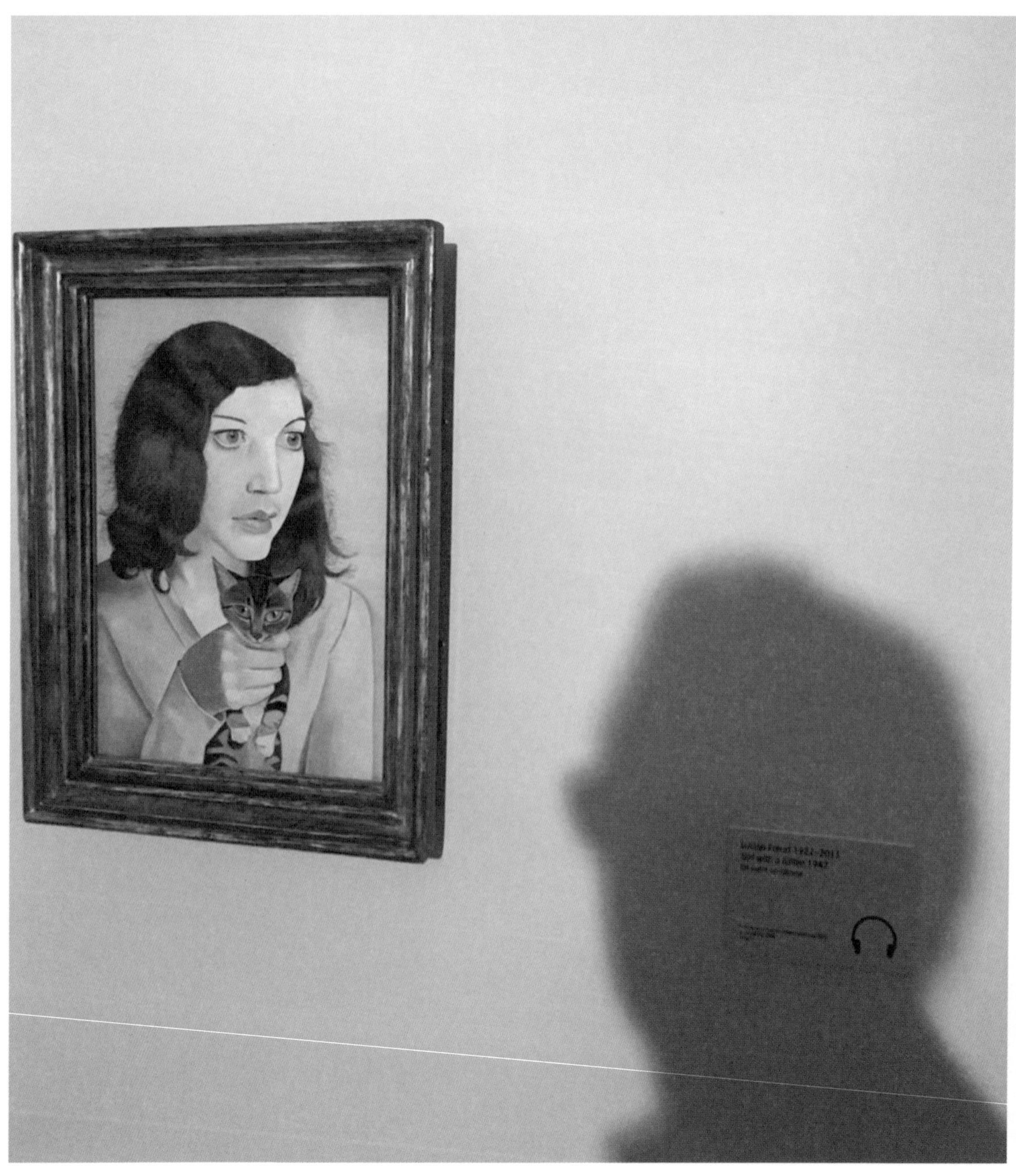

Waldemar Januszczak: Lucian Freud and me. Tate Liverpool.

Reading a screenful of information is quite a different thing from looking. It is a digital form of exploration in which the eye moves along an endless broken line. The relationship to the interlocutor in communication, like the relationship to knowledge in data-handling, is similar: tactile and exploratory. A computer-generated voice, even a voice over the telephone, is a tactile voice, neutral and functional. It is no longer in fact exactly a voice, any more than looking at a screen is exactly looking.

Aldo Rossi, *A Scientific Holiday*, 1981.

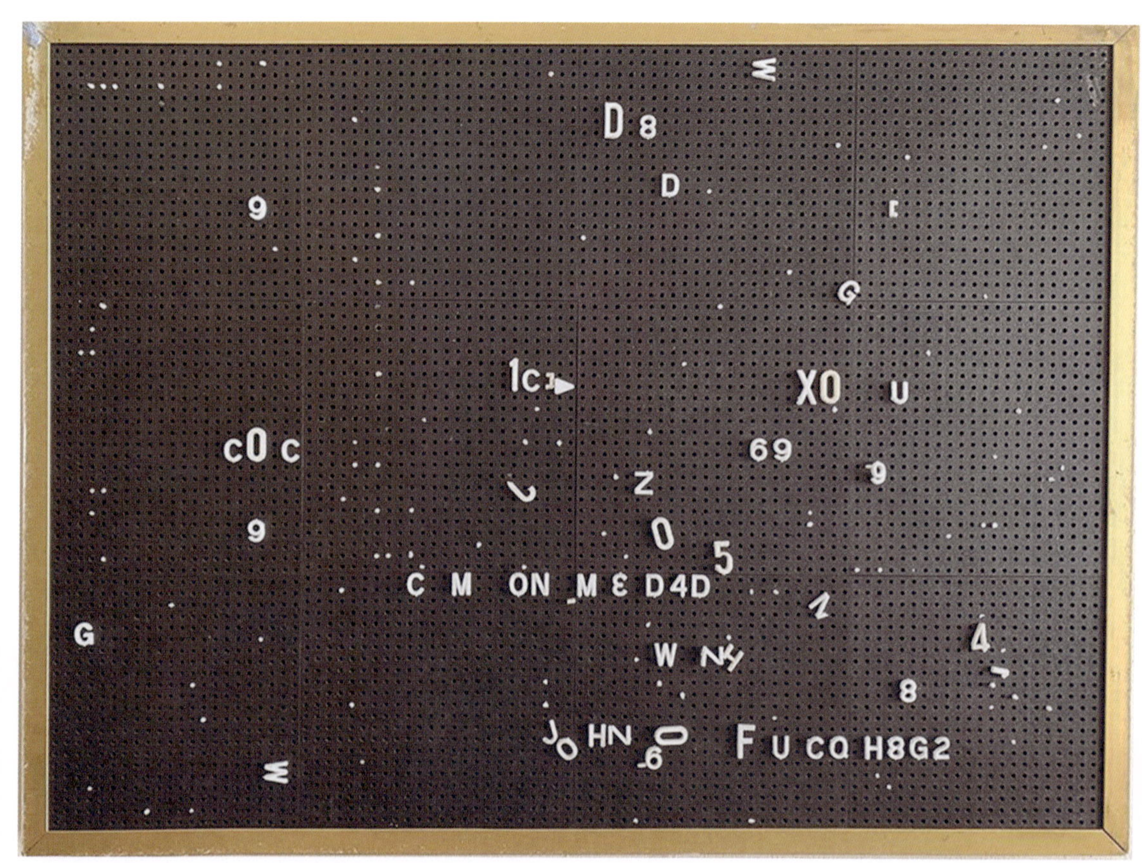

Carey Young: Drinks menu at the India Club bar, London.

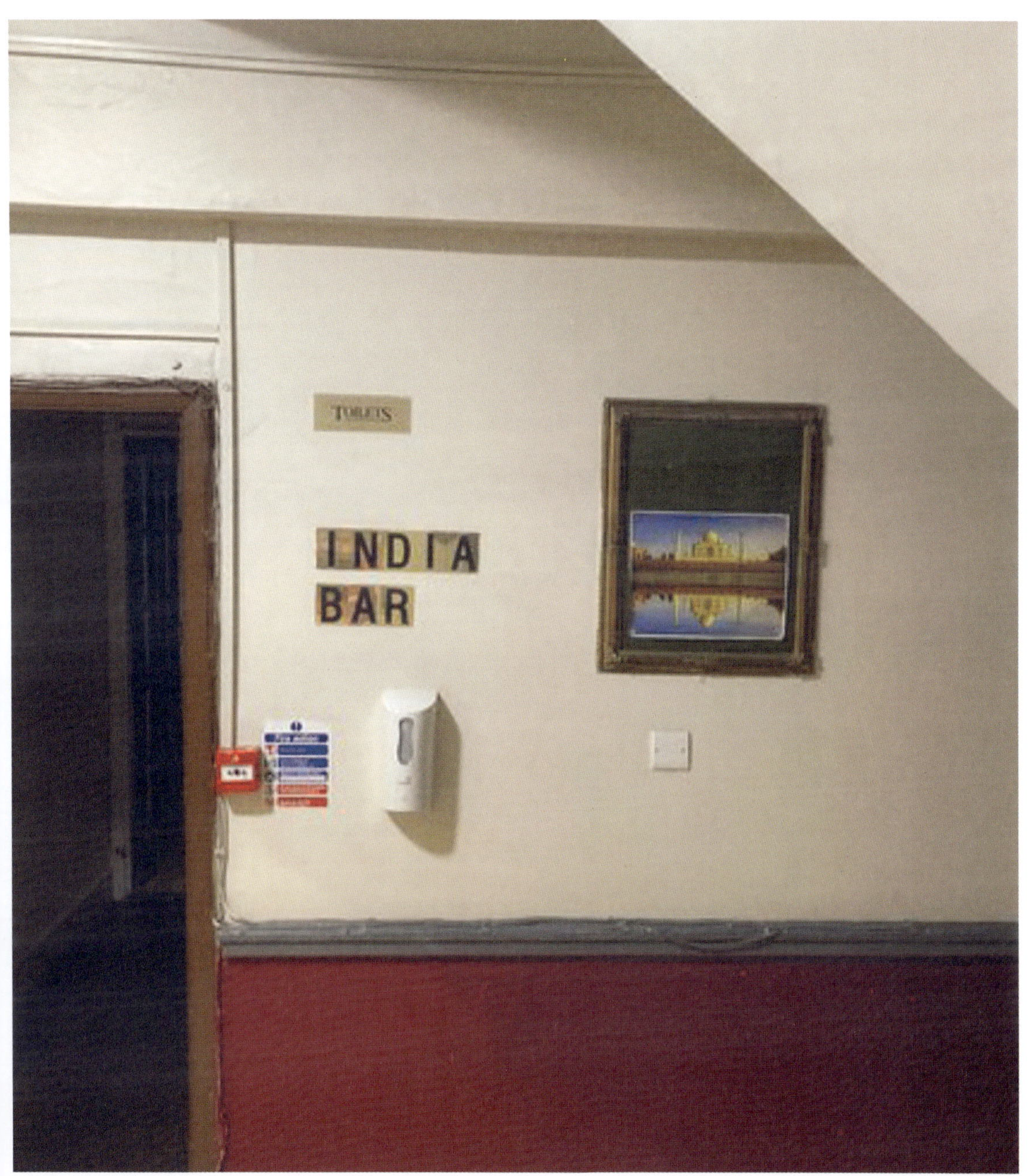

Bruno Wollheim: Going up to the India Club.

ATM Inside
ee Cash
Withdrawals
Free Balance
Enquiries
HARD ON

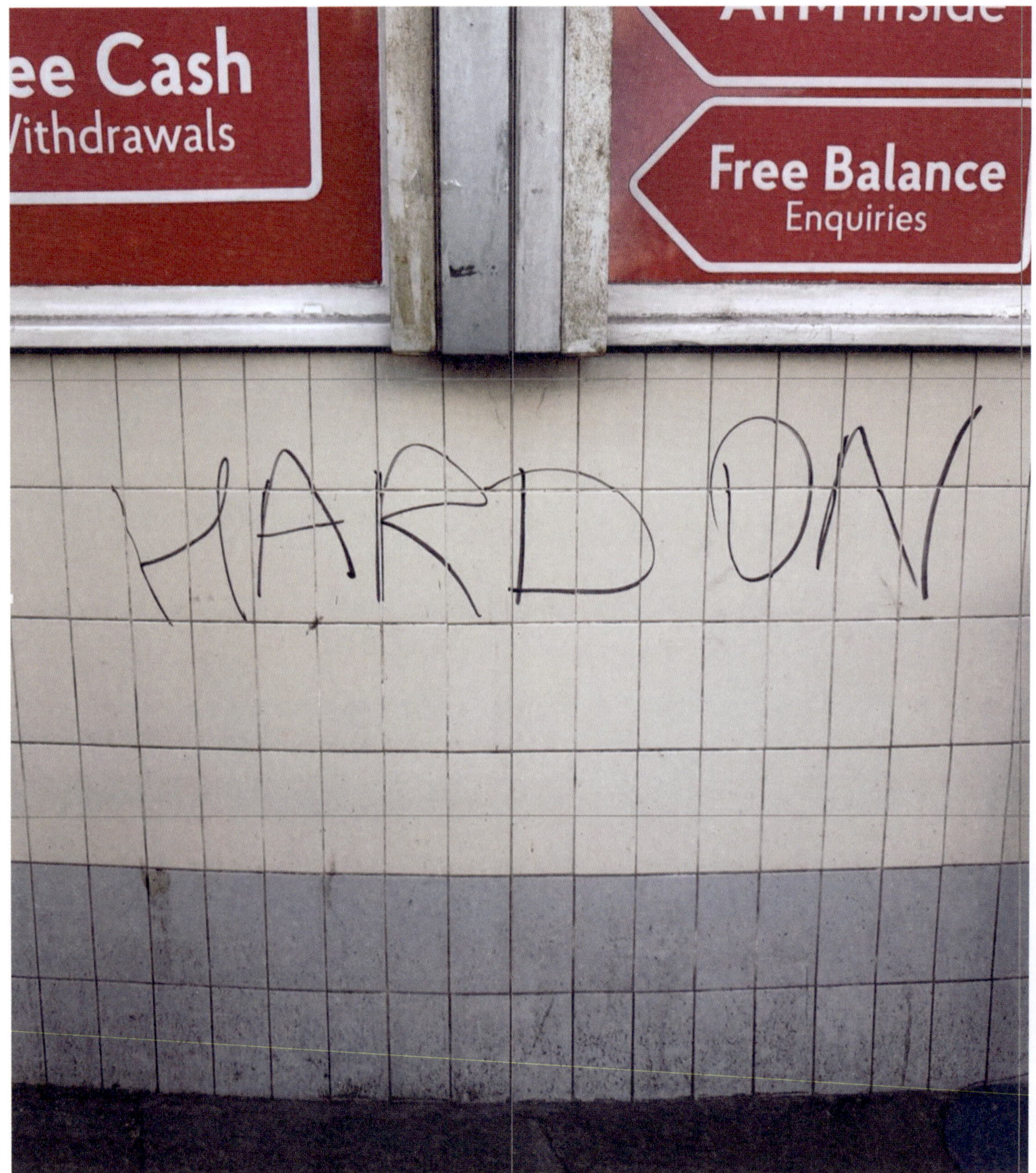

Rose Boyt.

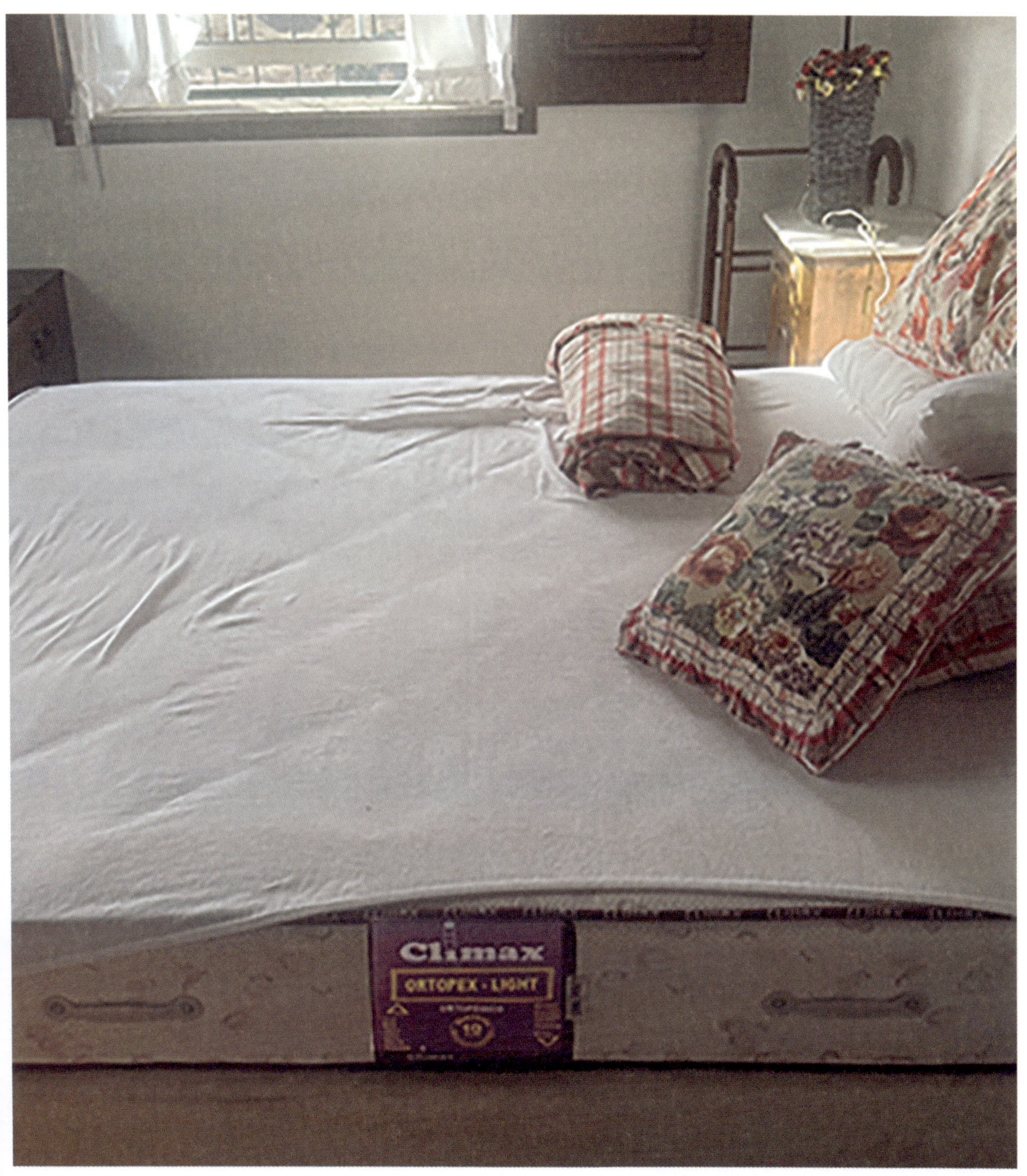

Rose Dempsey: Our hotel room in Lisbon.   31

I gave a thought to travel. Though the problem with travel is eventually you *arrive* – with your old self lagging behind a few hours or nights or days, and finally catching up with all the same shit on his mind – at which point all you can do is travel on to some other place.

Richard Ford, *Be Mine*, 2023.

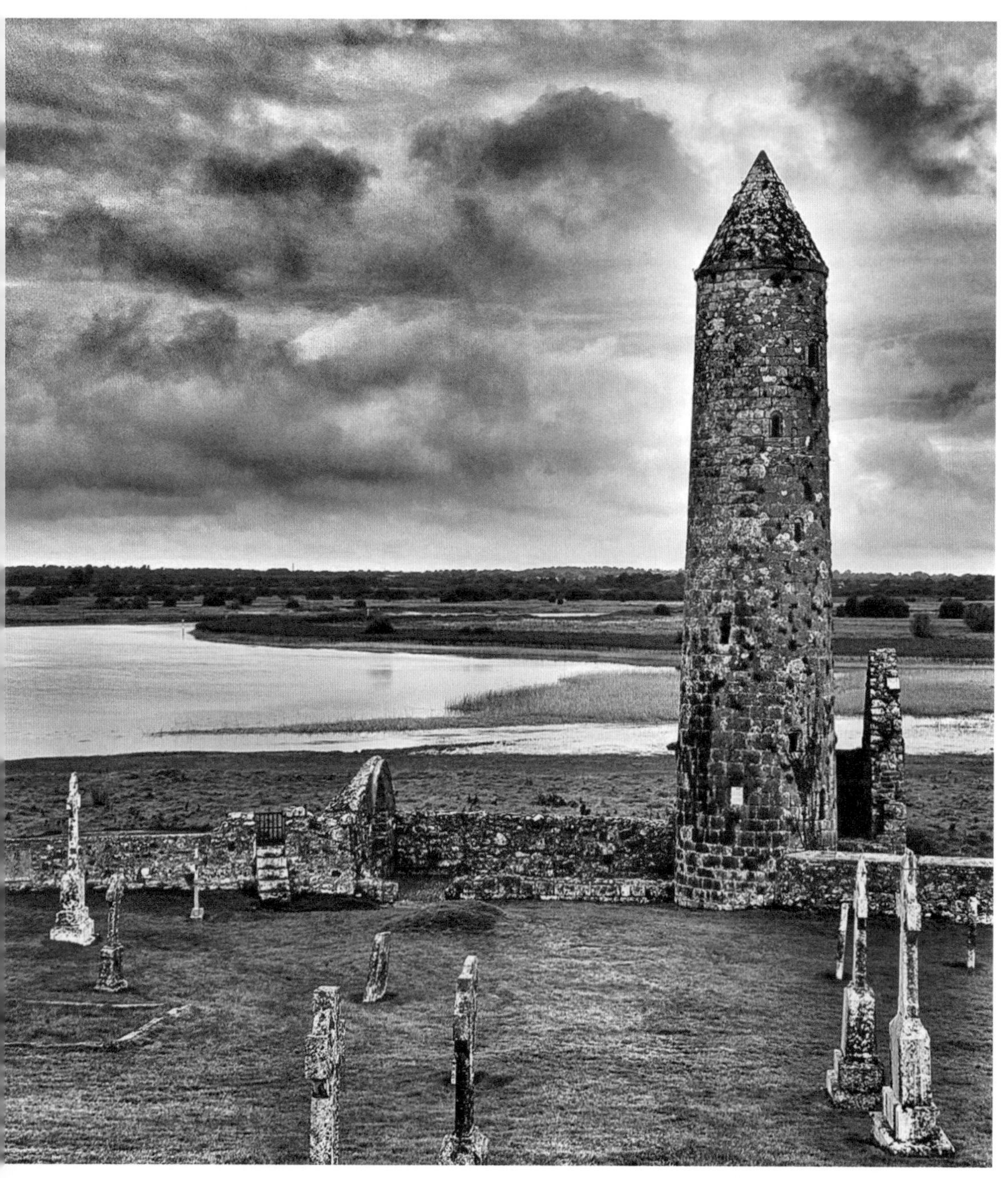

William Dalrymple: the Celtic monastery and tower of Clonmacnoisel, Ireland.

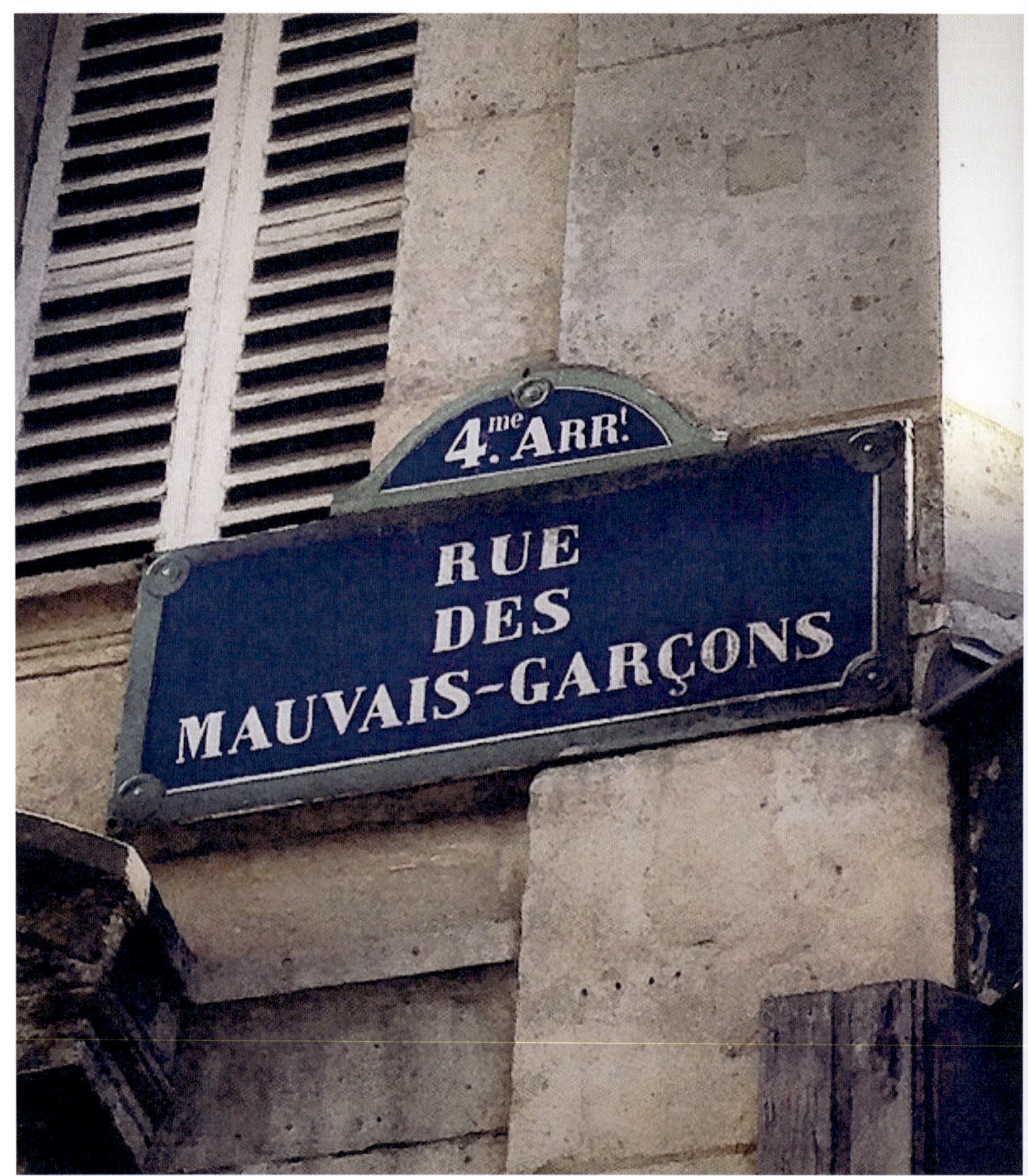
4.me ARR!
RUE
DES
MAUVAIS-GARÇONS

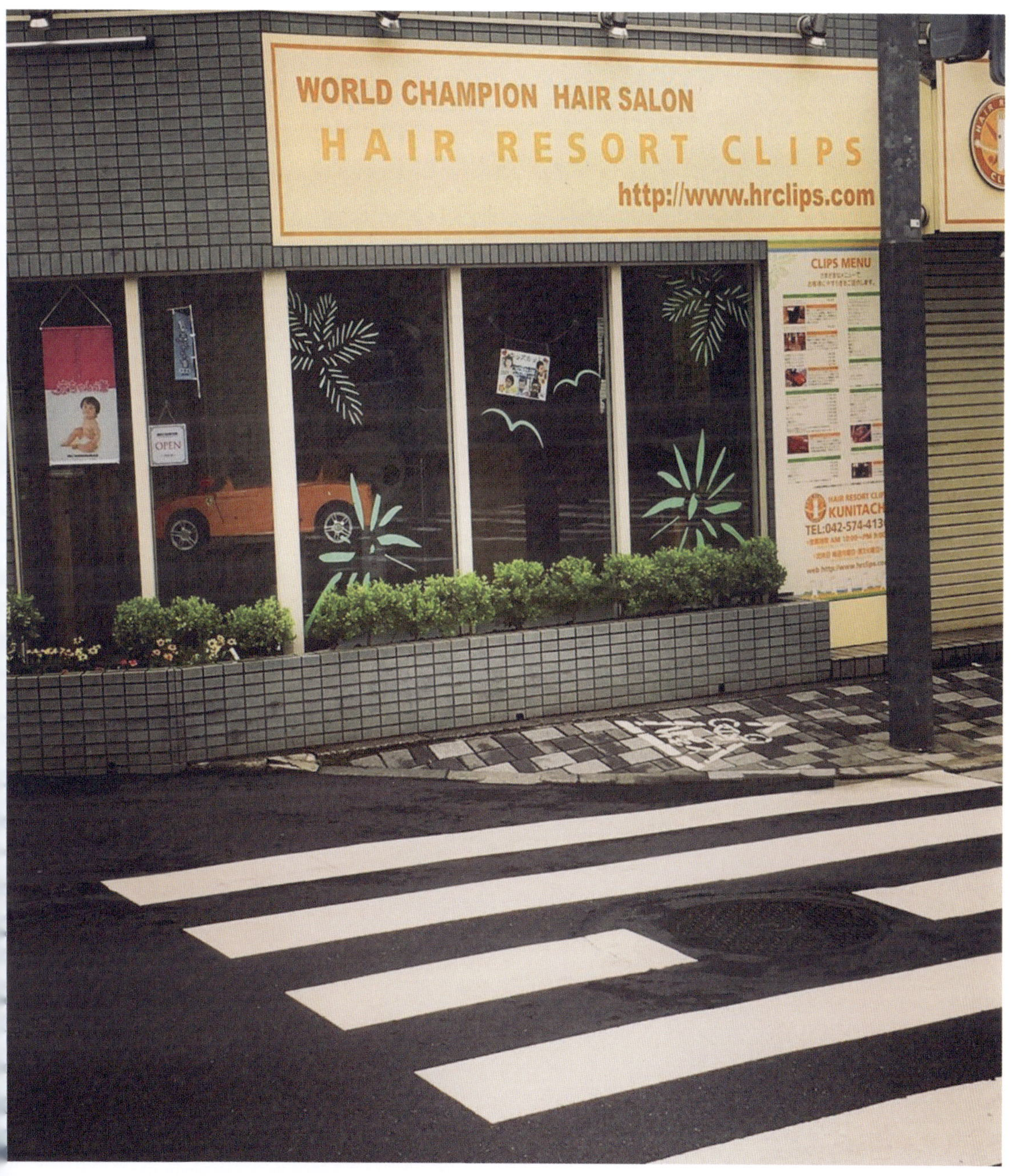

Waldemar Januszczak: When you're getting your hair cut, you go to the best! (Tokyo.)

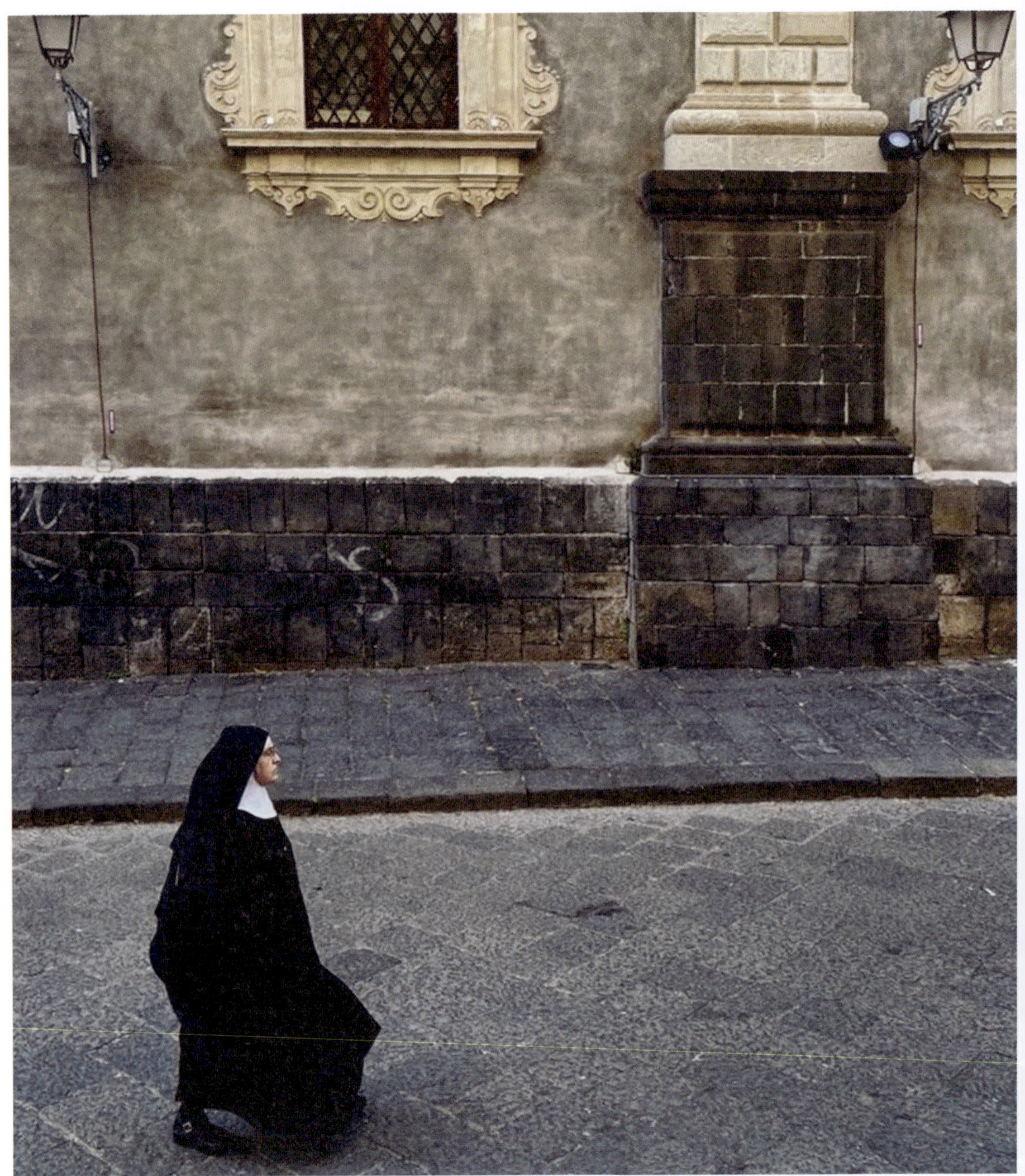

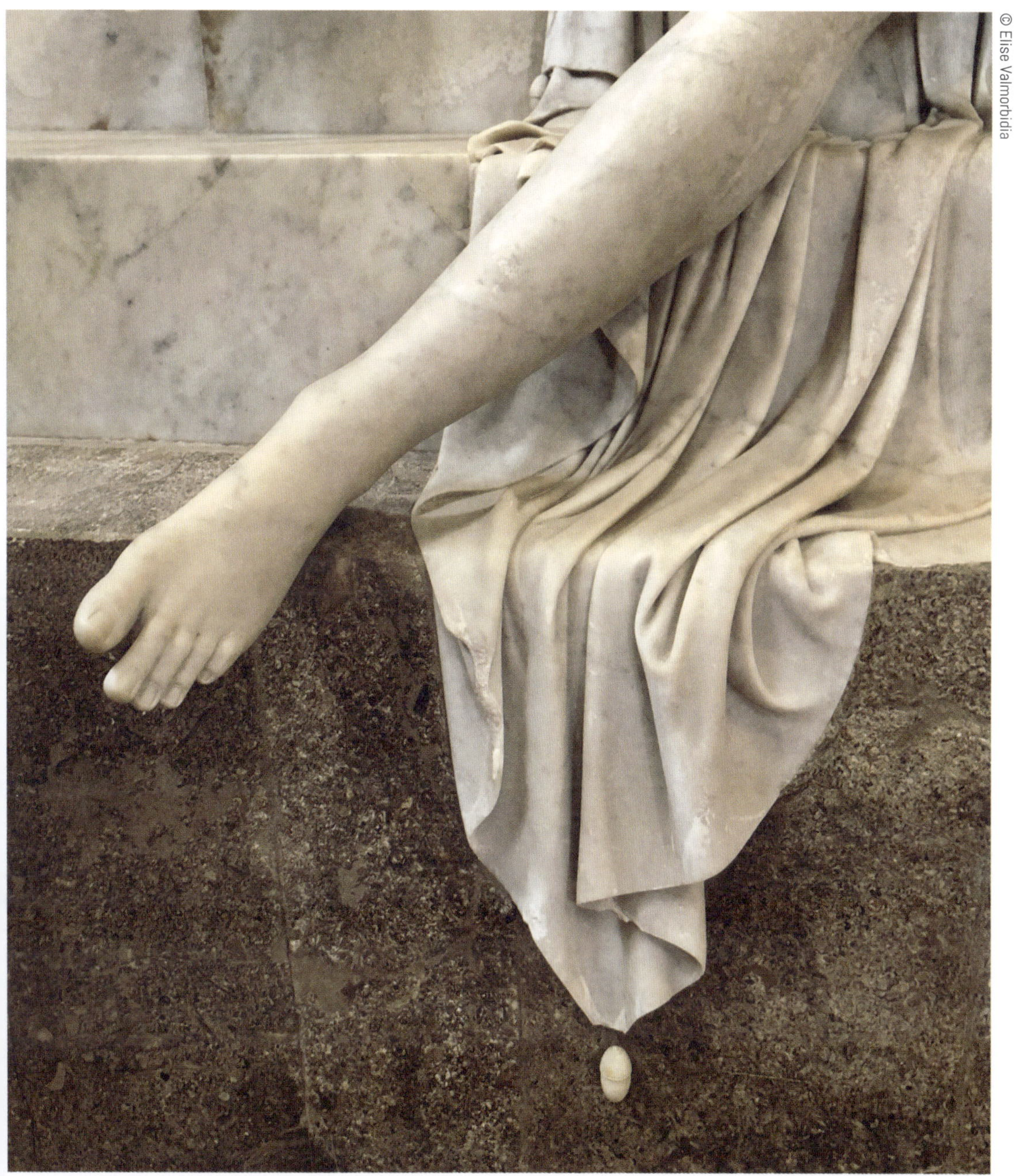

Elise Valmorbida: Marble breathing, draped, dripping, in Venice.   37

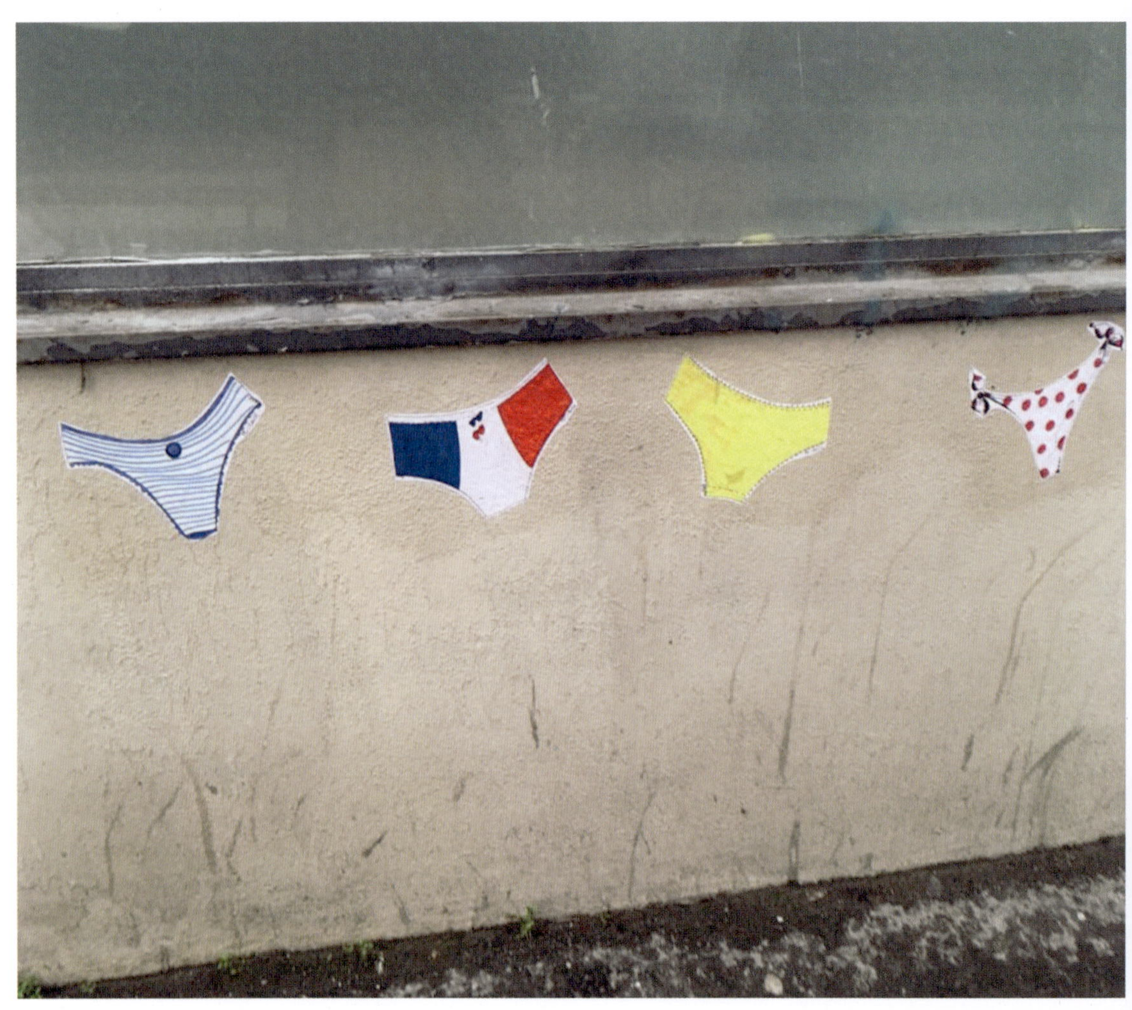

Susannah Clapp: By the way these graffiti pants are Parisian.

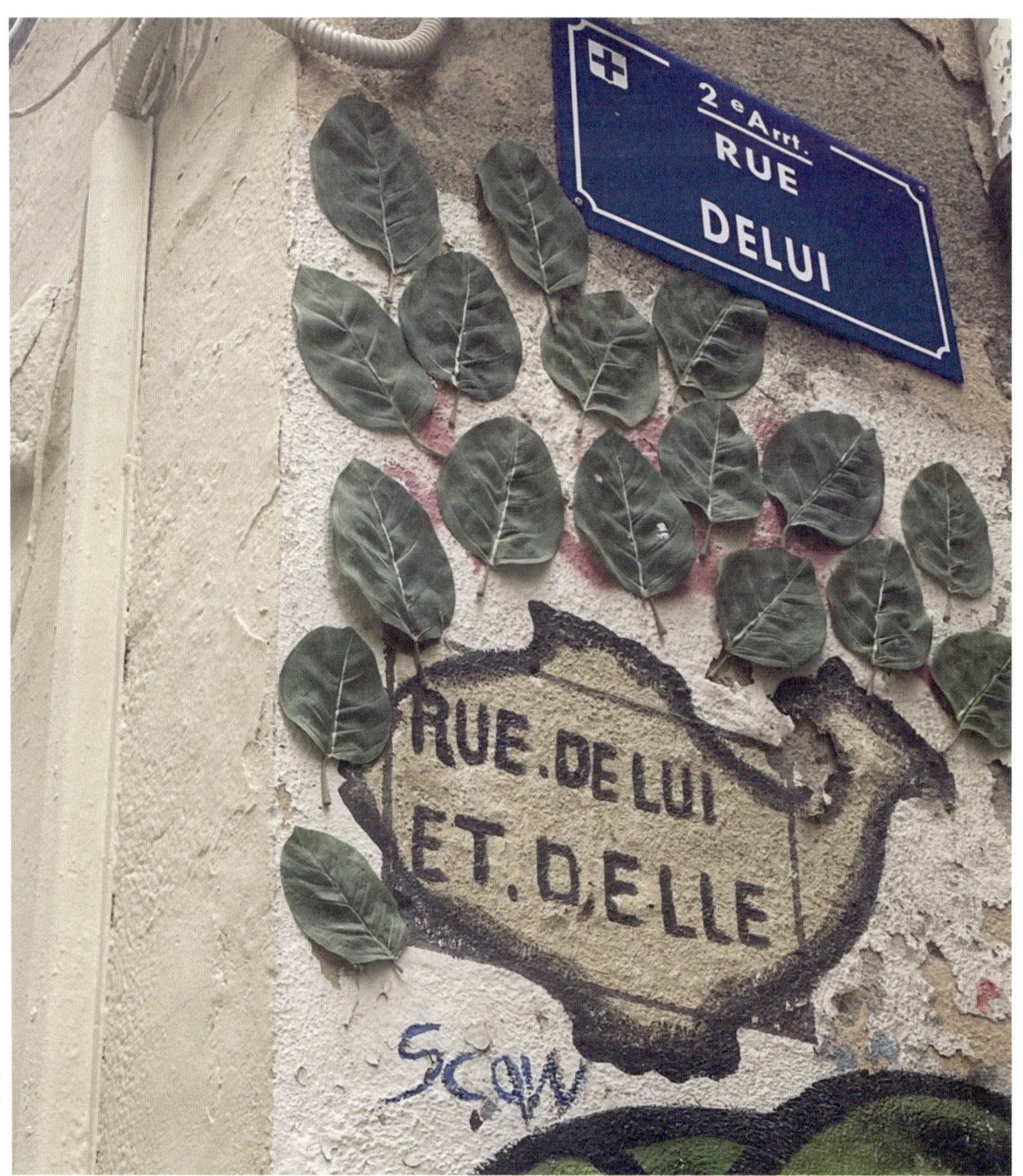

Susannah Clapp: Good graffiti in Marseille.   39

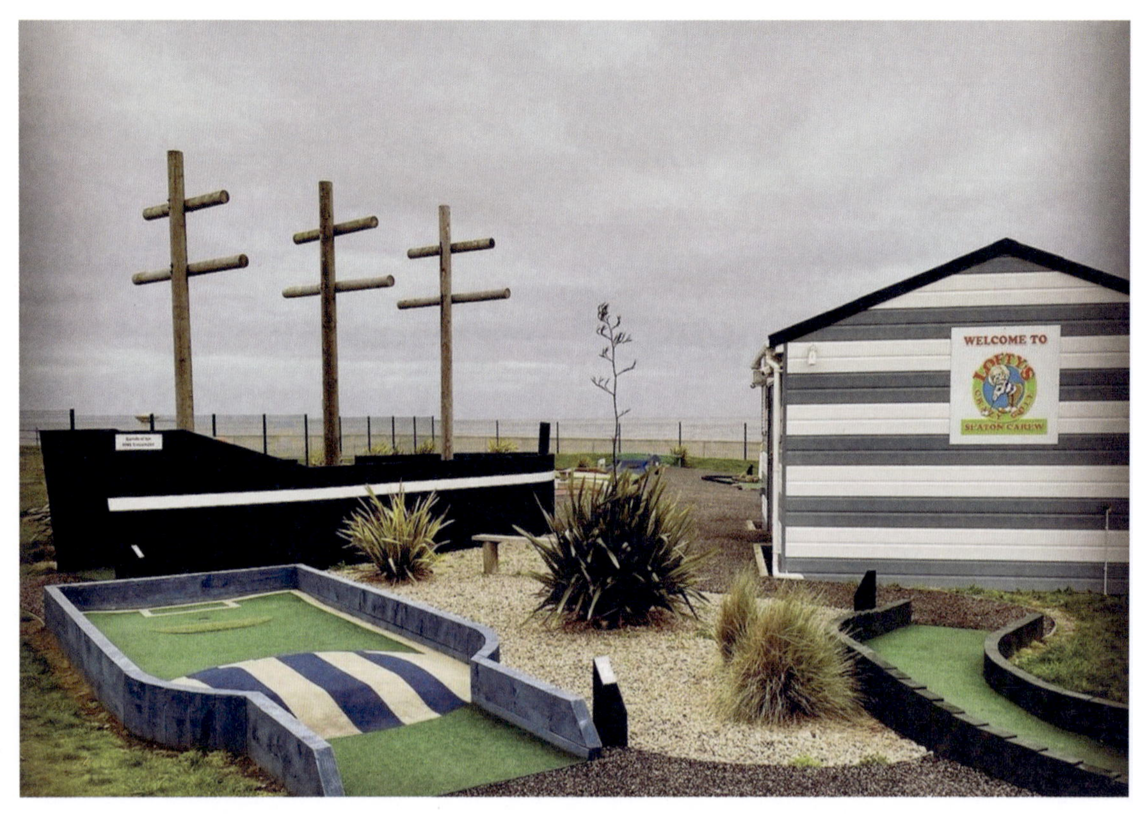

Suzannah Lipscomb: The "masts" of a ship in the crazy golf park have a particular resonance on Good Friday.

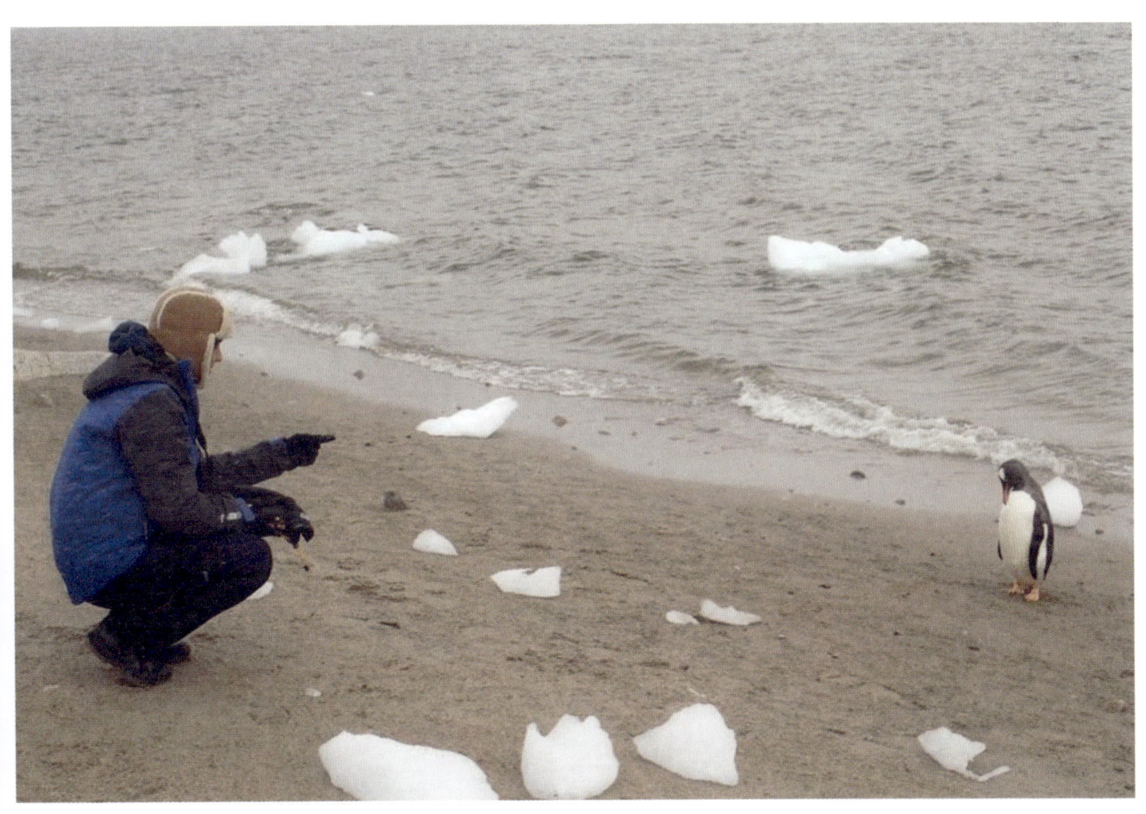

Kamila Shamsie: The time I admonished a penguin.

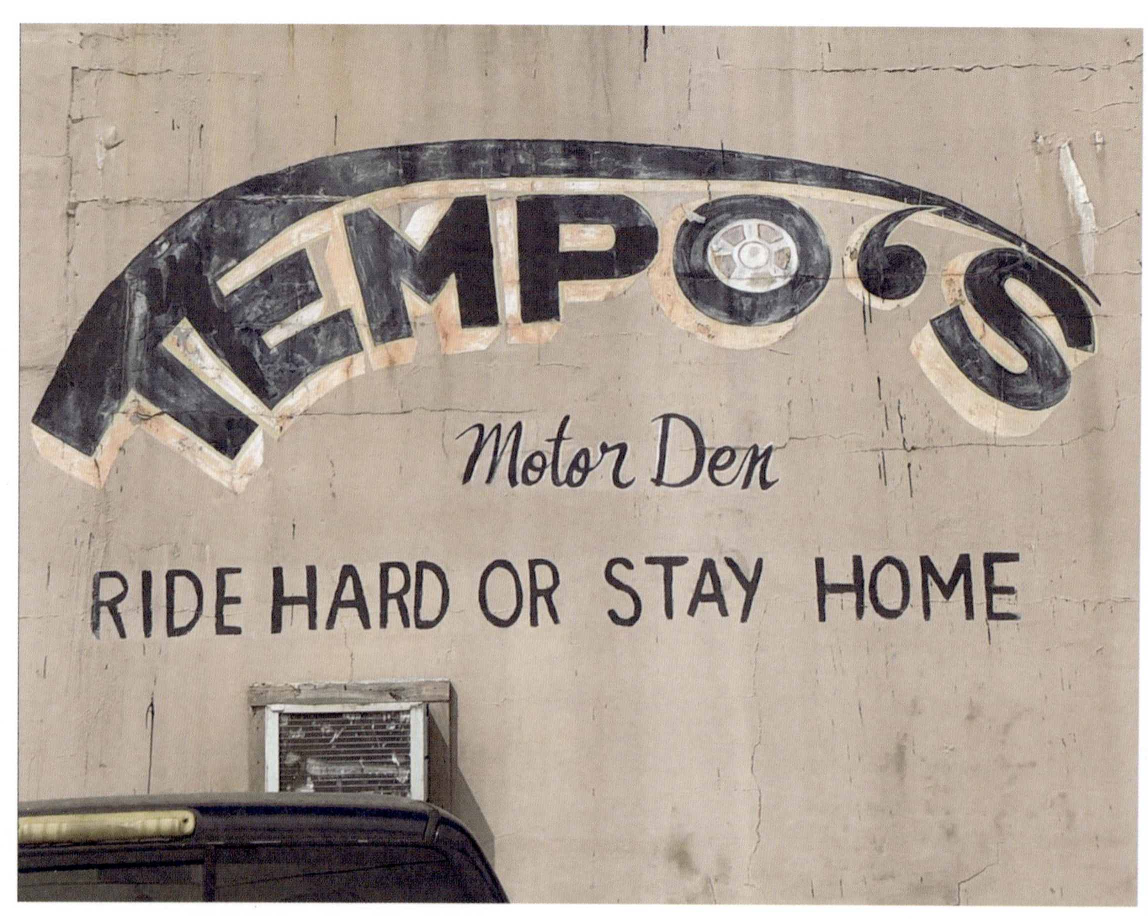

Mel Chin: Driving on Michigan Ave. in Mobile, Alabama, a timely message. Onward!

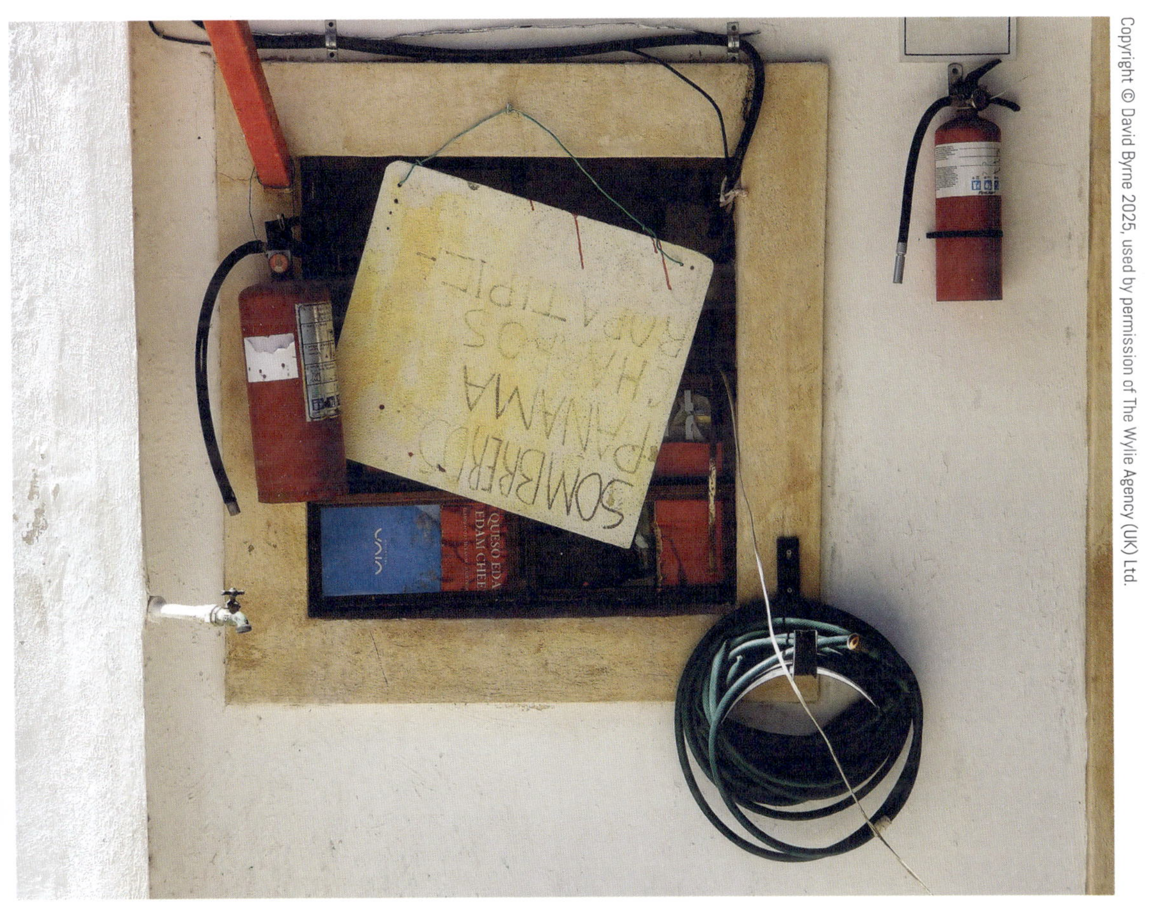

David Byrne: In a parking lot, Mérida, Mexico.

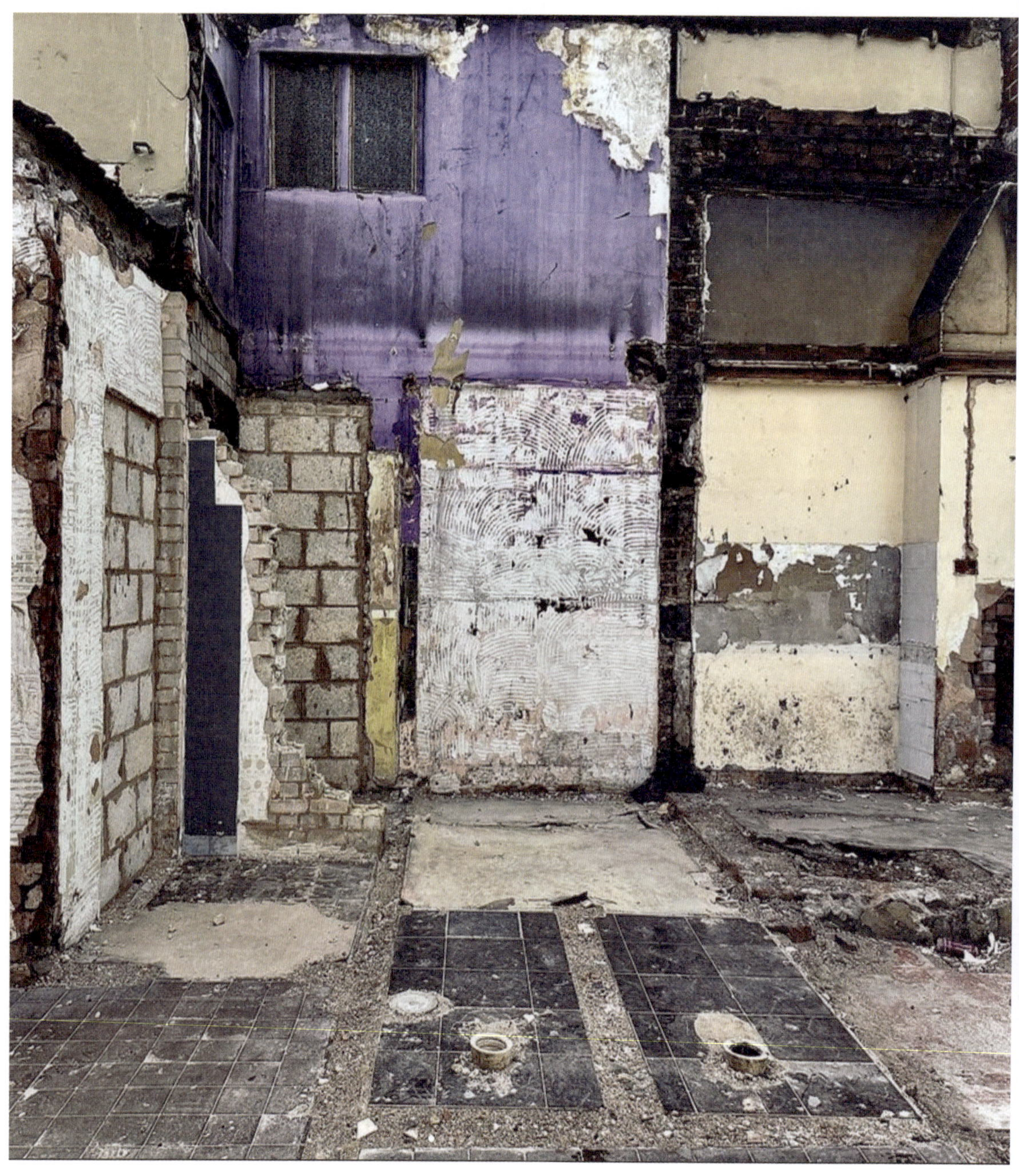

Simon Wallis: All that's now left of the boarded-up Grey Horse pub, Kirkgate, Wakefield.

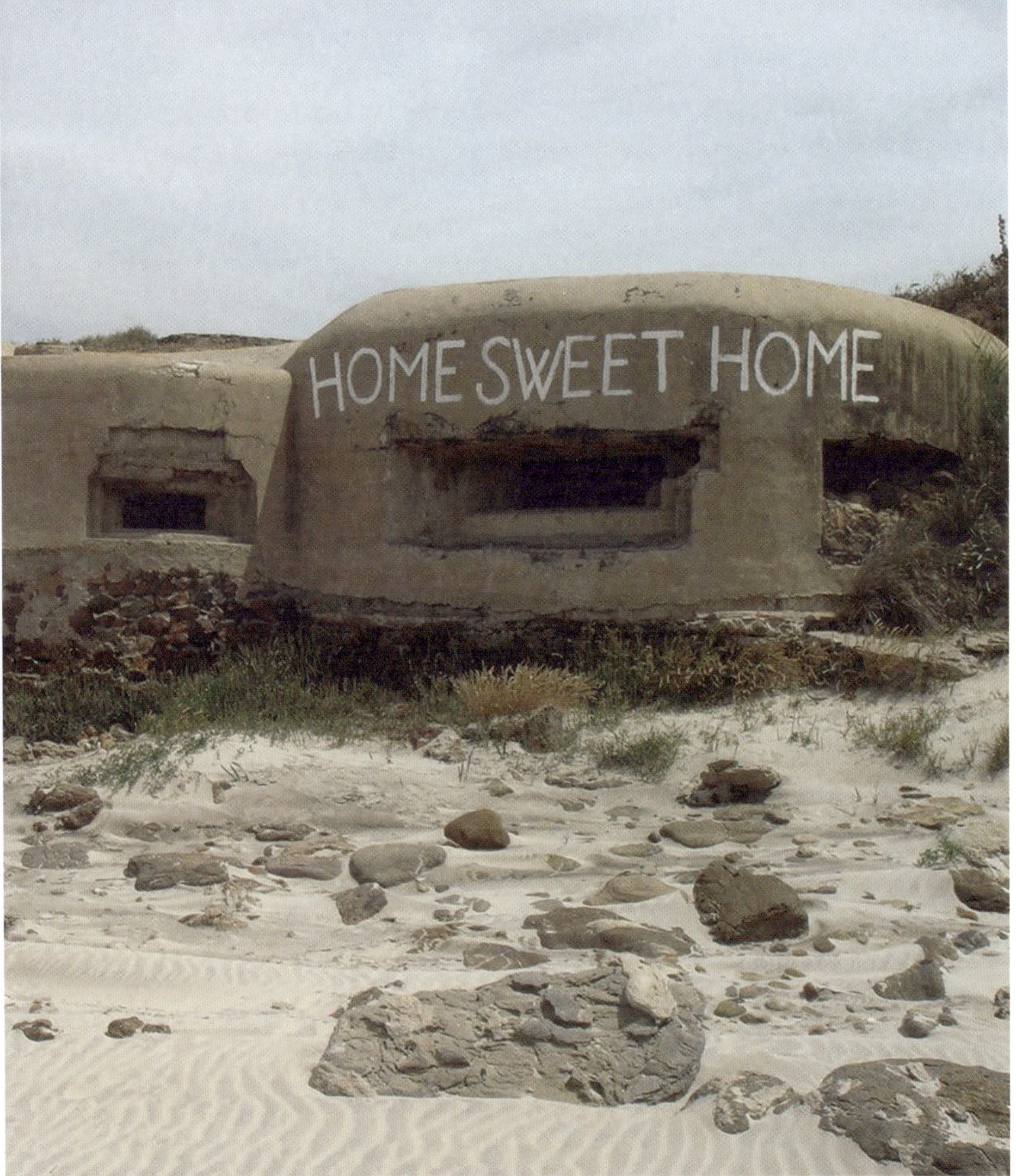

Rachel Whiteread: Two bunkers – Normandy, France, 2007.

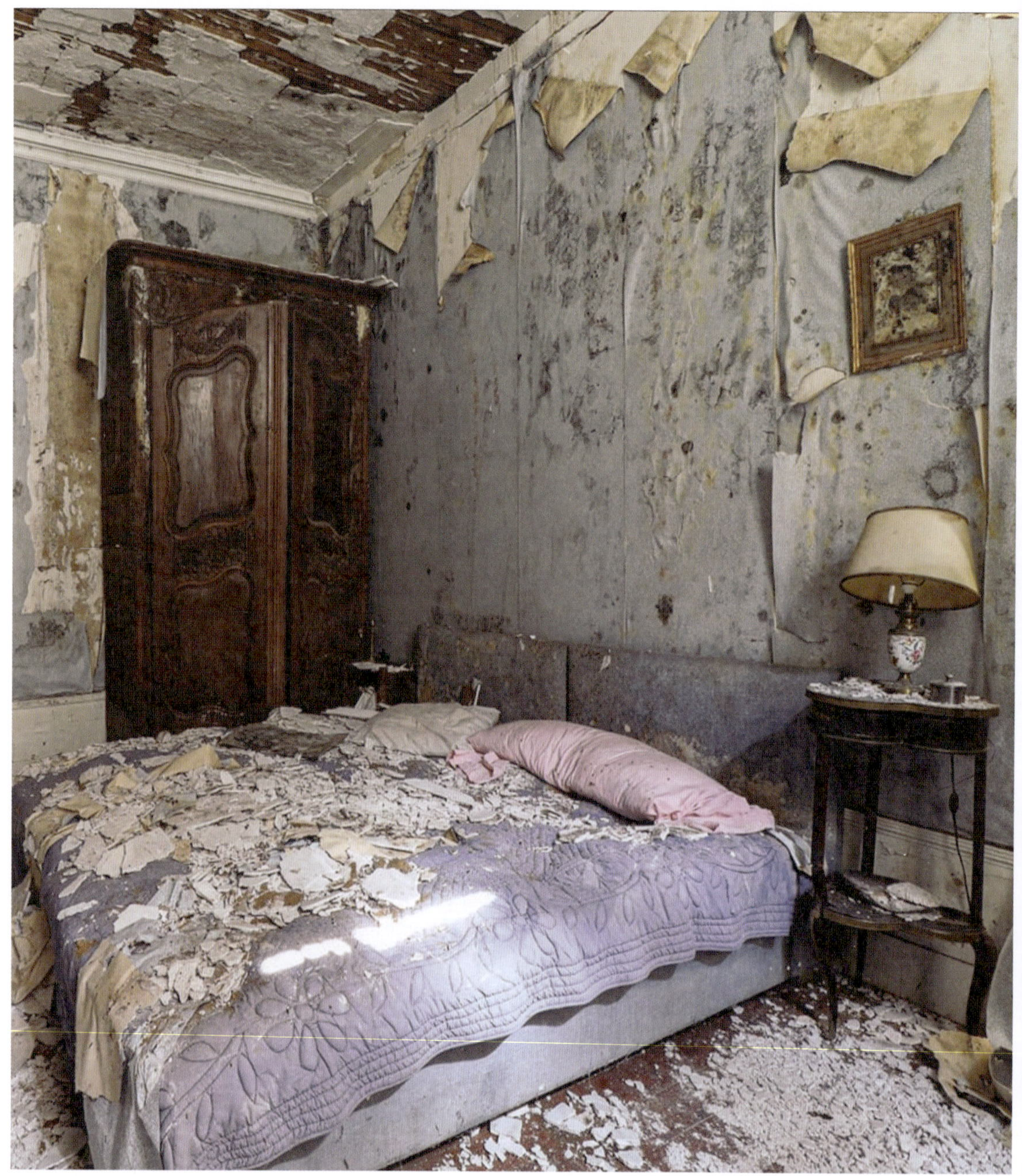

Keith McNally: Distressed to perfection.

Theirs was a difficult house, hard enough to live in if you knew how it all worked, and impossible for guests who didn't. The owners would tell you what you needed to know – where the frying pan lived, the knack for closing the bathroom door – though always with a little exclamation of surprise and irritation ("Oh! Didn't I tell you?") that conceded the oddity of their domestic arrangements (broken beds, bare light fittings, crumbling plaster) and scolded you for drawing attention to it.

Will Eaves, *The Inevitable Gift Shop*, 2016.

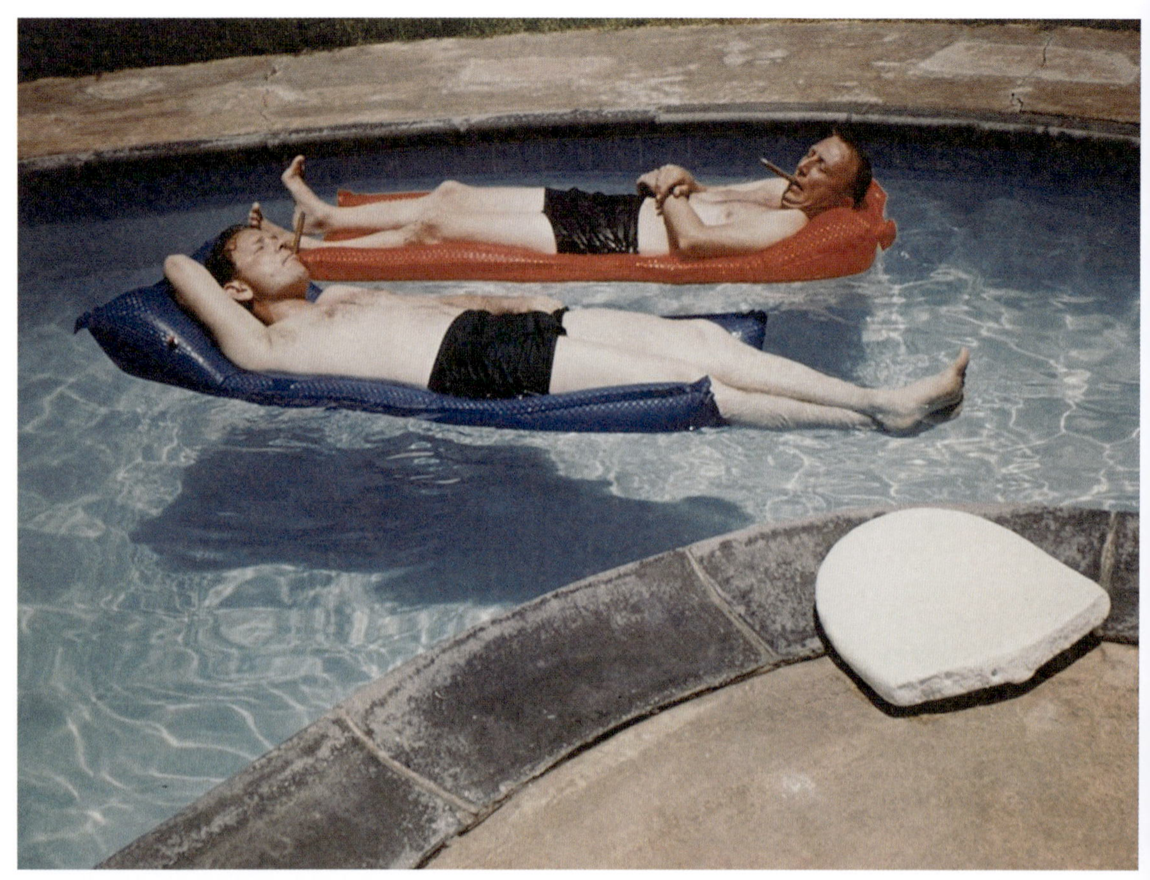

Lee Shulman.

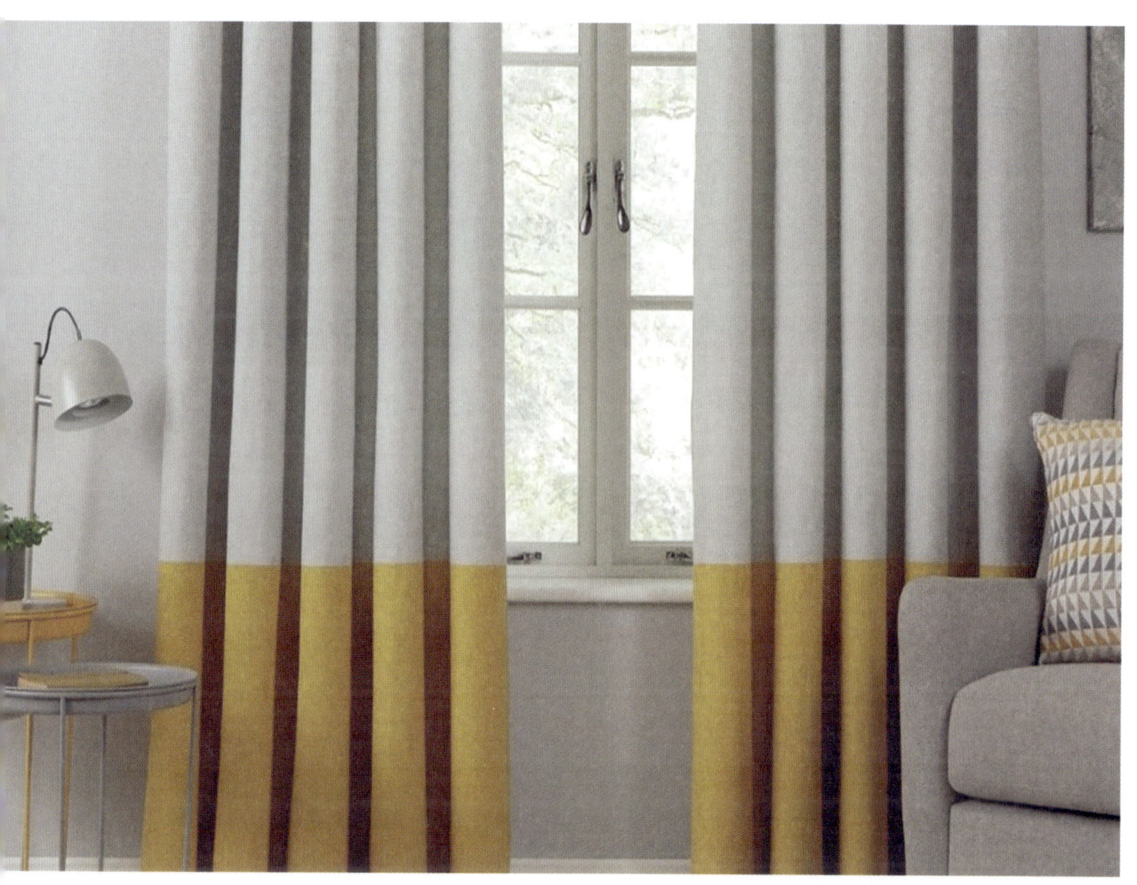

Andrew Still: Can you imagine trying to give up smoking only to come home and find your partner has bought these new curtains?

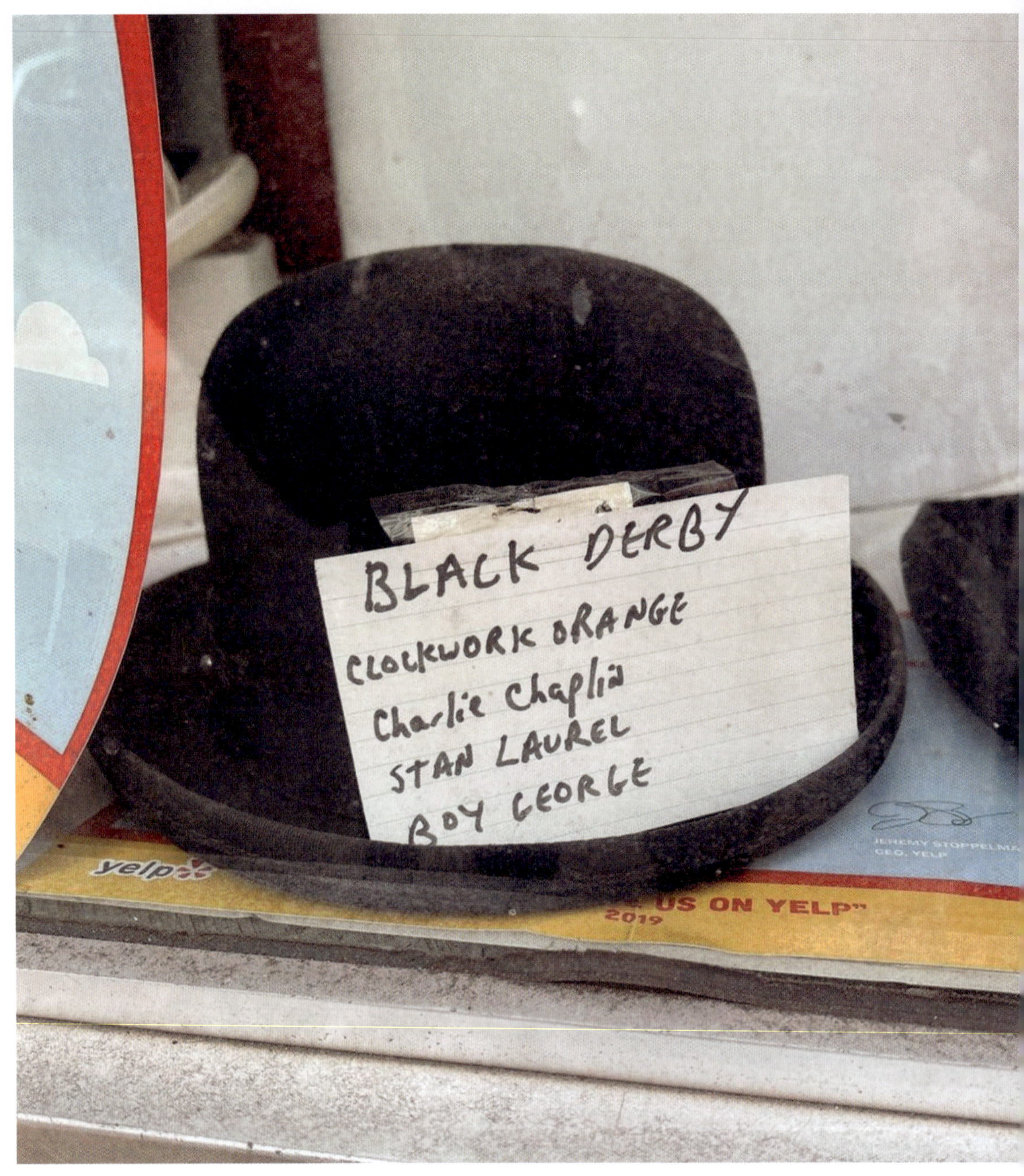

Mimi Thompson.

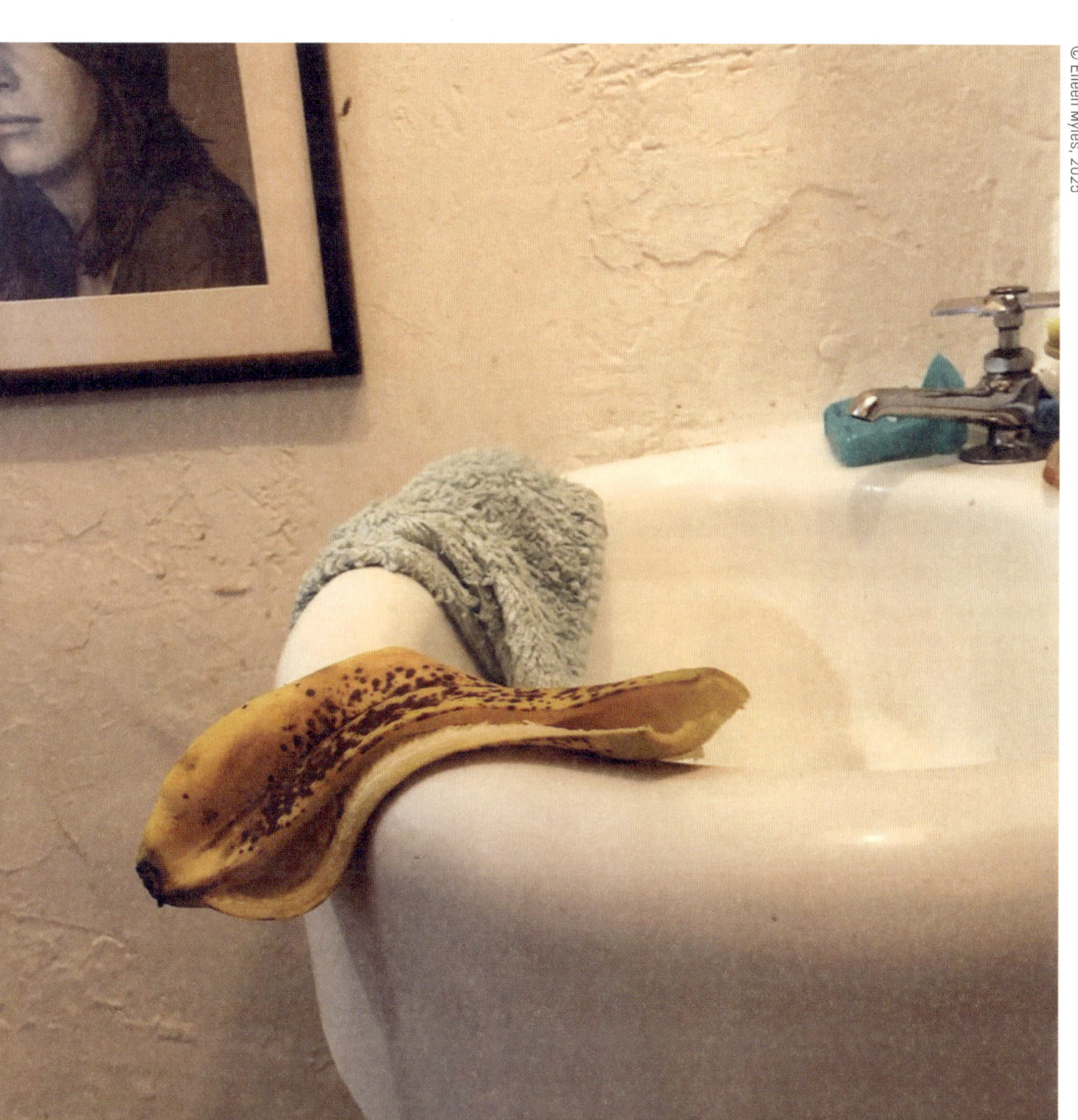

Eileen Myles.

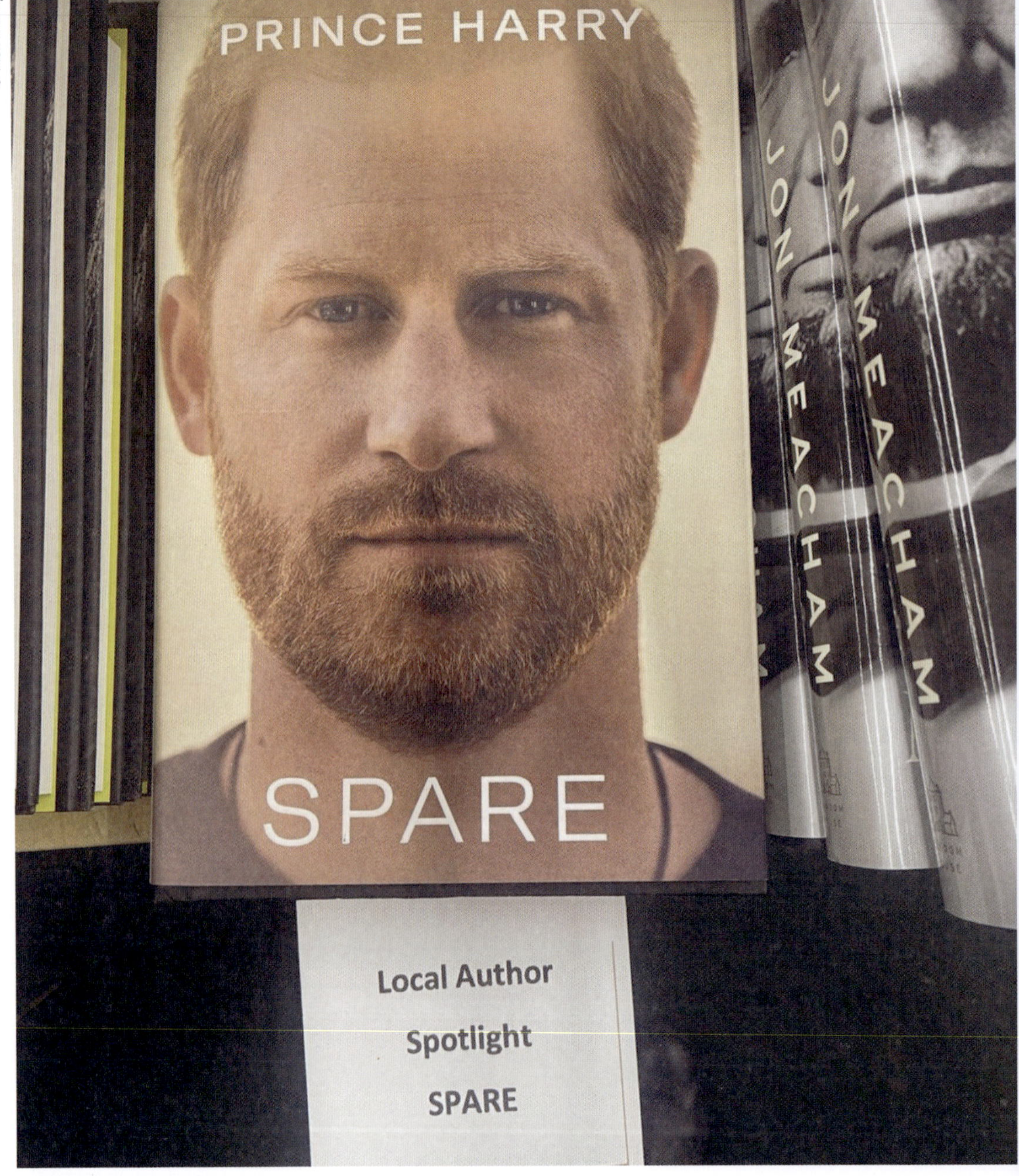

Nick Hornby: Chaucers Books in Santa Barbara.

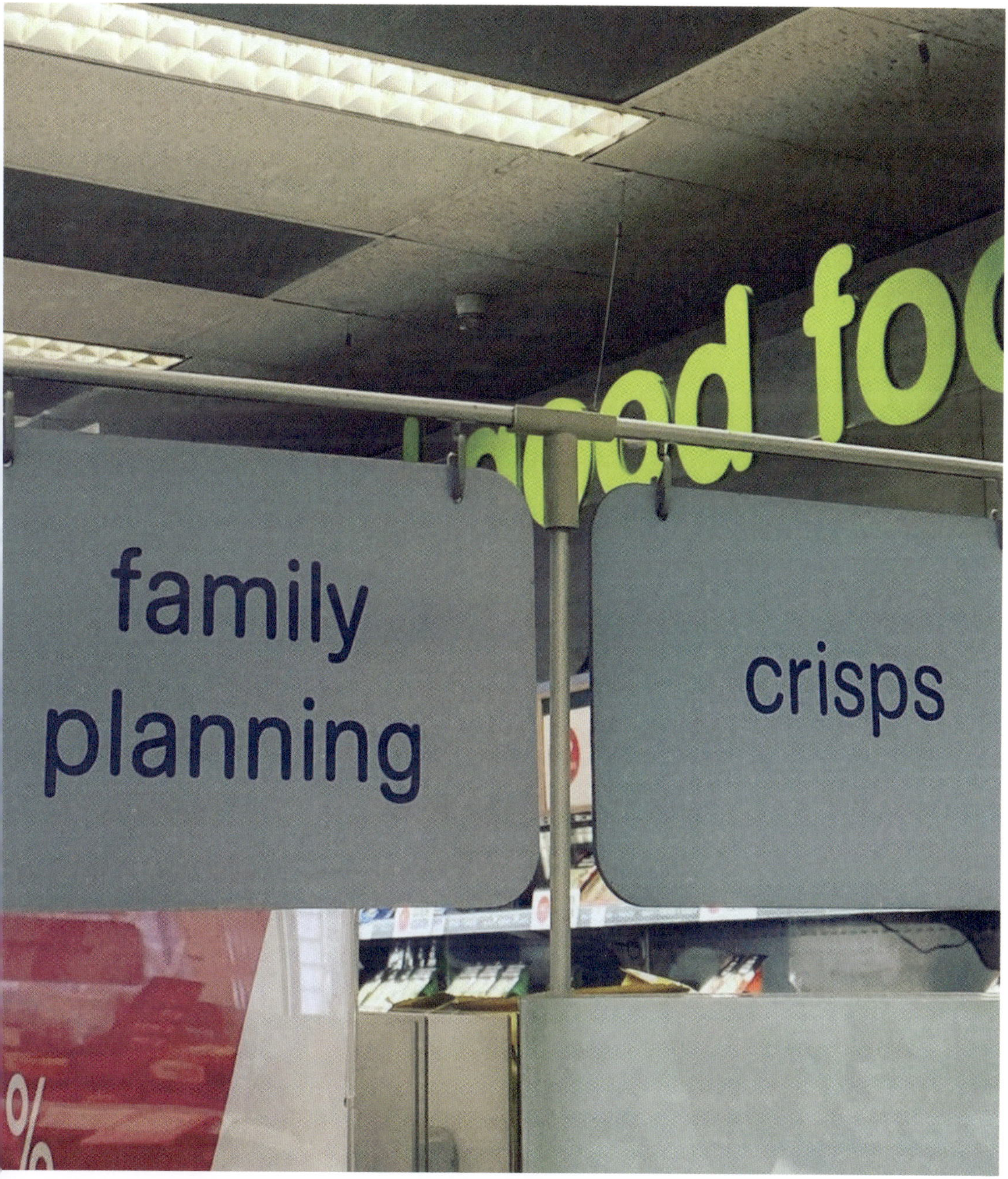

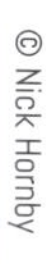

Nick Hornby: It's great to be of an age where you don't have to agonise for hours.

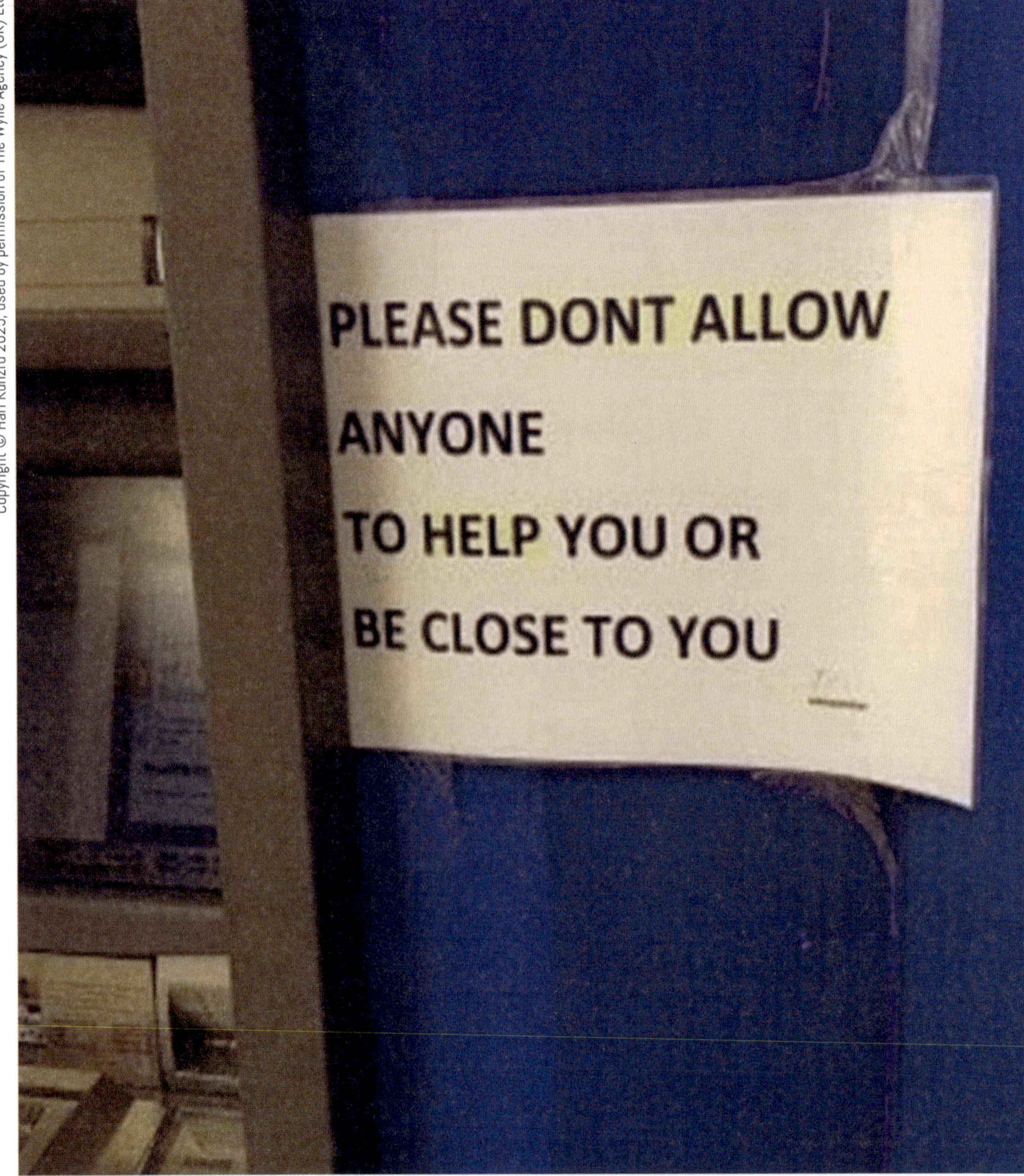

Hari Kunzru: There's no such thing as society when you're at the ATM. (Unknown photographer.)

2: CONTEMPLATING

FROM AVEEK SEN'S INSTAGRAM

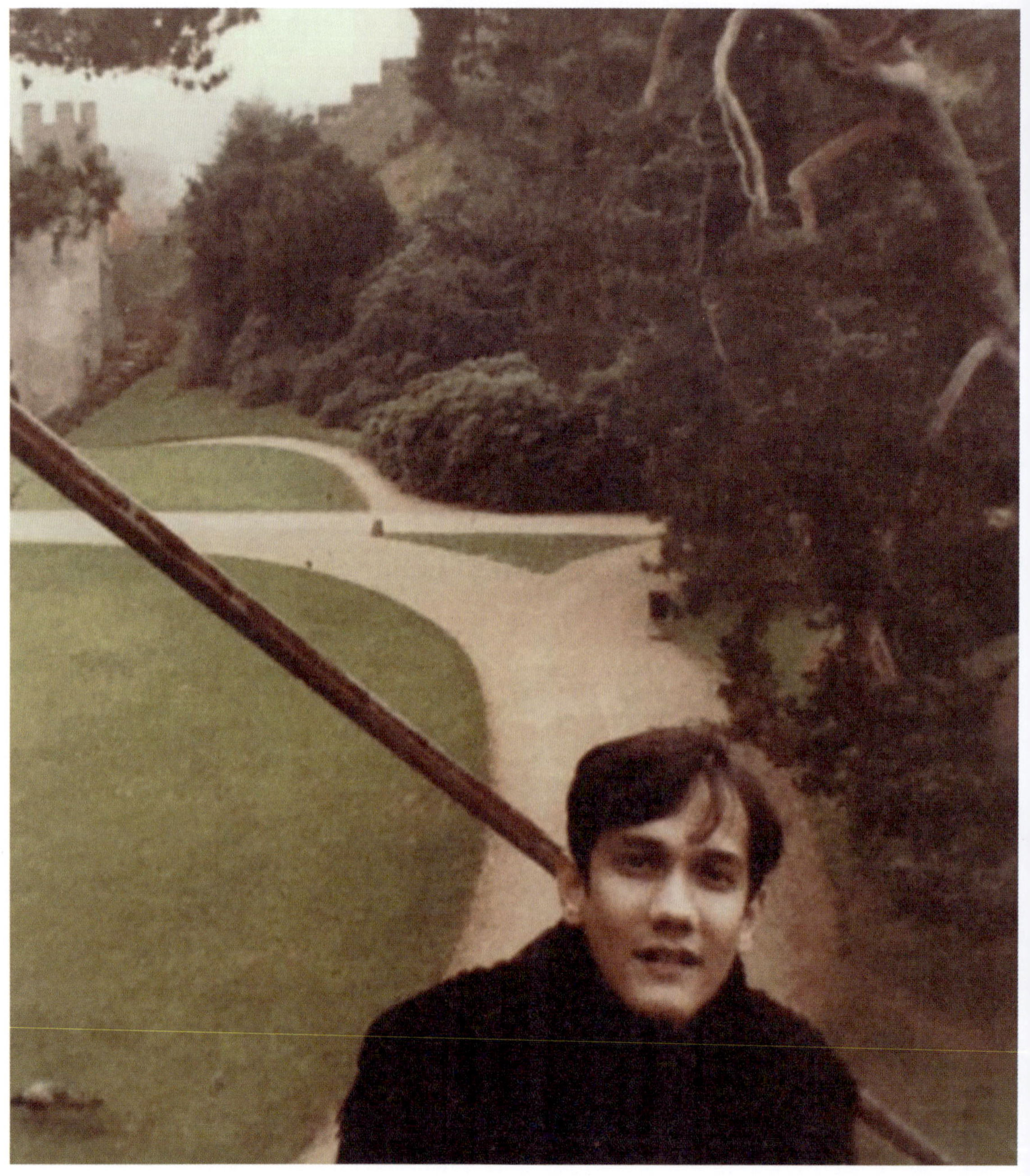

The camera is an instrument that teaches people how
to see without a camera.

Dorothea Lange.

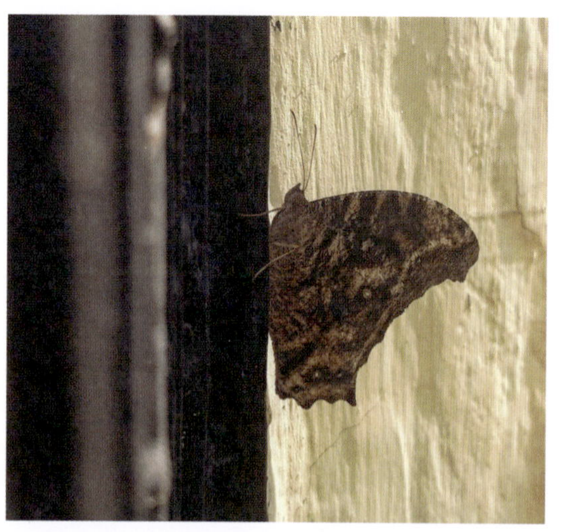

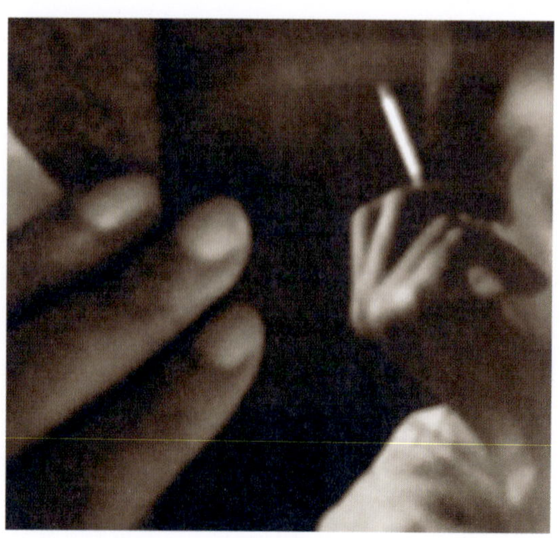

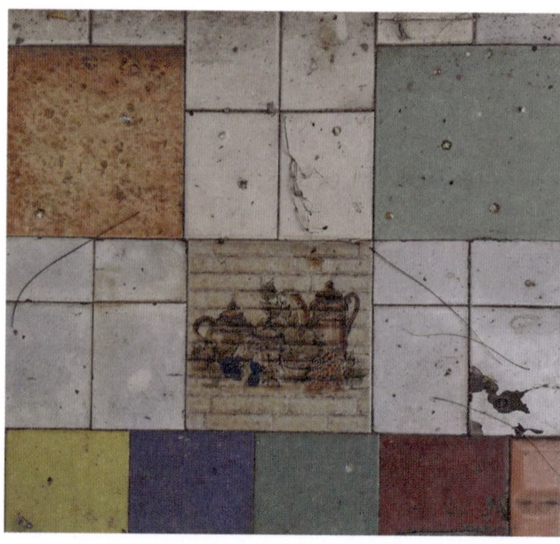

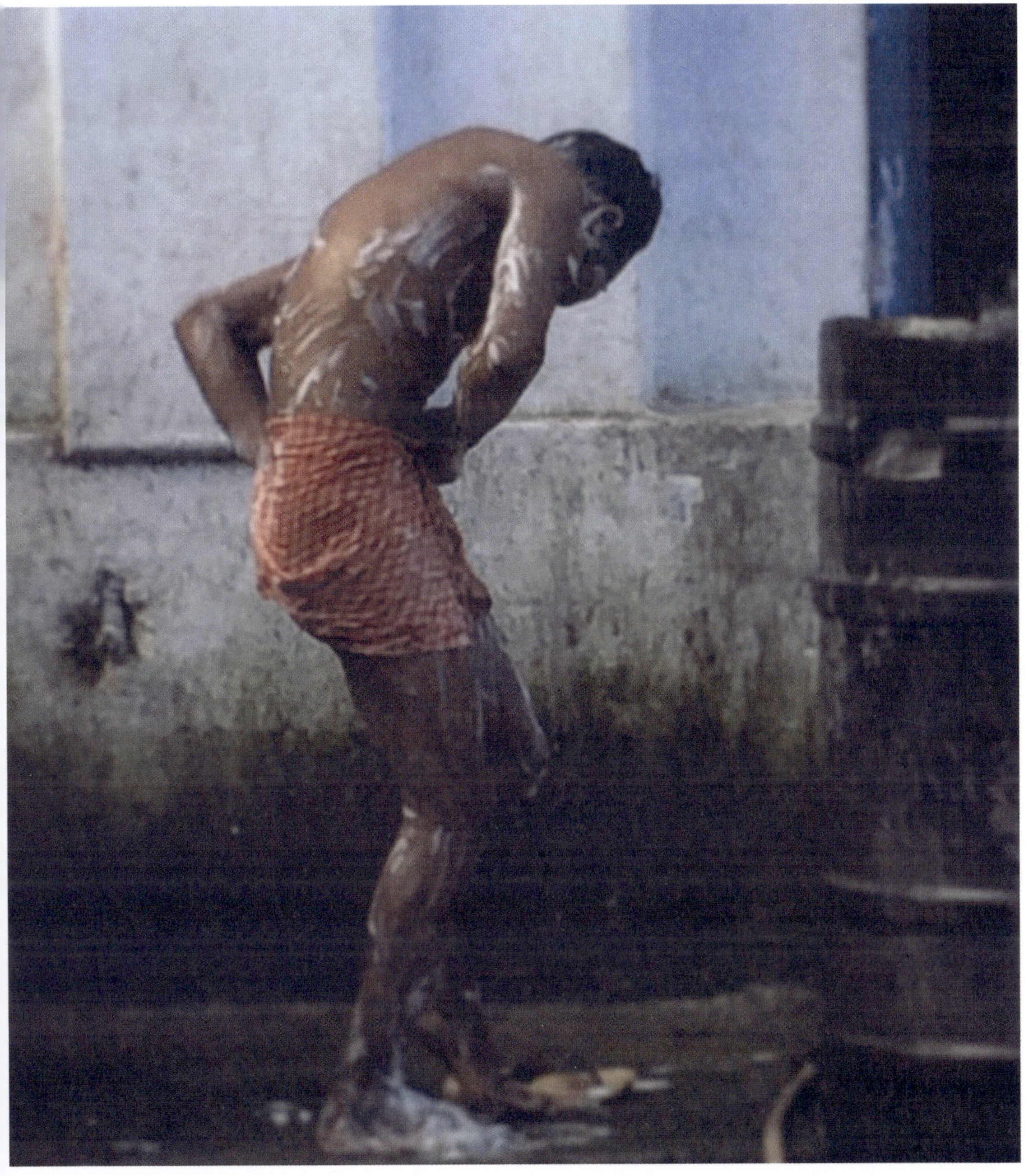

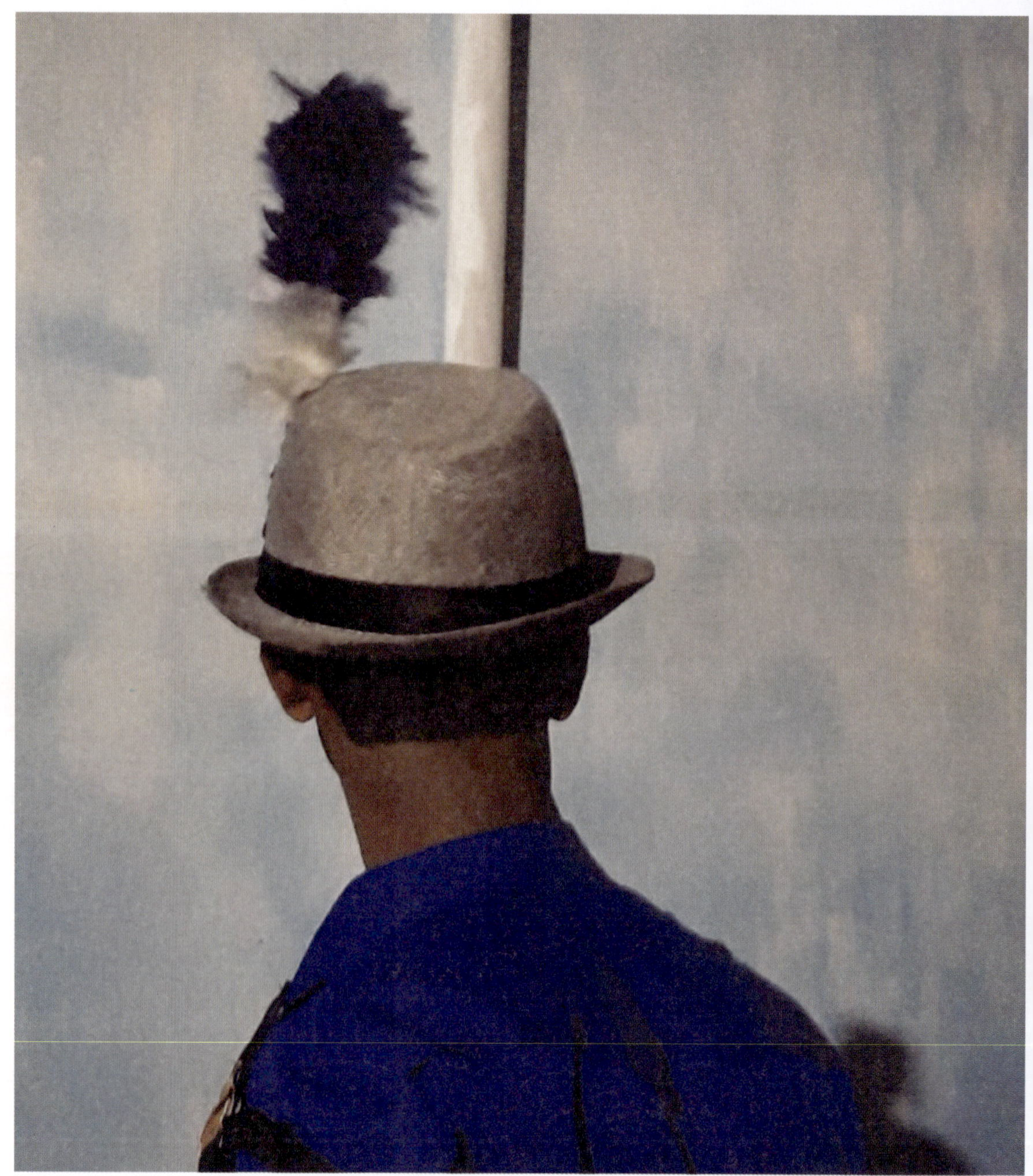

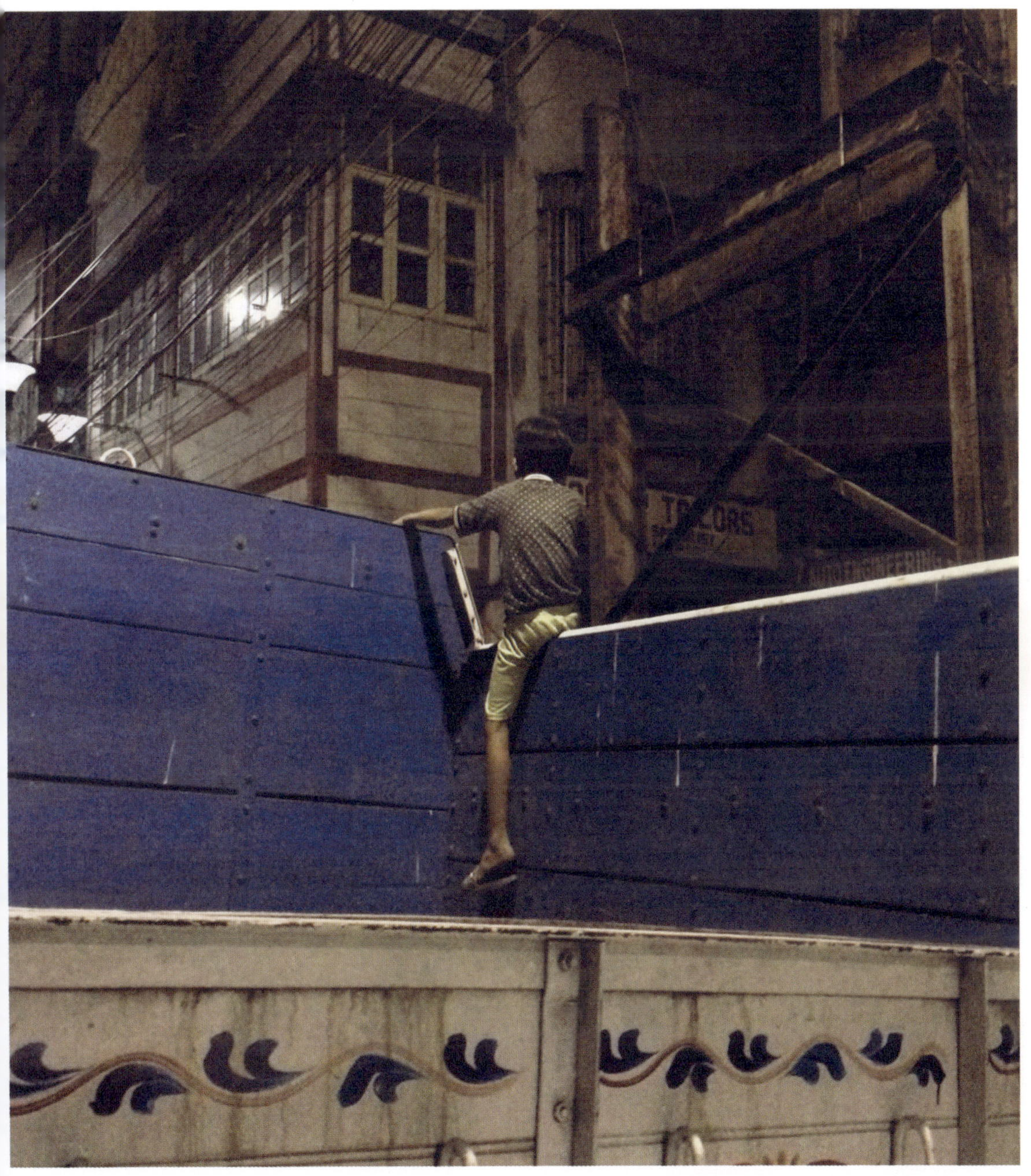

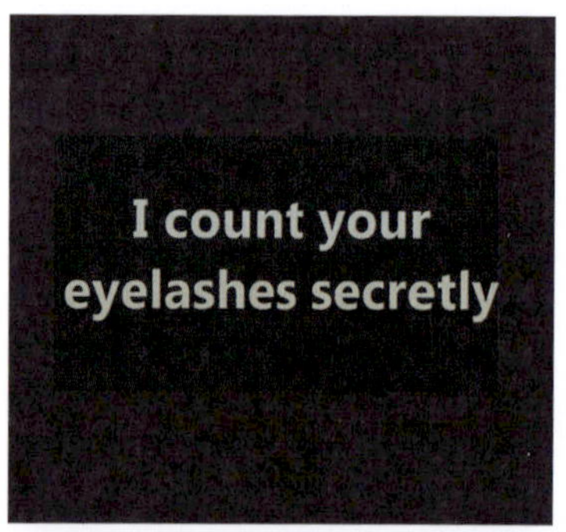
I count your
eyelashes secretly

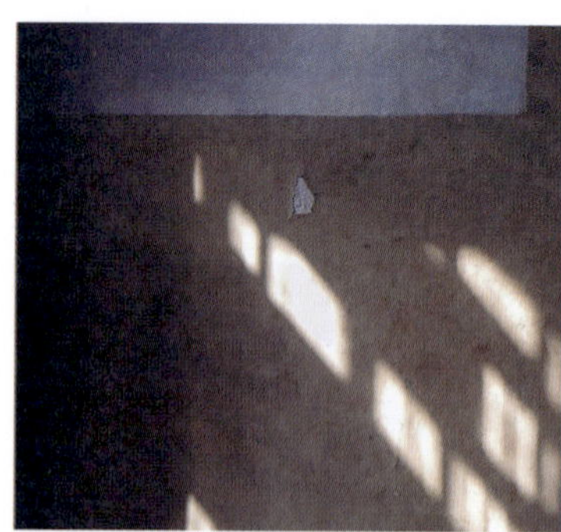

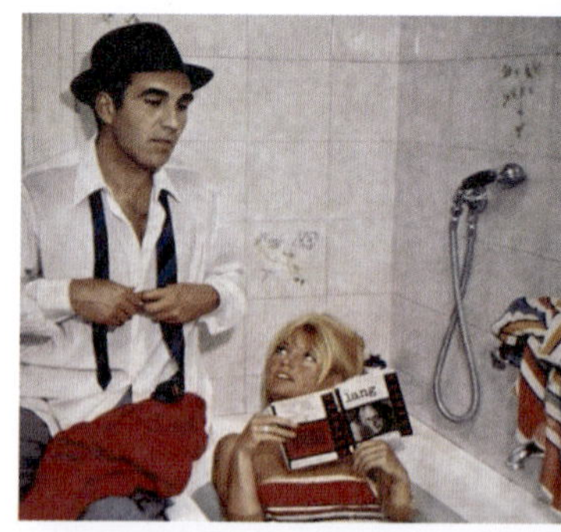
lang

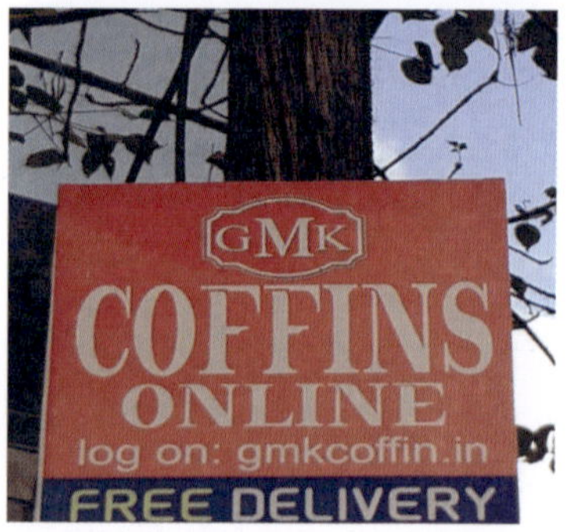
GMK
COFFINS
ONLINE
log on: gmkcoffin.in
FREE DELIVERY

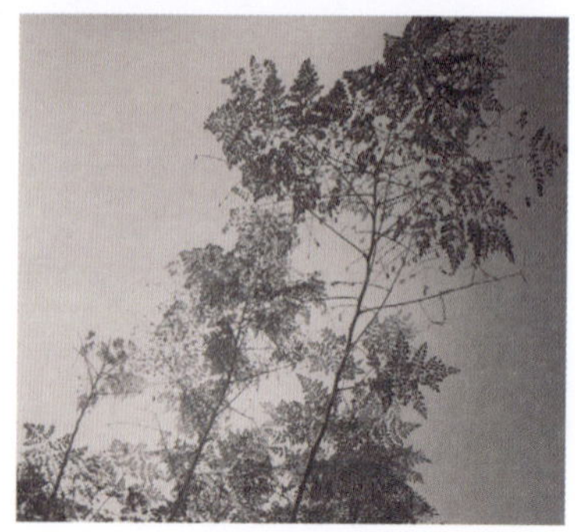

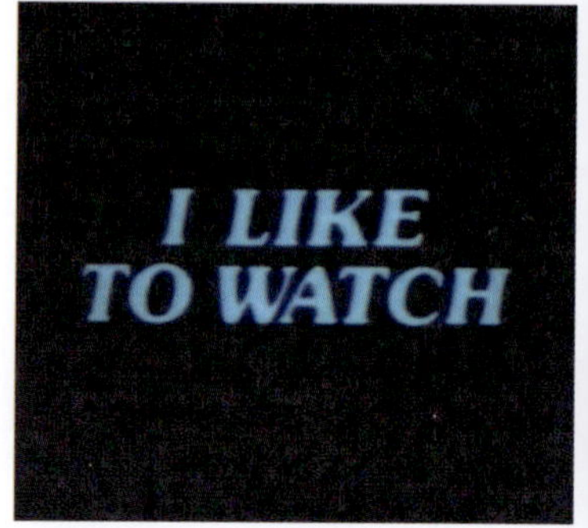
I LIKE
TO WATCH

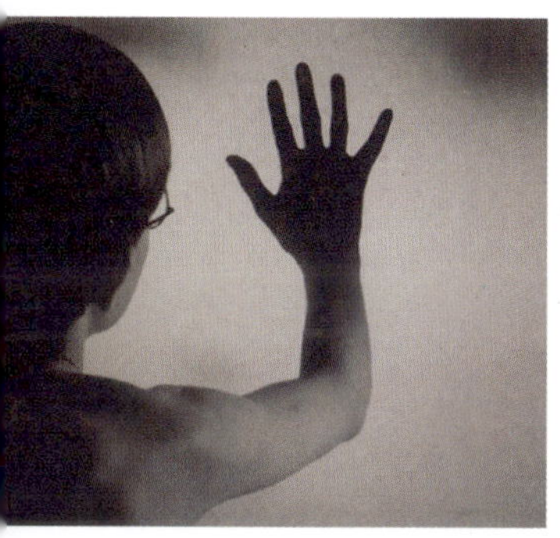

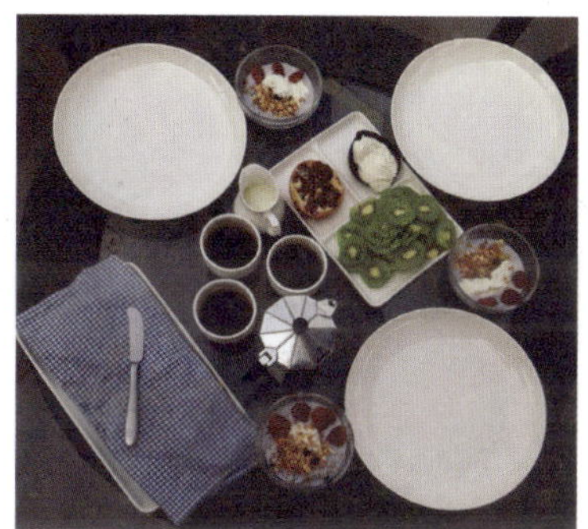

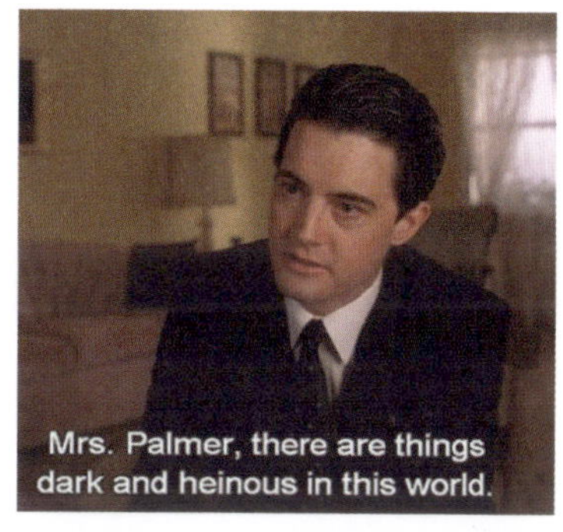
Mrs. Palmer, there are things dark and heinous in this world.

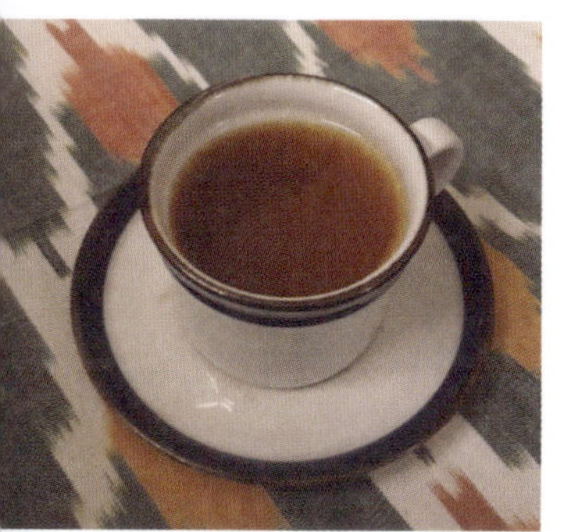

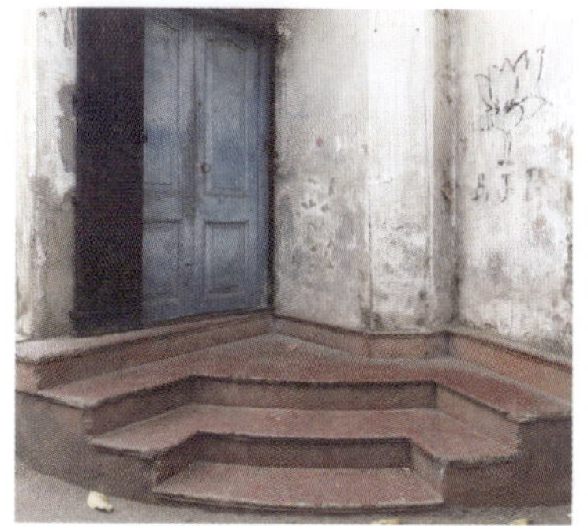

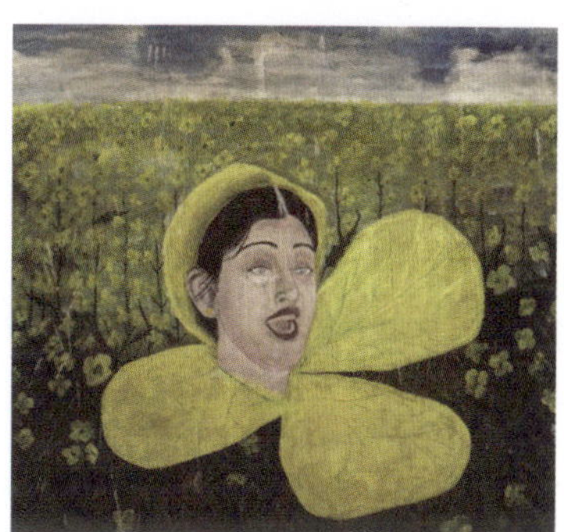

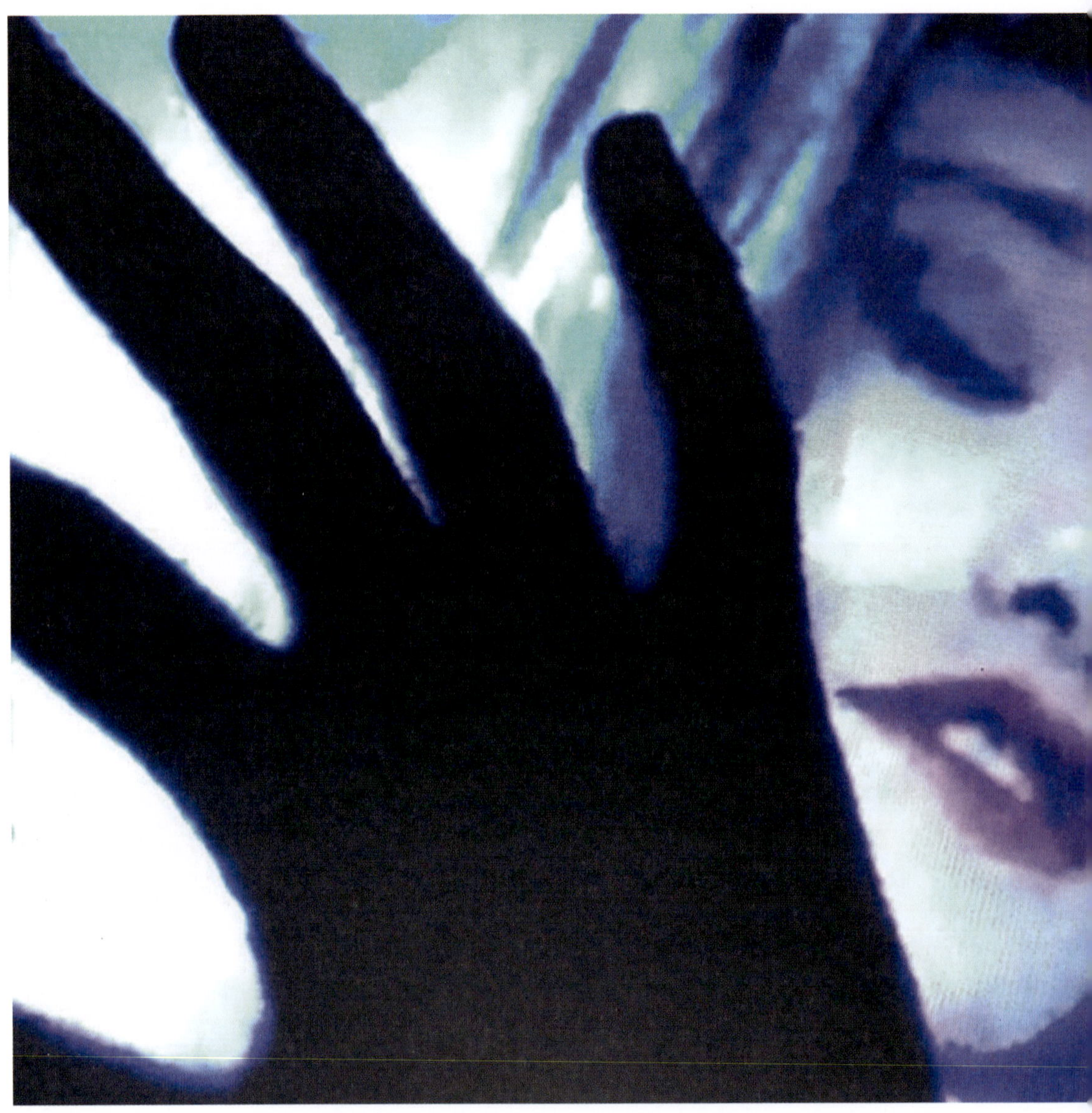

I first saw Hal Hartley's *Amateur* as a student in 1994..loved it and have been wanting to see it again ever since.

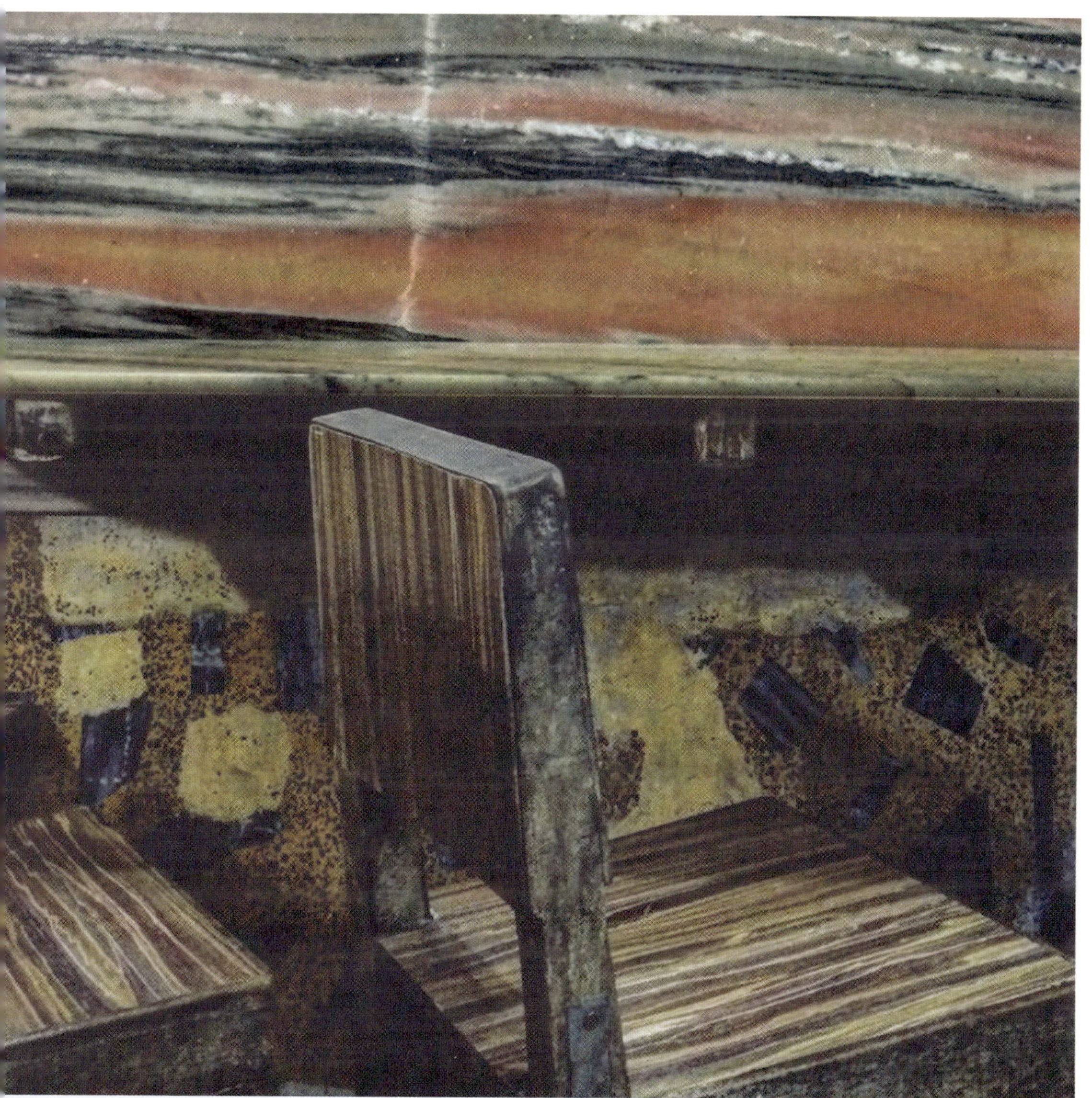

White Cube boredom – why do we always go in for the clinically minimal global high art look when many of the richest and most enduring spaces of aesthetic, sensory and emotional savouring in our immediate environment are so beautifullly different and contrary?

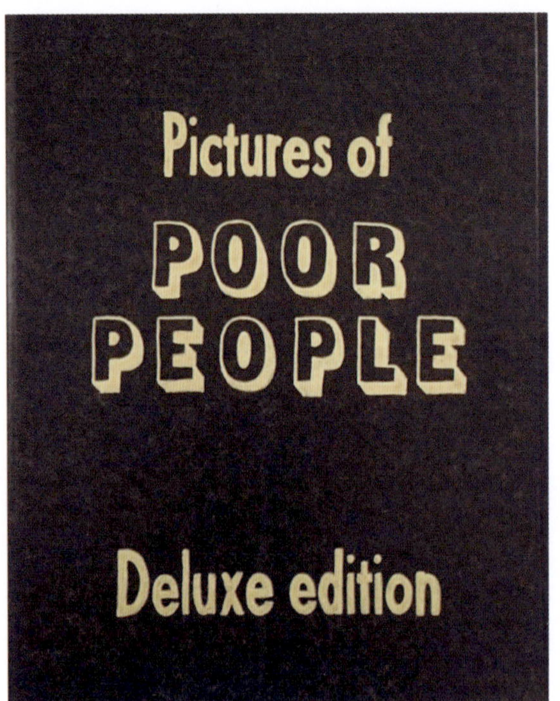

Pictures of POOR PEOPLE

Deluxe edition

By Johan Deckmann. Love this work: gives us, especially photographers and writers on photography, a great deal to think about. Photographers will have to teach themselves to think harder through the pitfalls of photographic "empathy" when trying to bridge every kind of distance and difference – of course, without throwing the baby out with the bathwater. It's a difficult job, as it should be; and just reading Susan Sontag won't help.

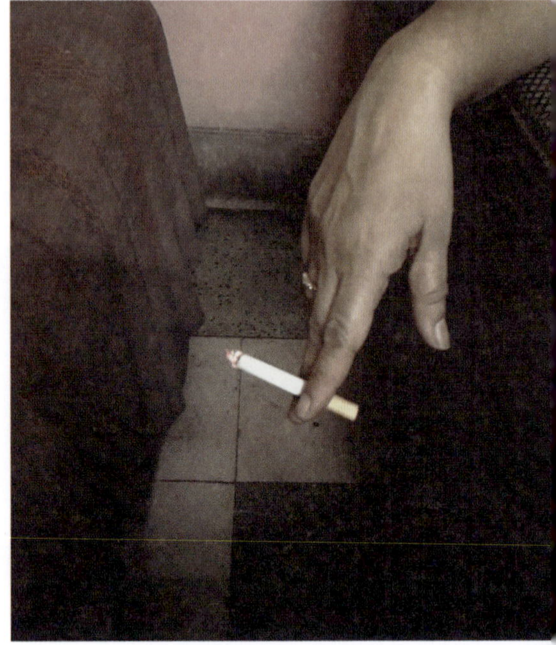

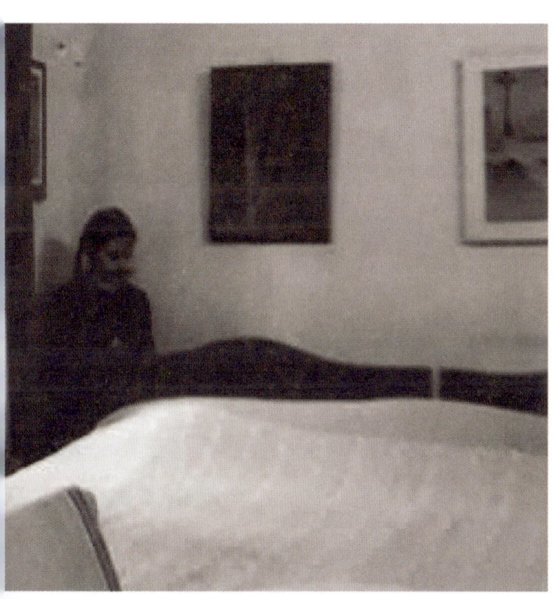

For Anjana Kothamachu, who sent me the most wonderful book on sadness. How did you know?

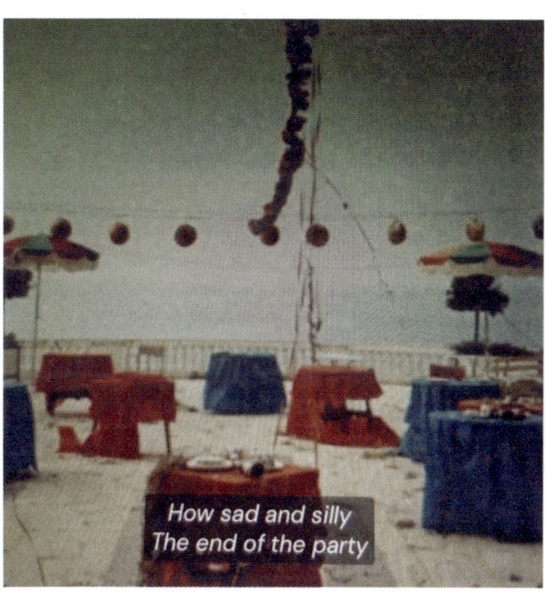

Agnes Varda. Who else?

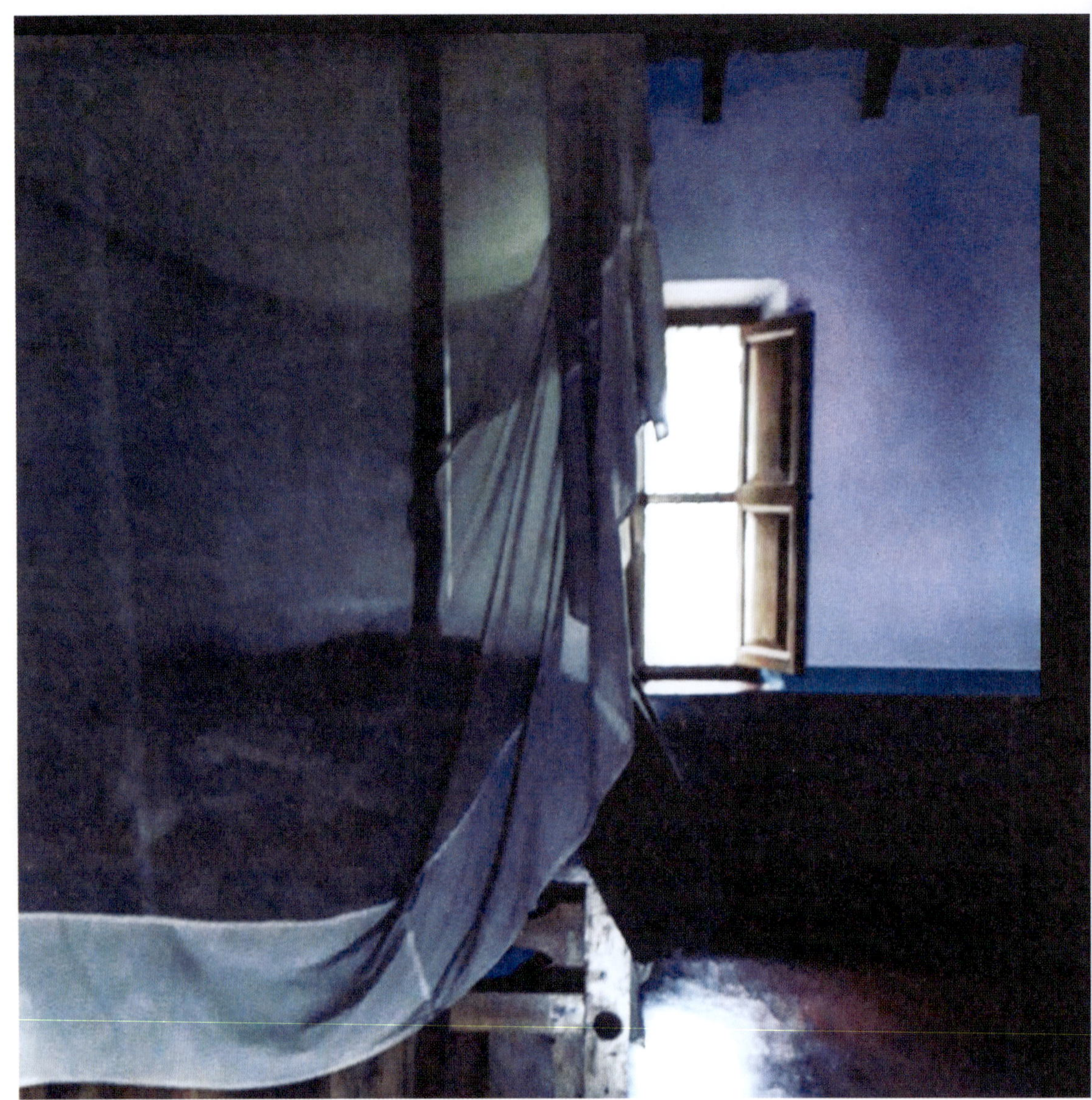

3: STARING

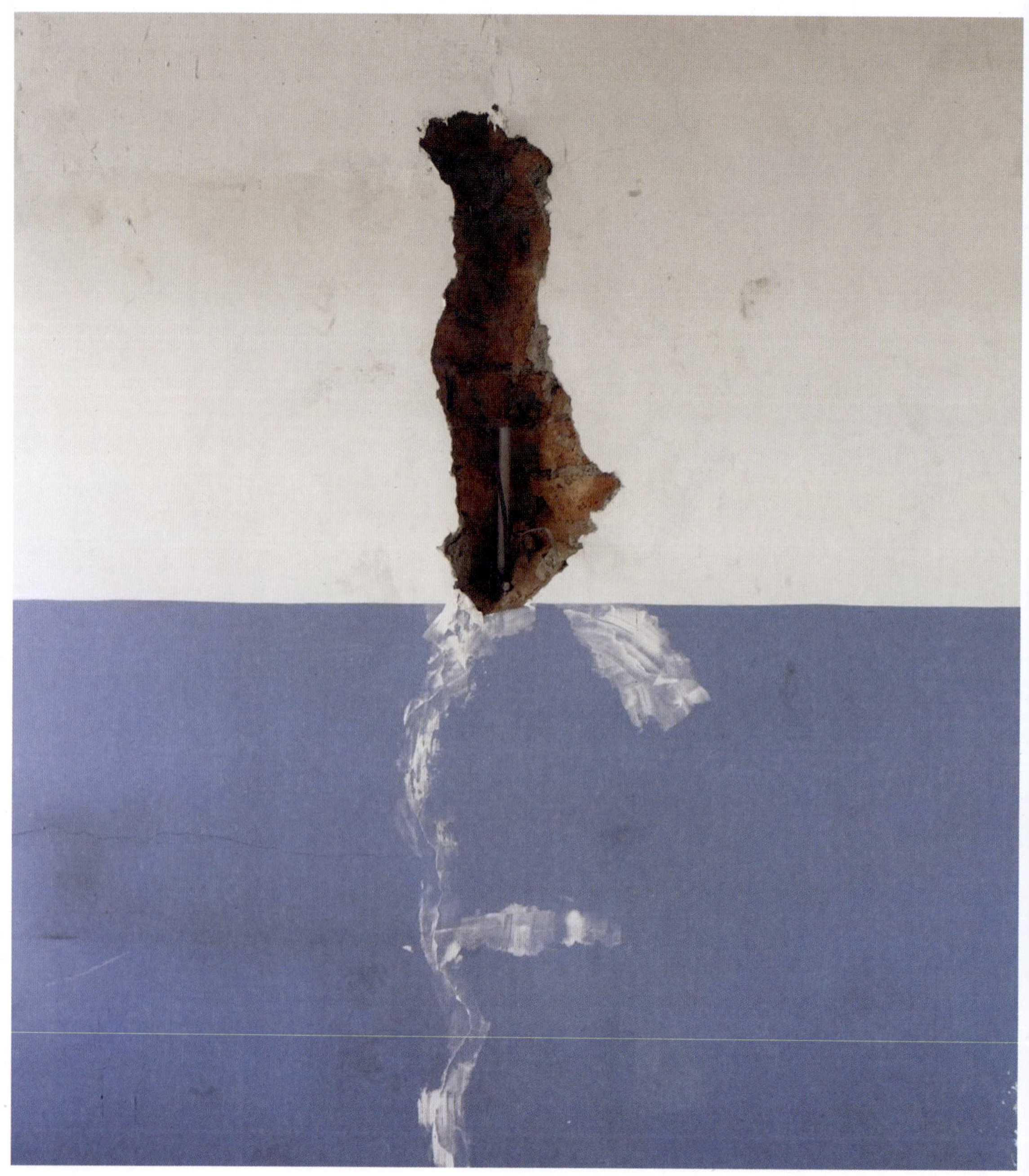

Hemali Bhuta.

That was the whole thing, there was nothing remarkable about it
whatsoever, it was an utterly ordinary thing — and yet for some unknown
reason she kept staring at it, and falling, again for some unknown reason,
into a kind of trance.

Mieko Kanai, *Mild Vertigo*, translated by Polly Barton, 2023.

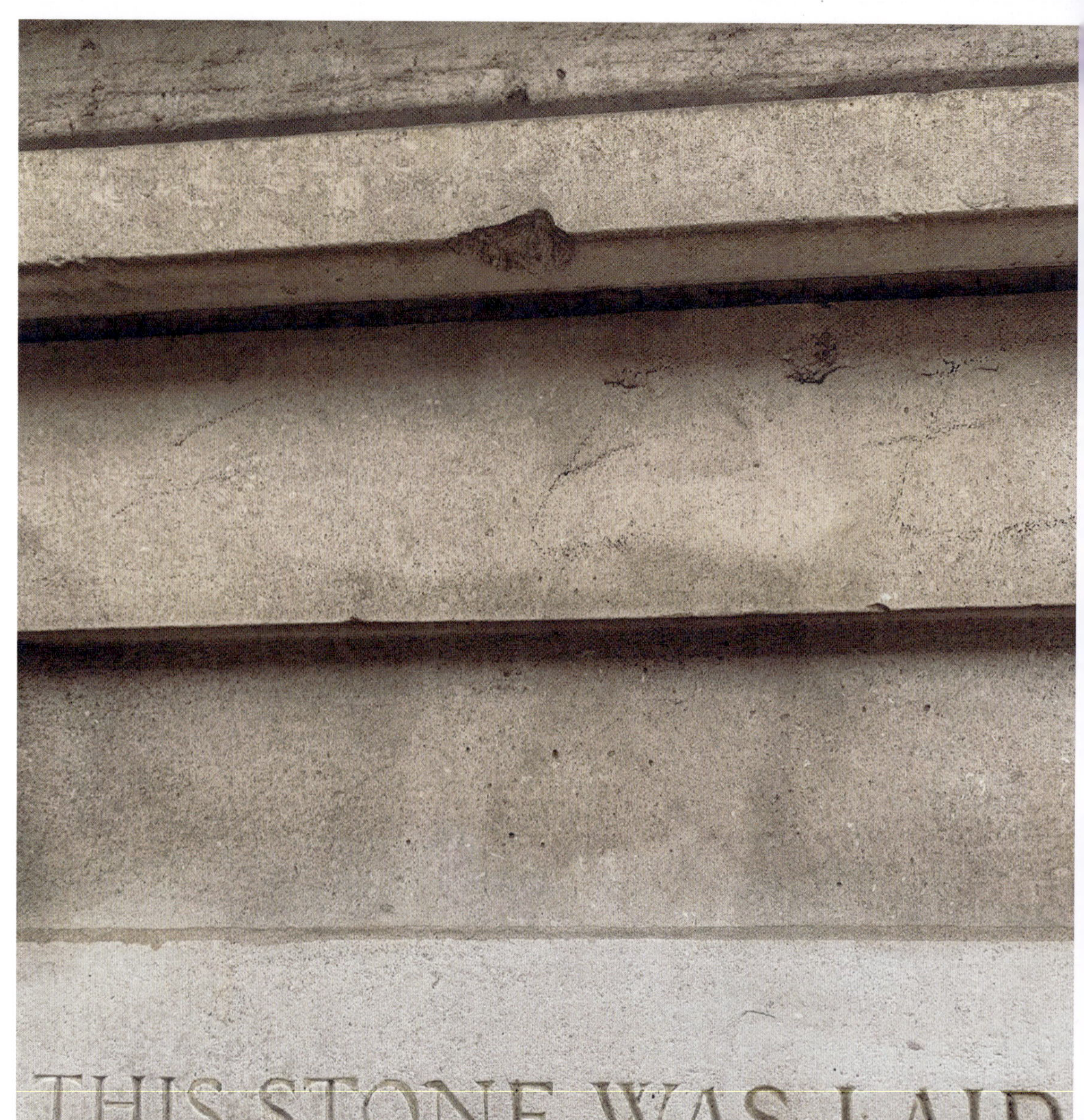

Olivia Sudjic: Hot stone summer.

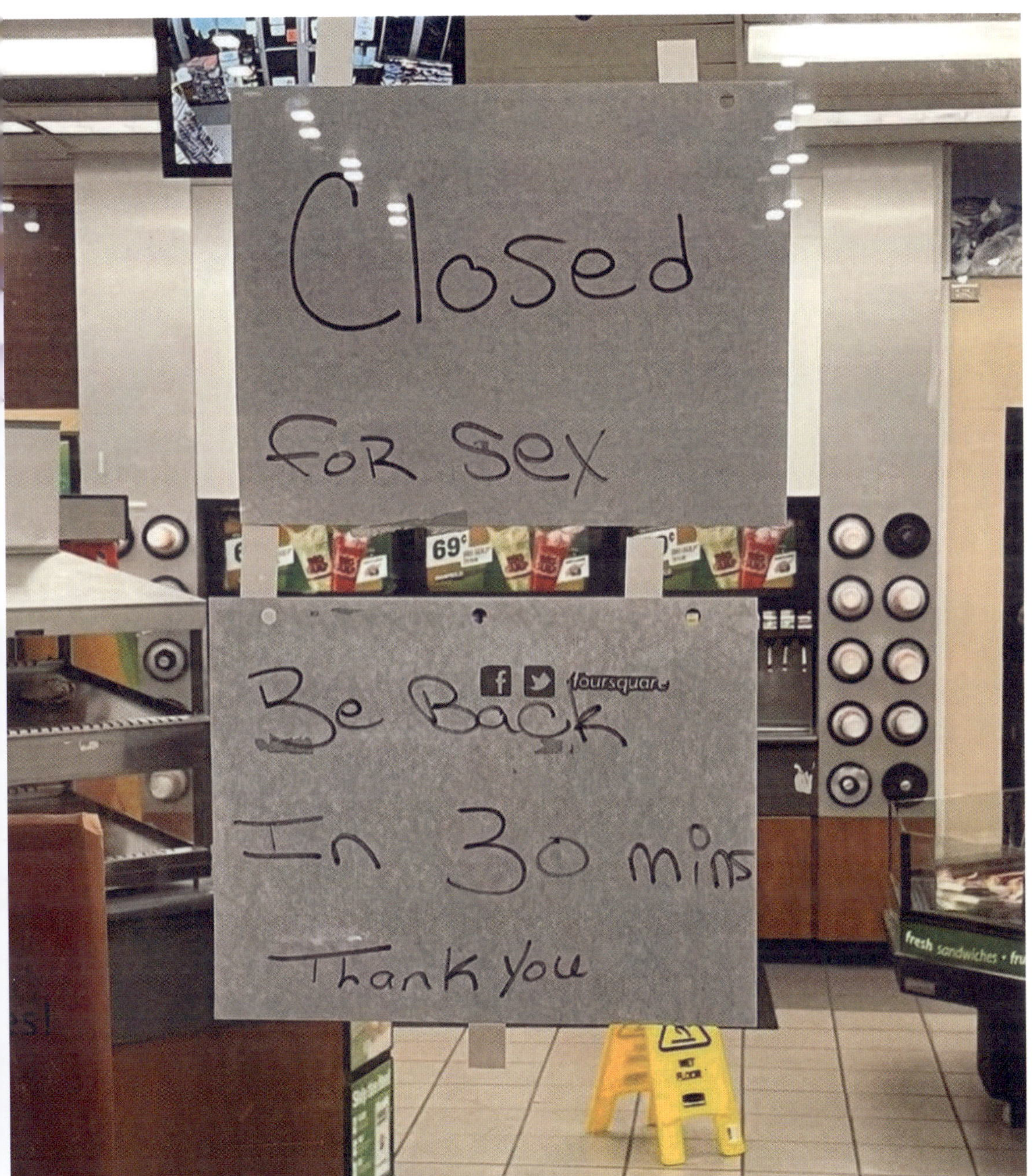

Rick McGuire.

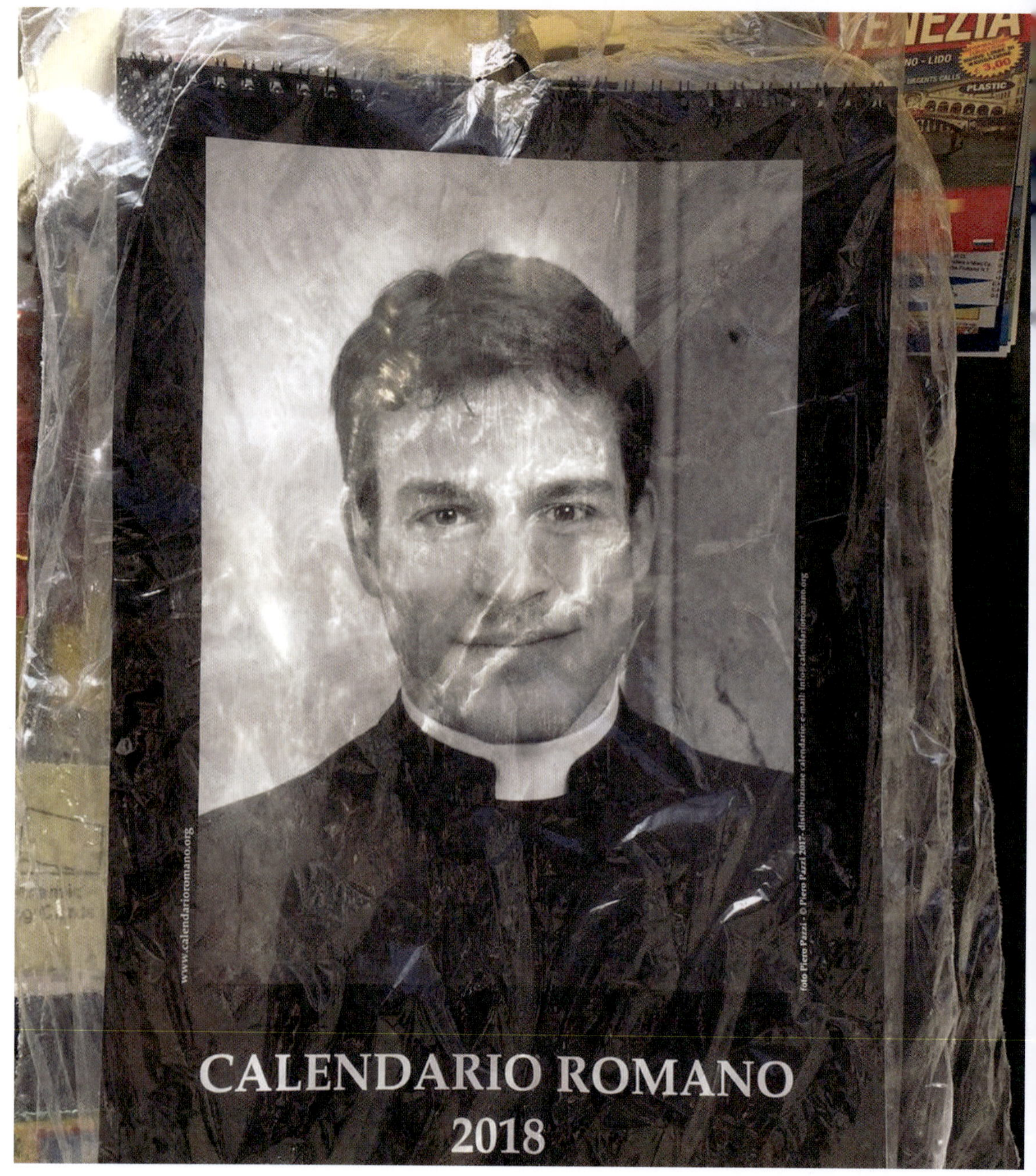

CALENDARIO ROMANO
2018
www.calendarioromano.org
foto Piero Pazzi - © Piero Pazzi 2017; distribuzione calendario; e-mail: info@calendarioromano.org

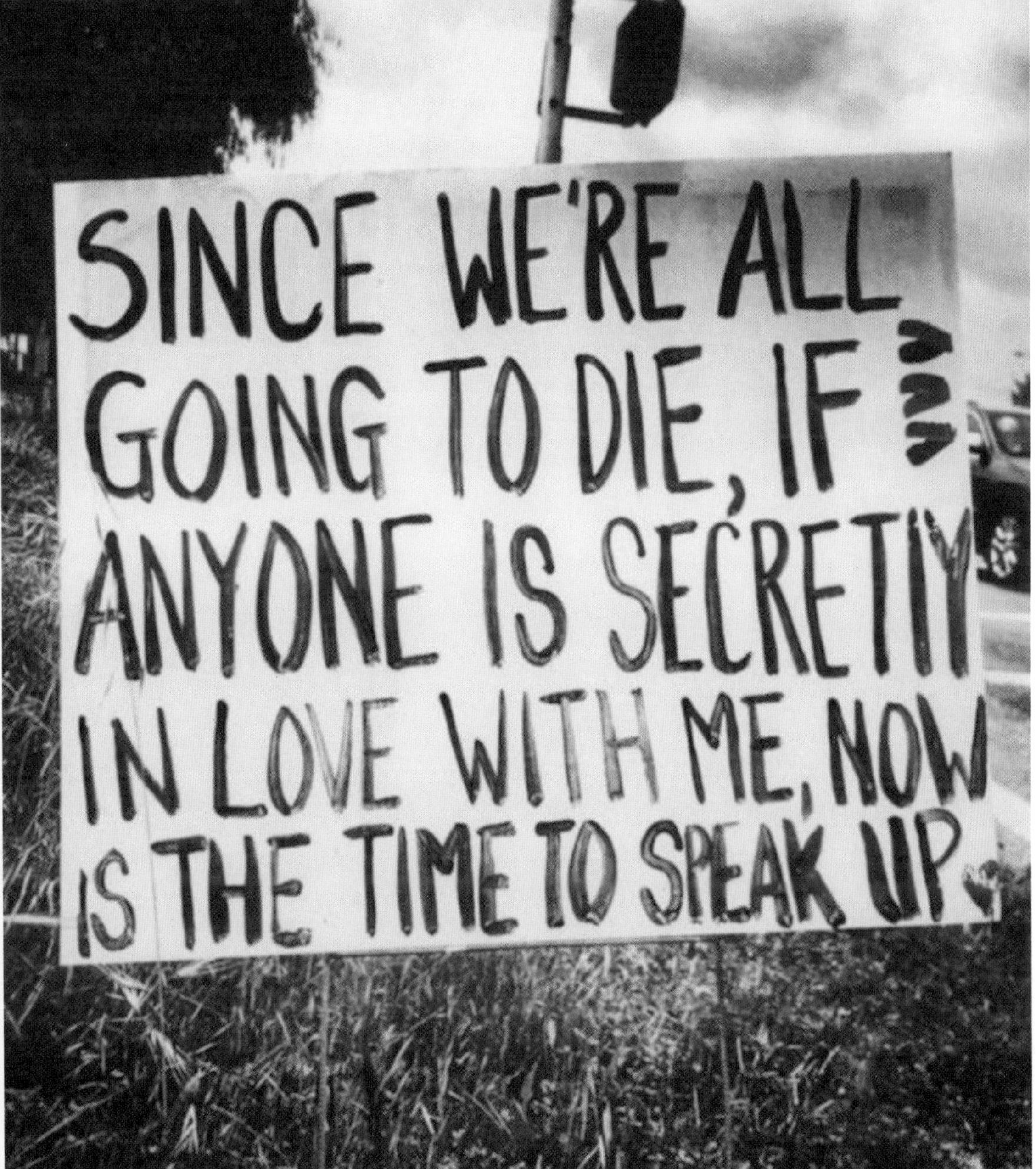

Keith McNally. (Unknown photographer)

They will all vanish at the same time, like the millions of images that lay behind the foreheads of the grandparents, dead for half a century, and of the parents, also dead. Images in which we appeared as a little girl in the midst of beings who died before we were born, just as in our own memories our small children are there next to our parents and schoolmates. And one day we'll appear in our children's memories, among their grandchildren and people not yet born. Like sexual desire, memory never stops. It pairs the dead with the living, real with imaginary beings, dreams with history".

Annie Ernaux, *The Years*, translated by Alison L. Strayer, 2008.

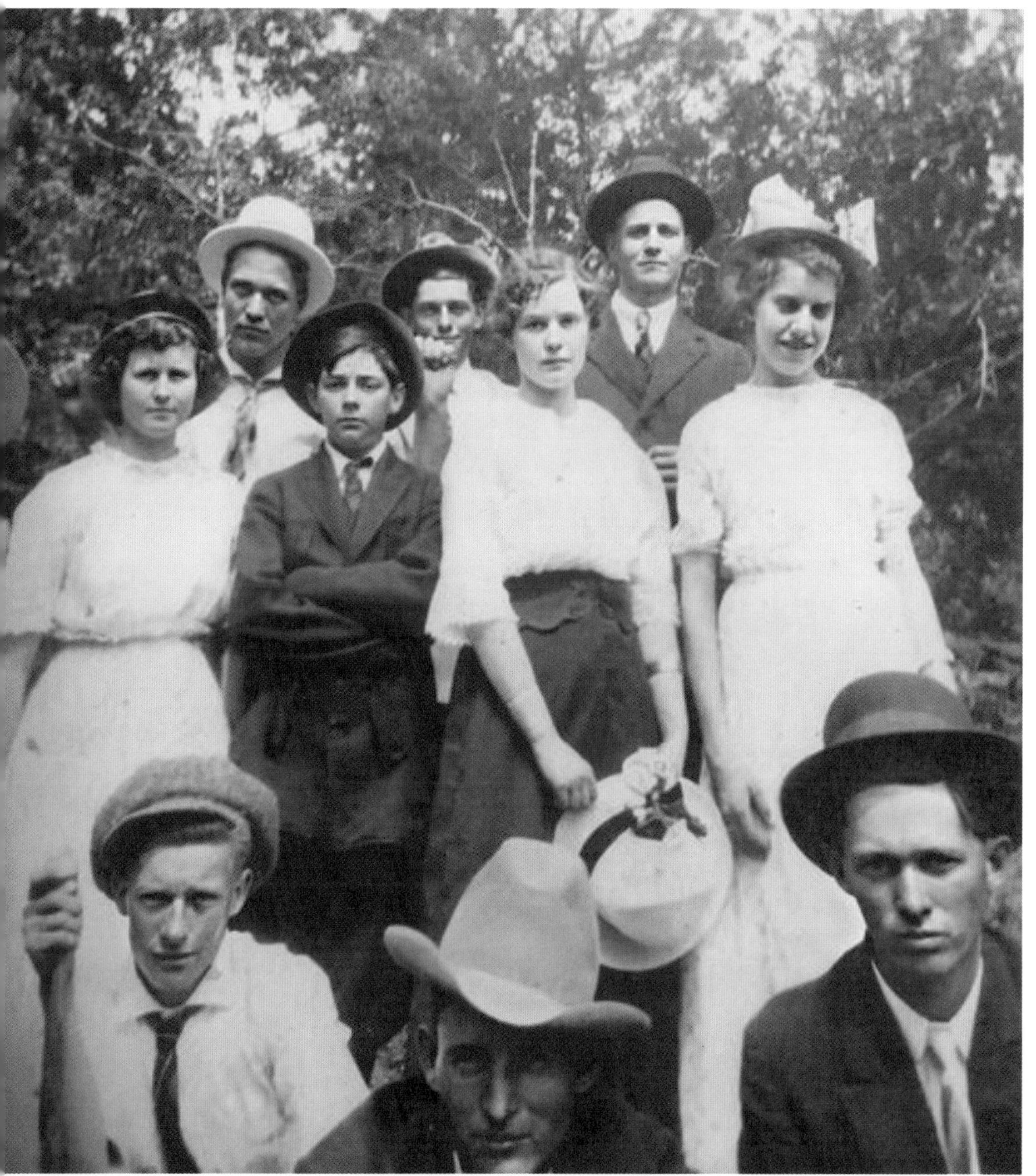

Clark and Booth family.

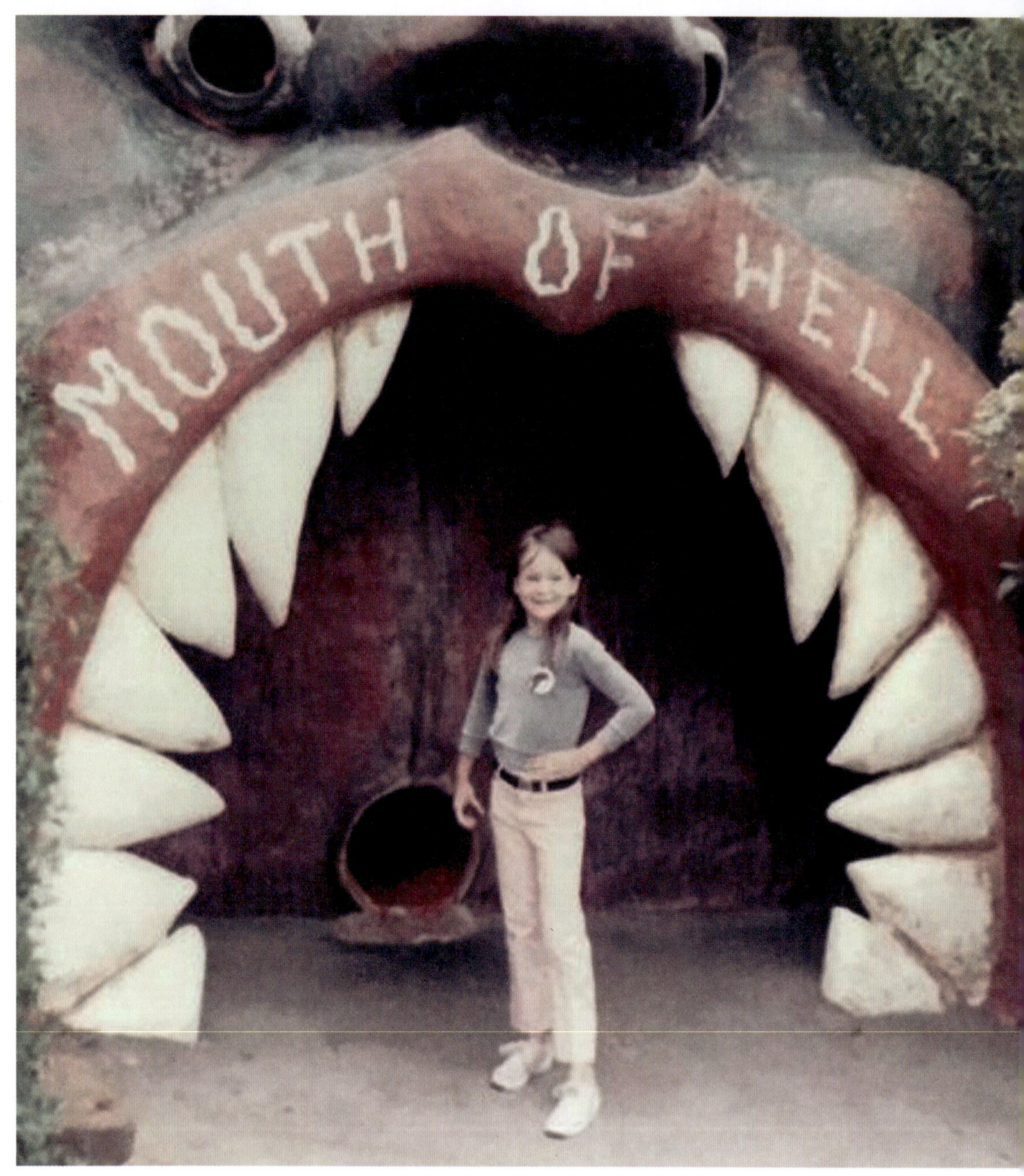

Olivia Laing: Peaked on the author pic in 1983.

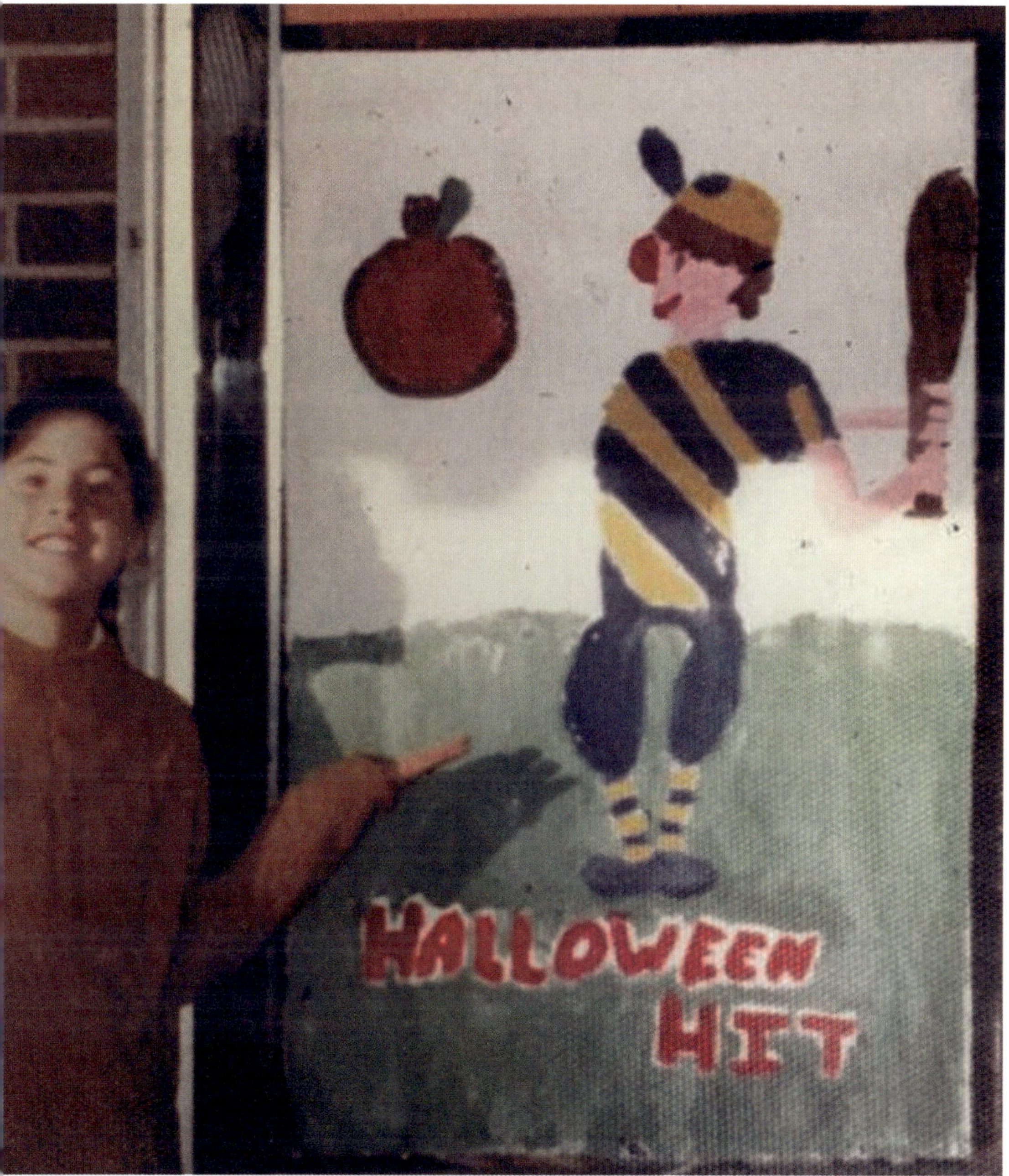

Nicole Eisenman: Early work.

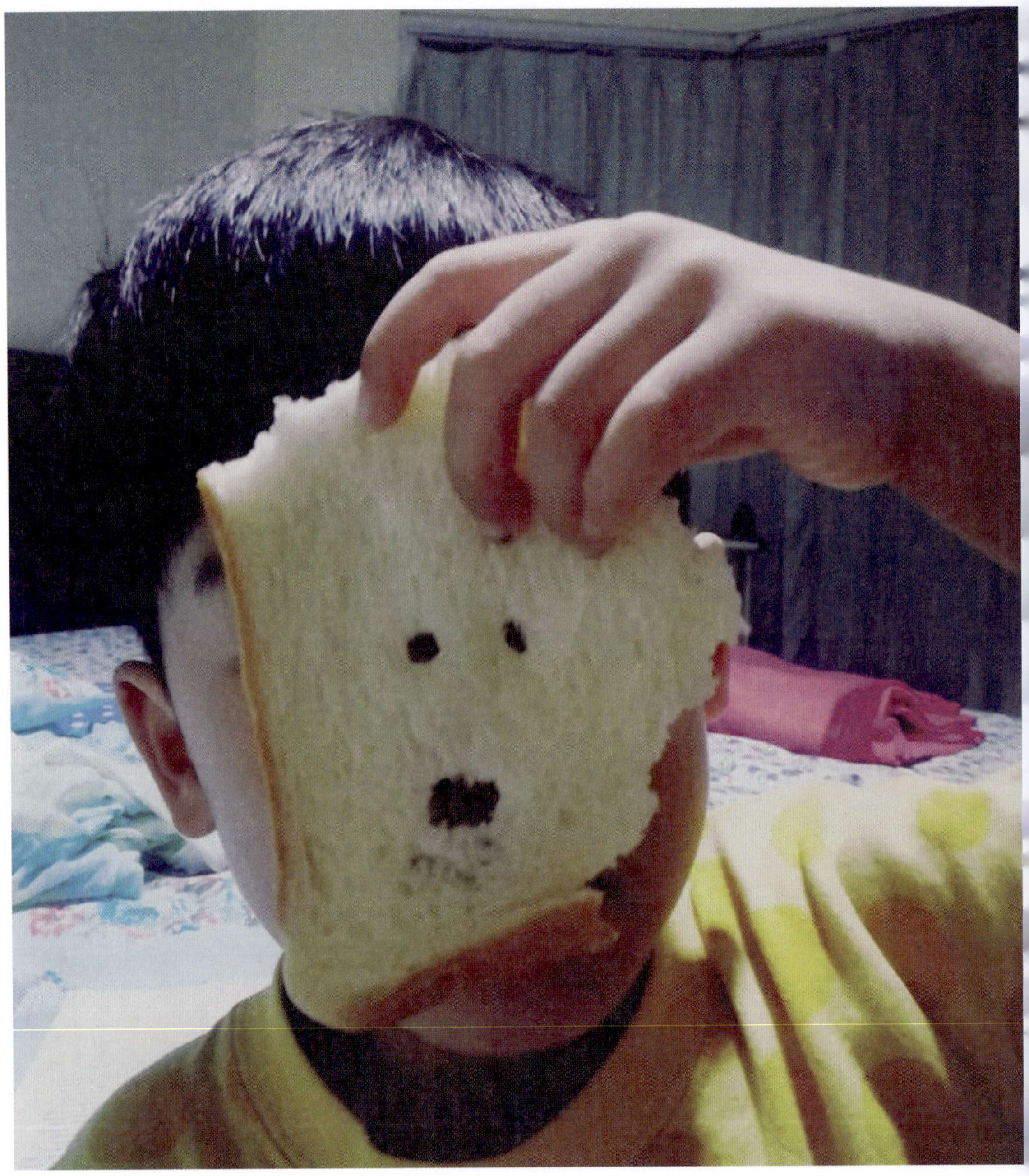

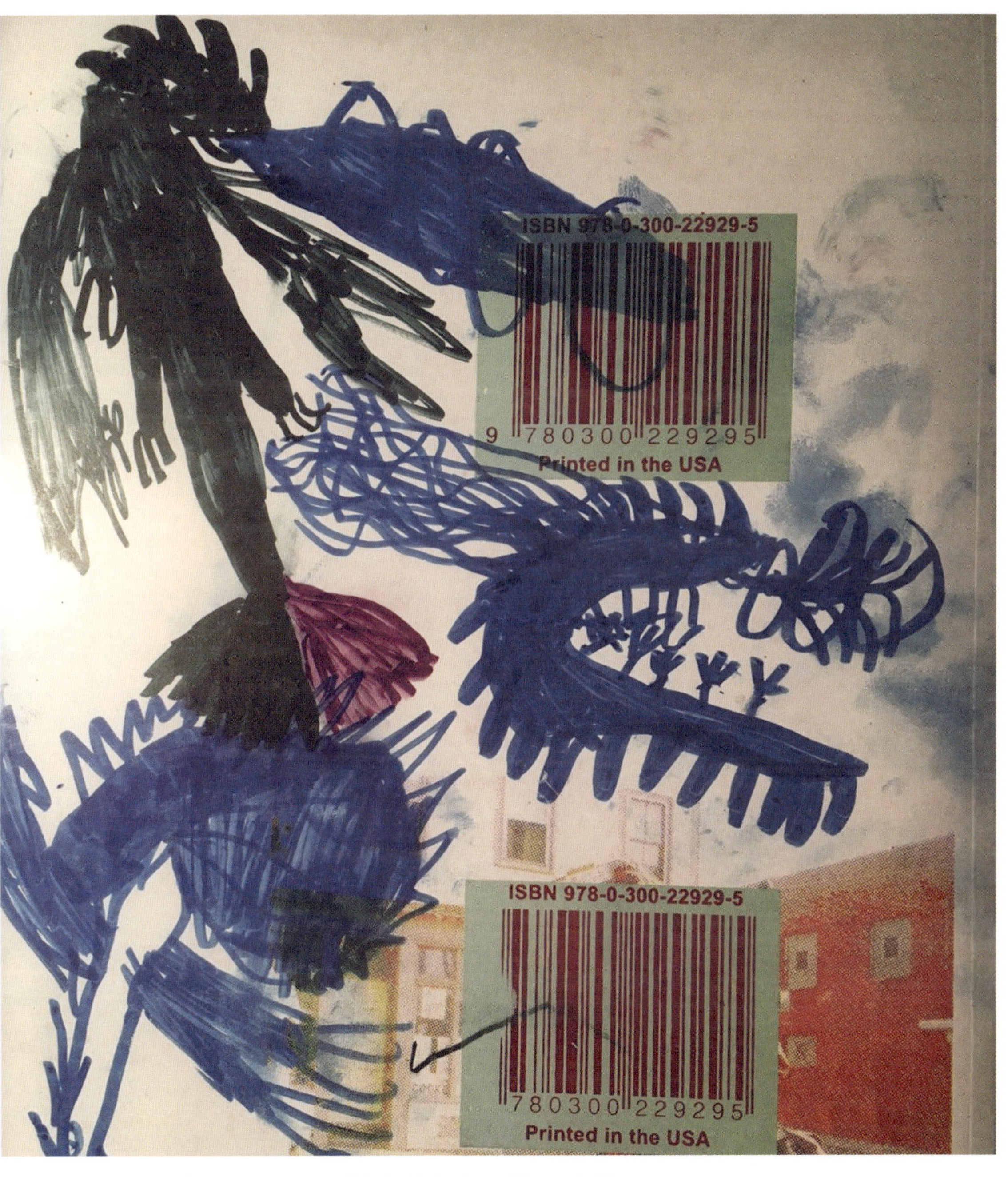

Joseph Grigely: The Laura Owens catalogue embellished with drawings of dragons by Girma.

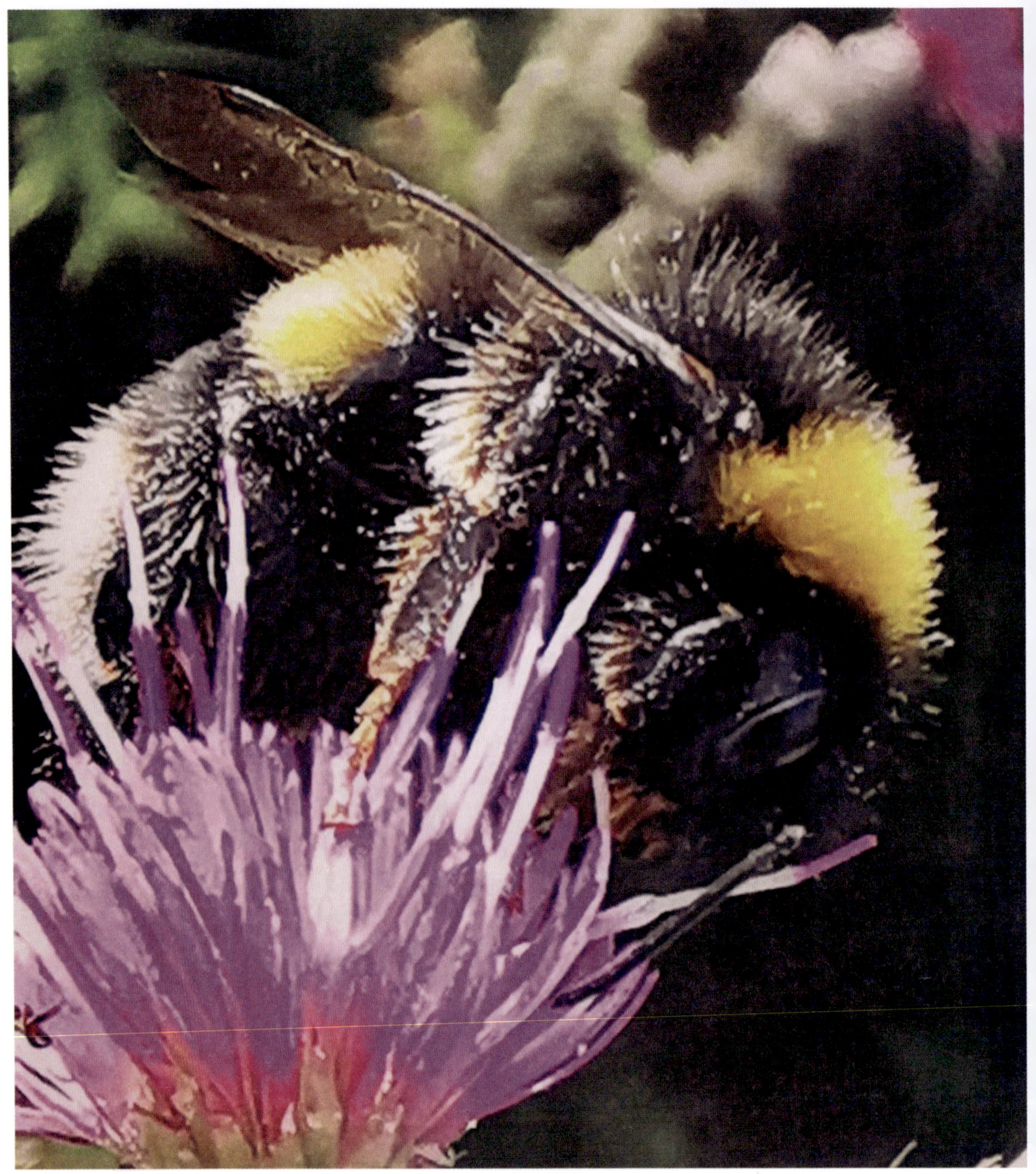

Chad Wollen.

In a world myriad as ours, the gaze is a singular act: to look at something is to fill your whole life with it, if only briefly.

Ocean Vuong, *On Earth We're Briefly Gorgeous*, 2019.

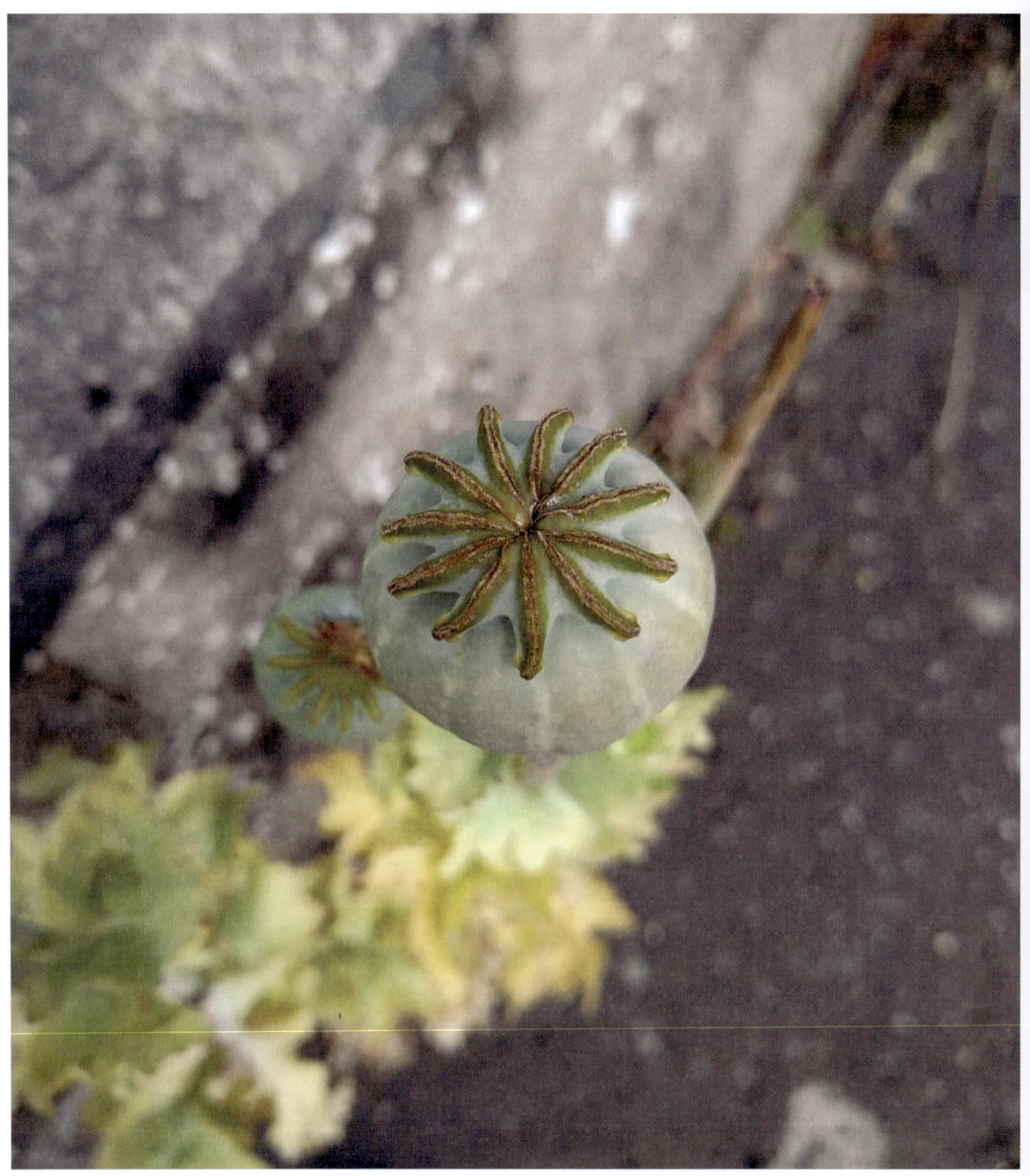

Henry Noltie, *Papaver somniferum.*

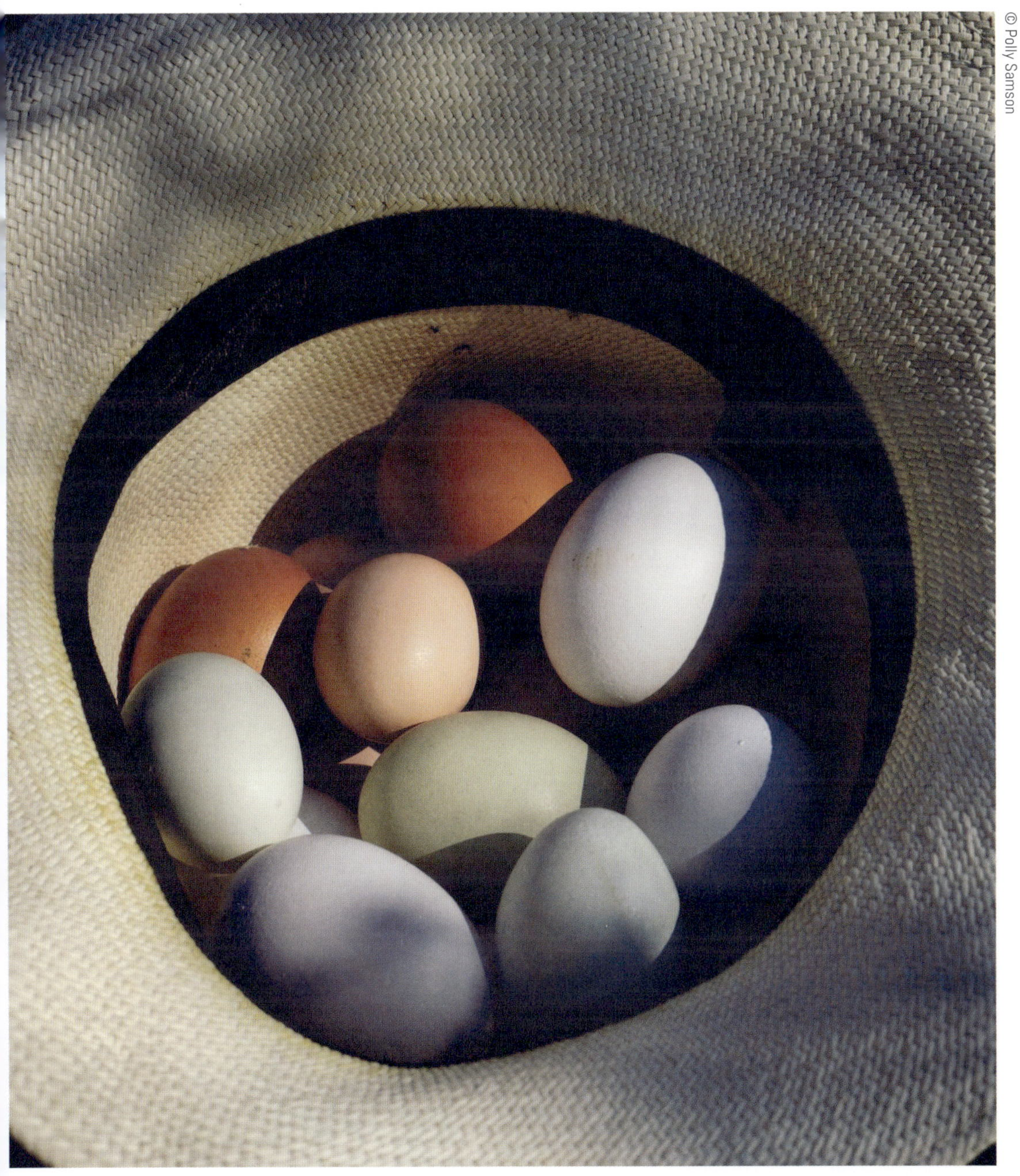

Polly Samson.

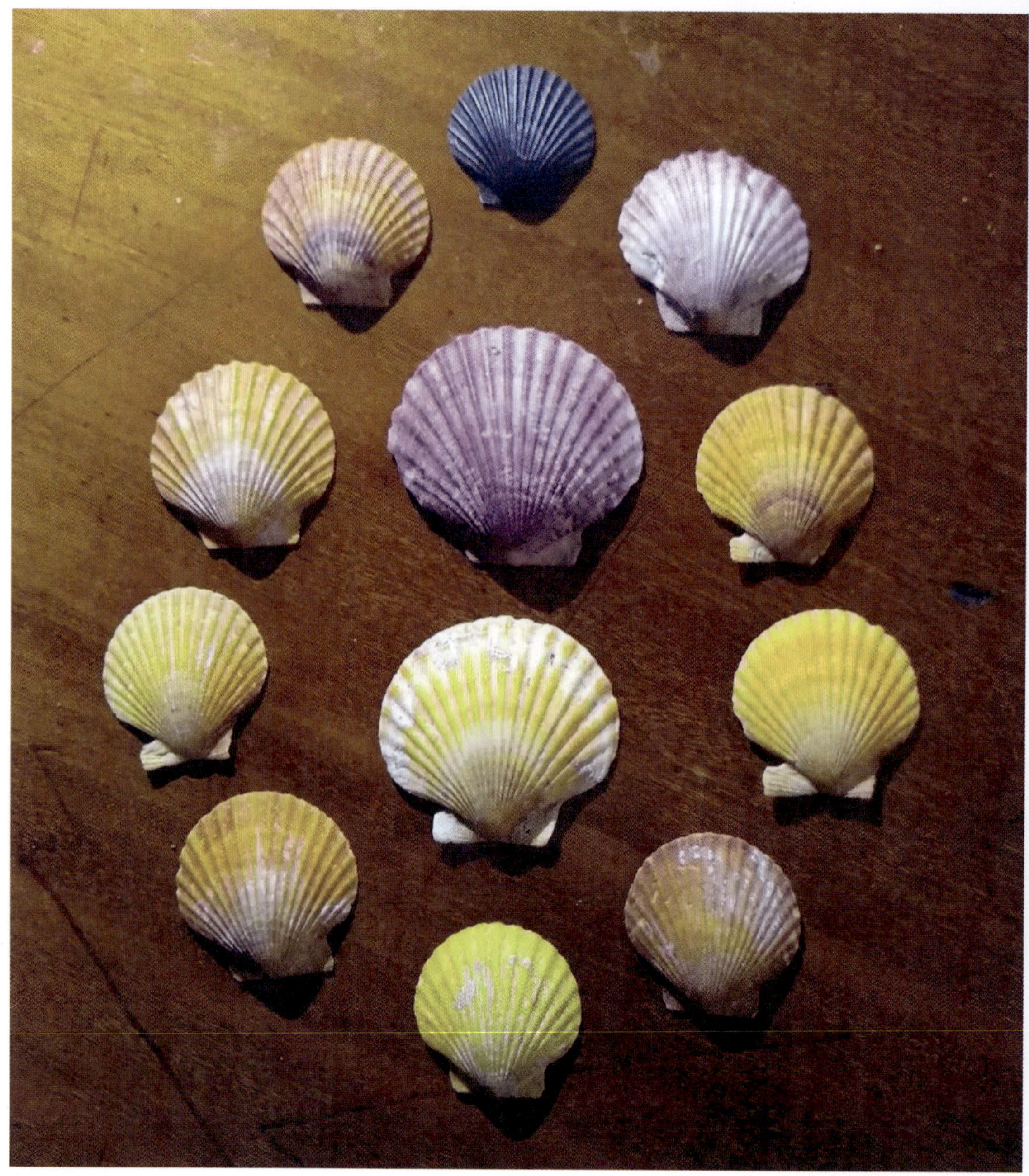

Henry Noltie.

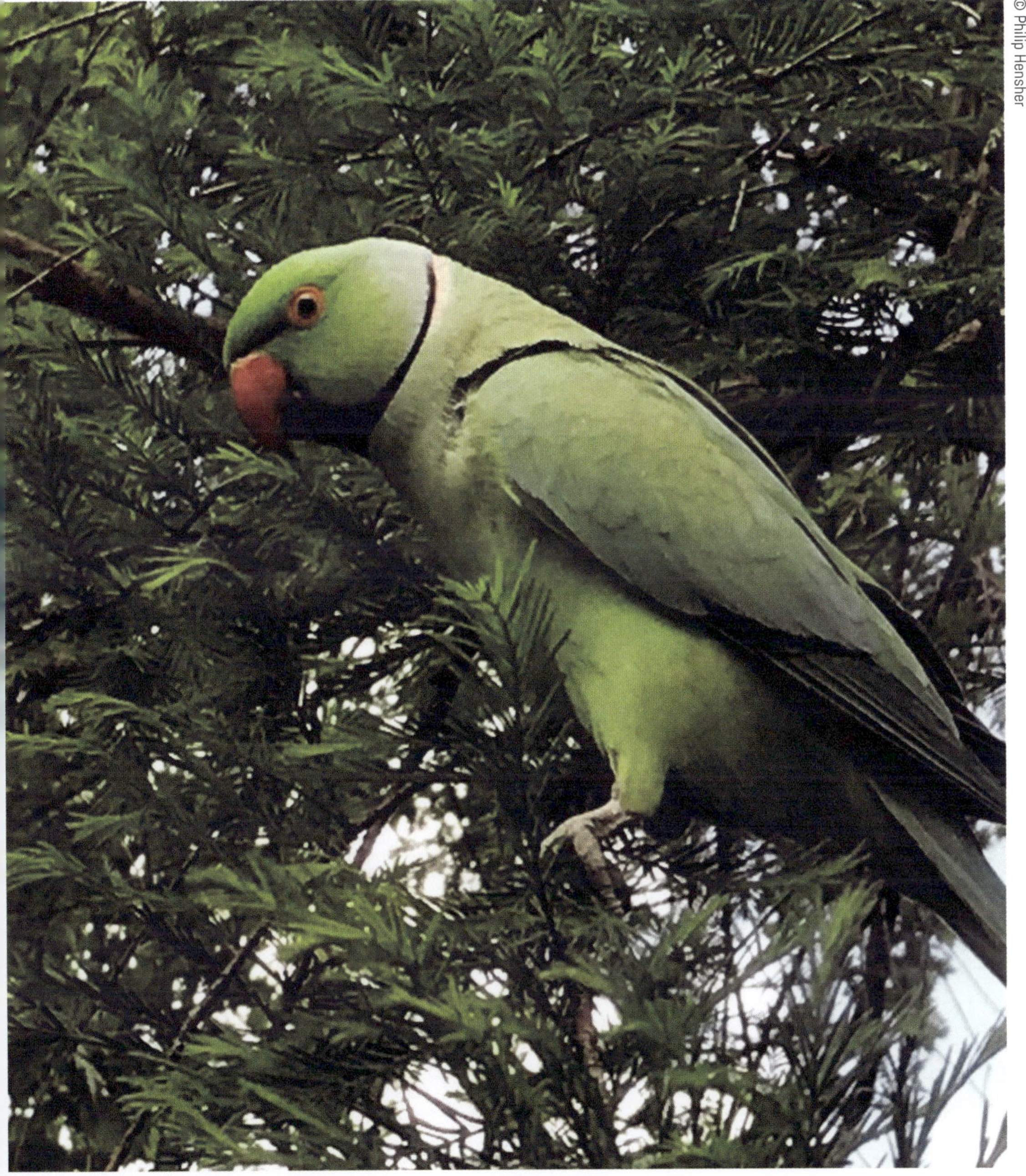

Philip Hensher: These newish additions to the London stock of birds, the ring-necked parakeet.

Standing there on the embankment, staring into the current, I realized that —
in spite of all the risks involved — a thing in motion will always be better than
a thing at rest; that change will always be a nobler thing than permanence; that
that which is static will degenerate and decay, turn to ash, while that which is
in motion is able to last for all eternity.

Olga Tokarczuk, *Flights*, translated by Jennifer Croft, 2007.

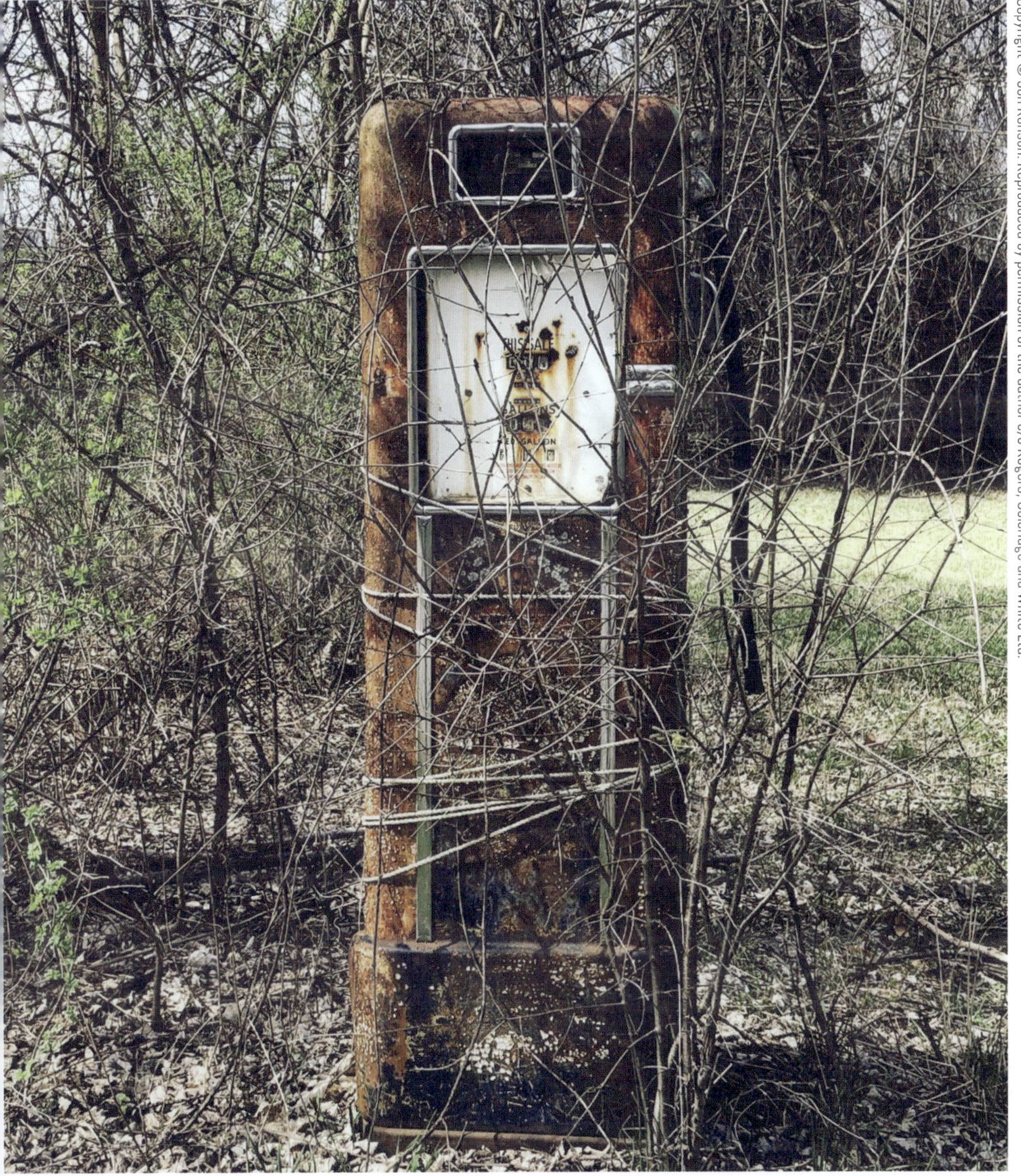

Jon Ronson.

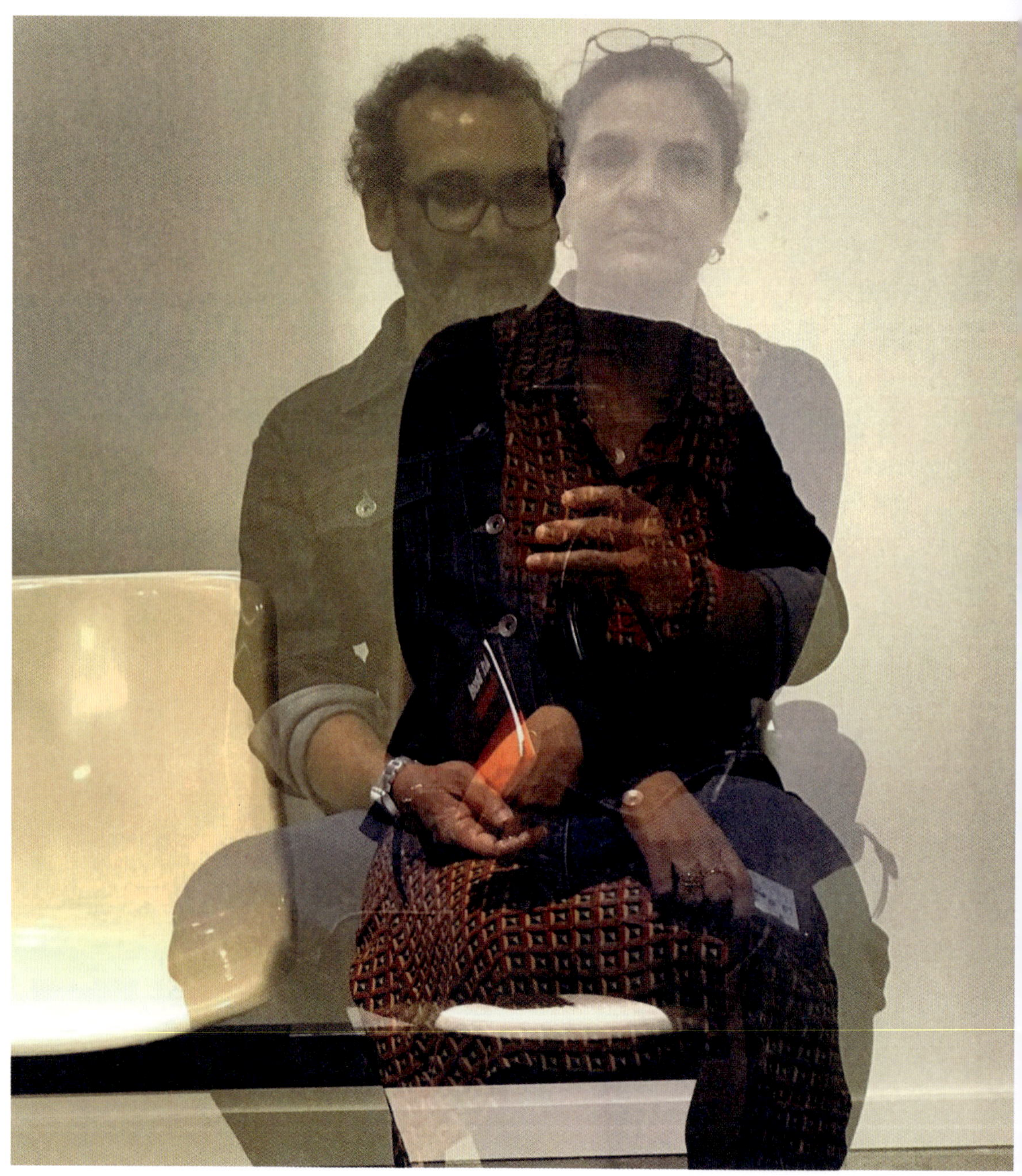

Subodh Gupta: Self portrait.

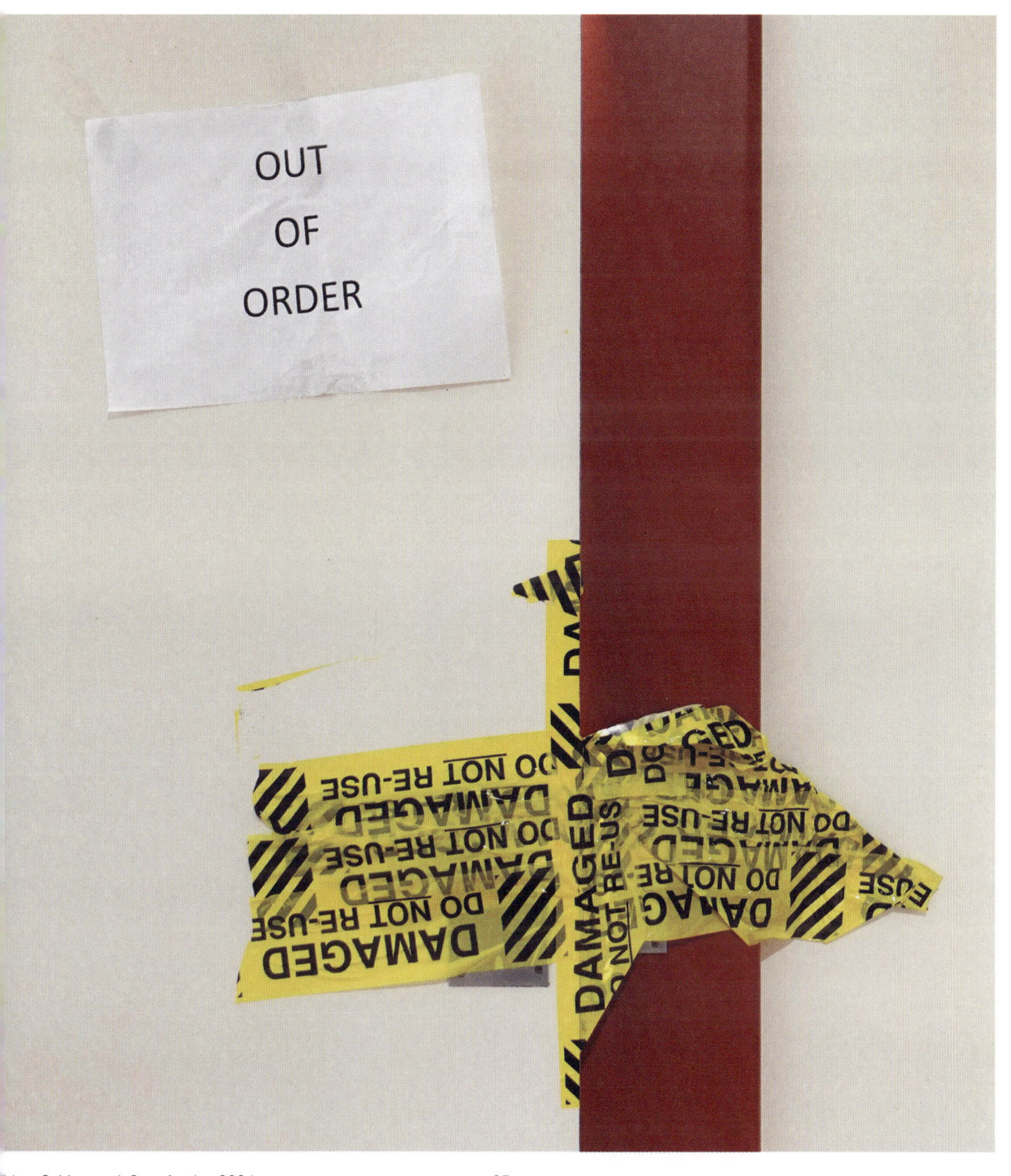

Matt Calderwood: Out of order, 2024.

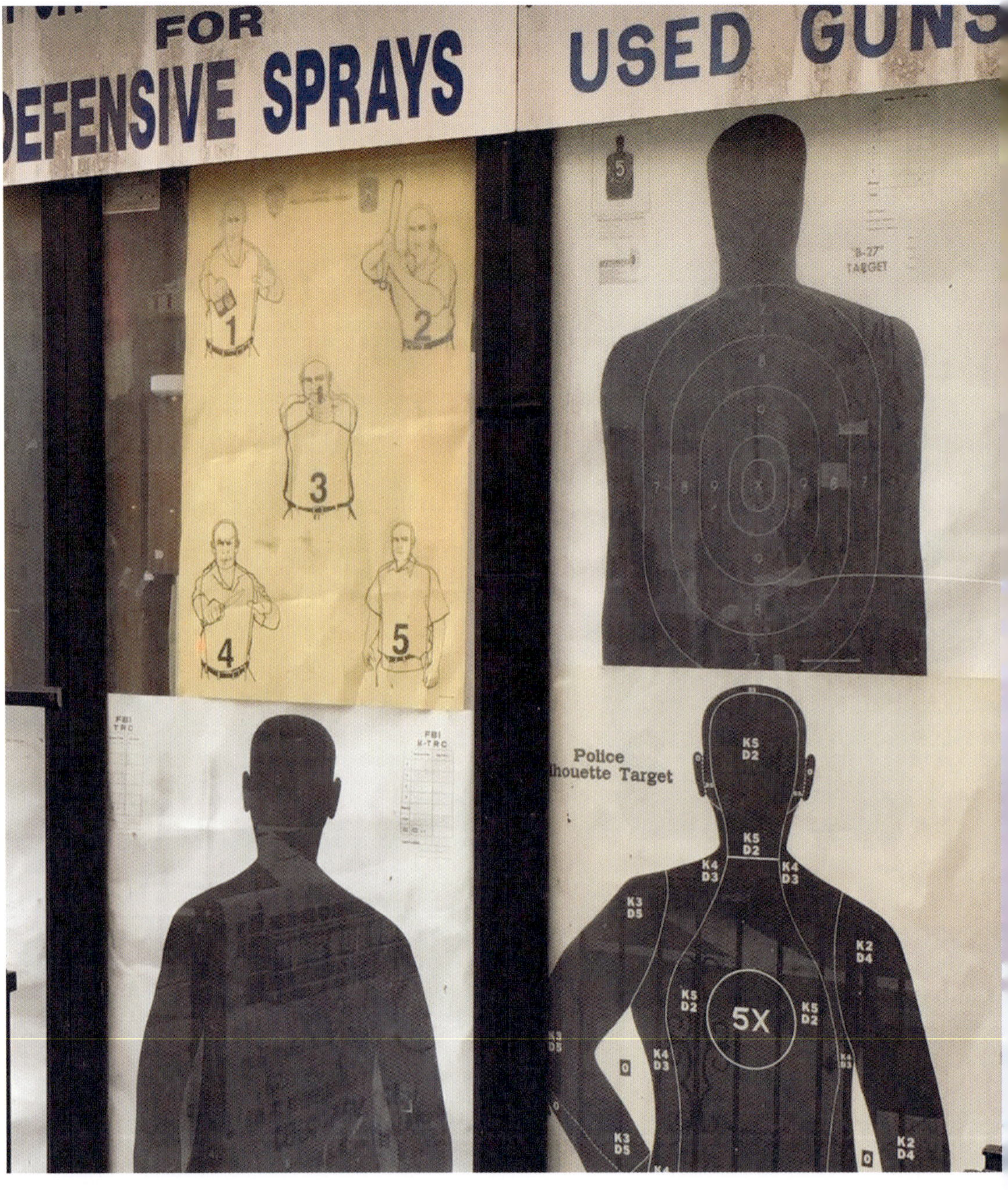

Hurvin Anderson: Gun store in New York.

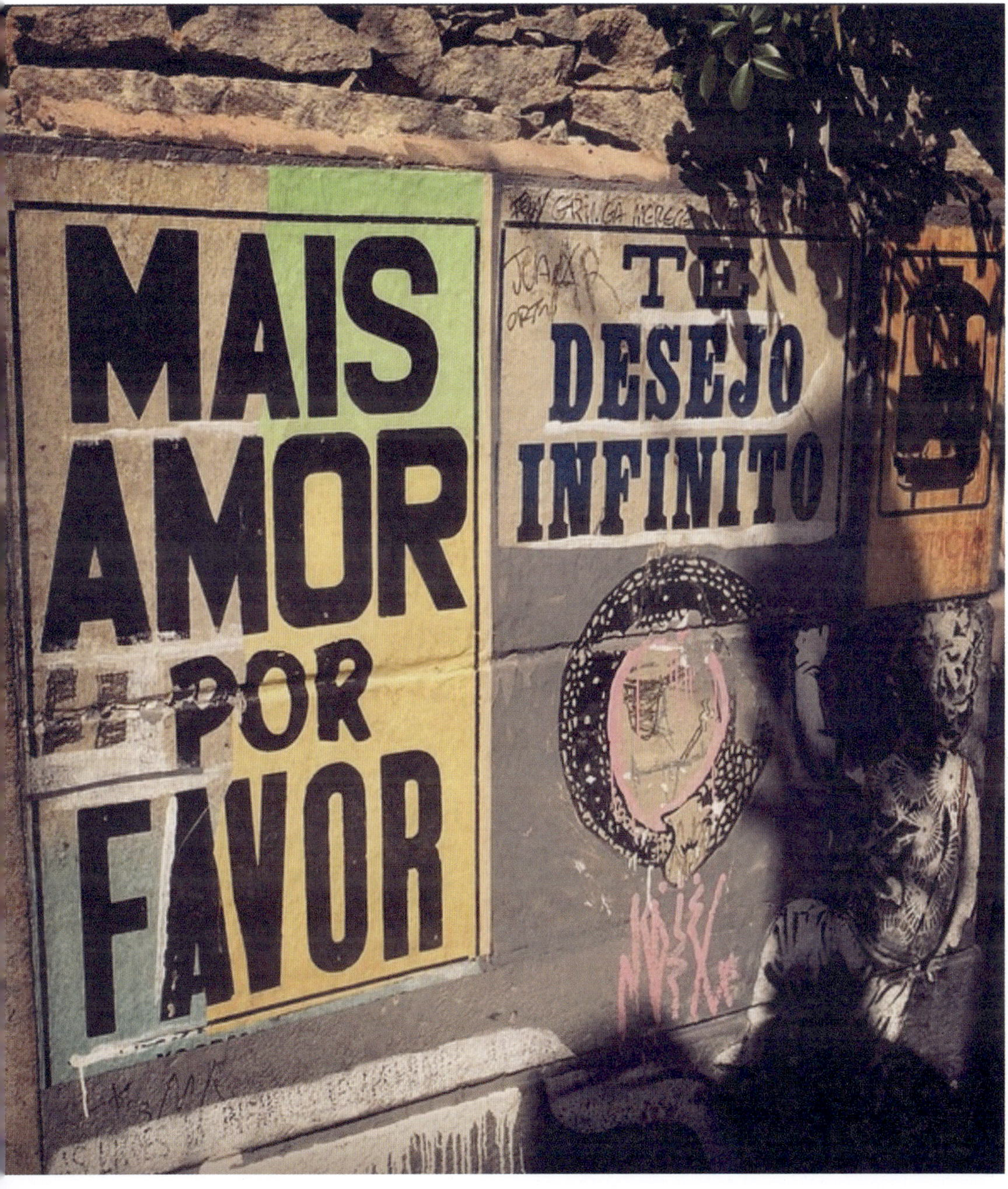

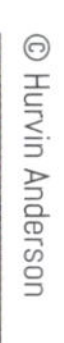

Hurvin Anderson: More Love Please, Rio de Janeiro.

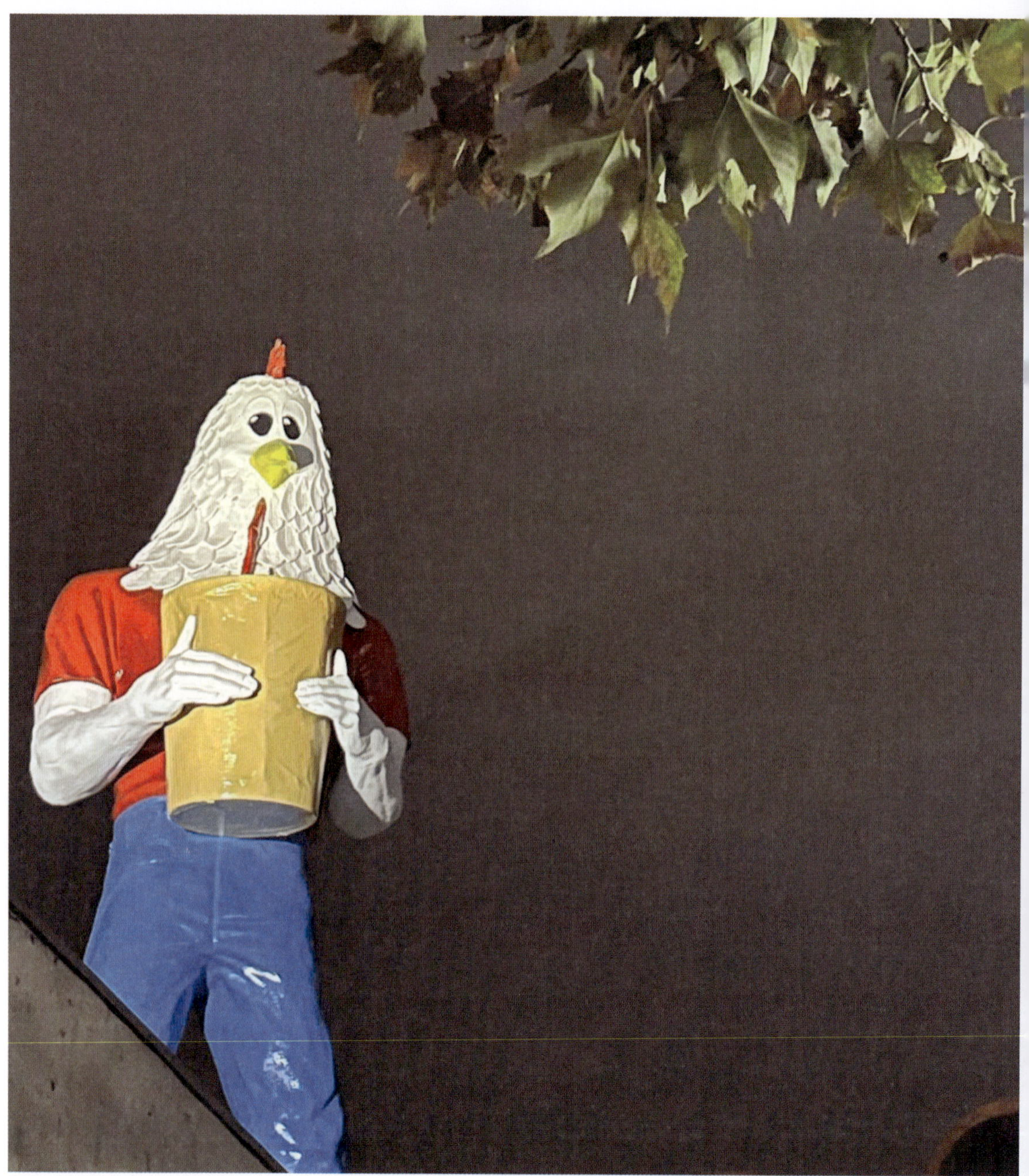

Kamila Shamsie: Oh, hello Mr Chicken Man.   98

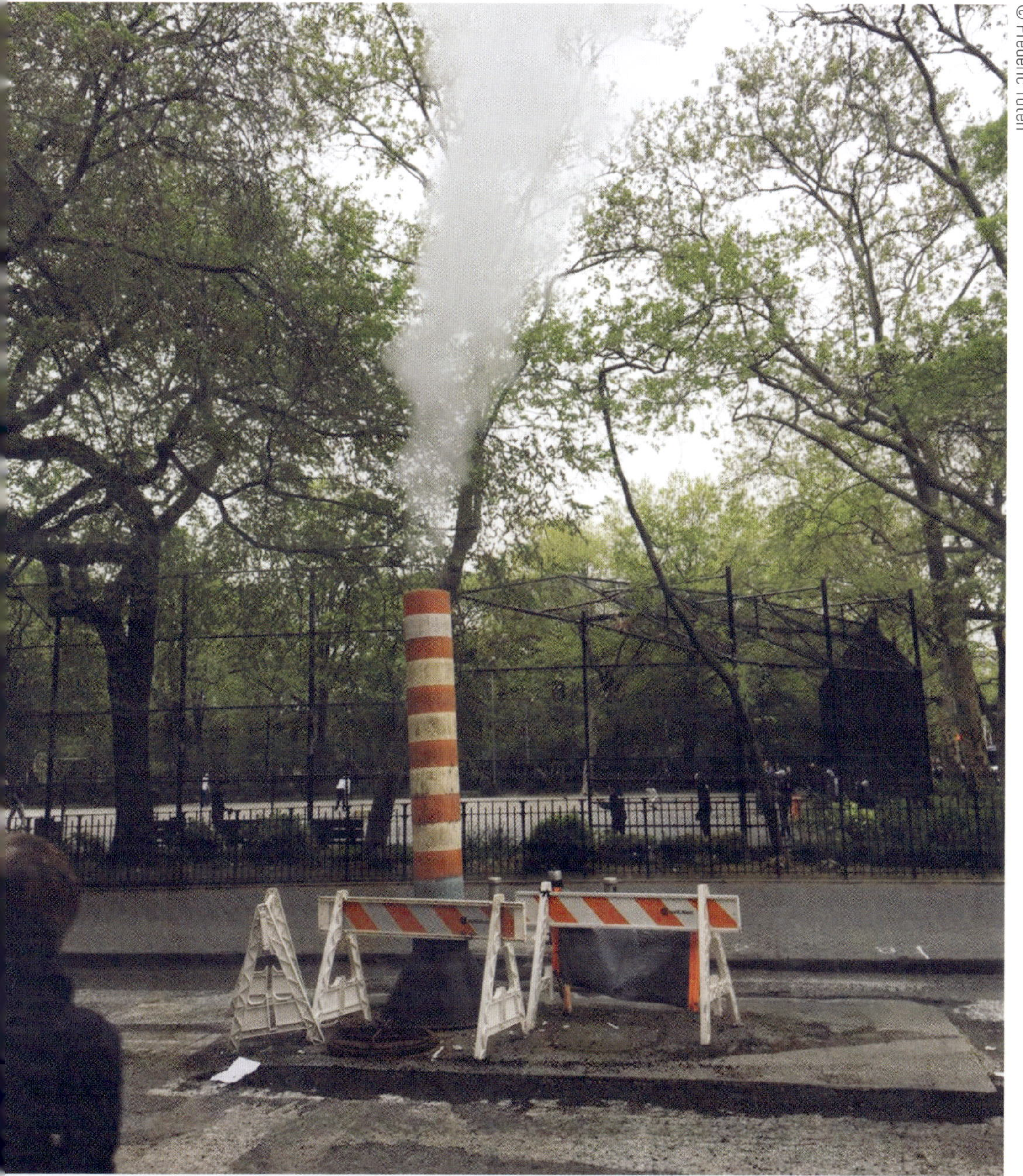

Frederic Tuten: Found sculpture, Tompkins Square Park.

One reason that extremists think the world is out to get them is that the world really is out to get them.

David Runciman, "Dealing with Extremism", in *Extremes*, edited by Duncan Needham and Julius Weitzdörfer, 2019.

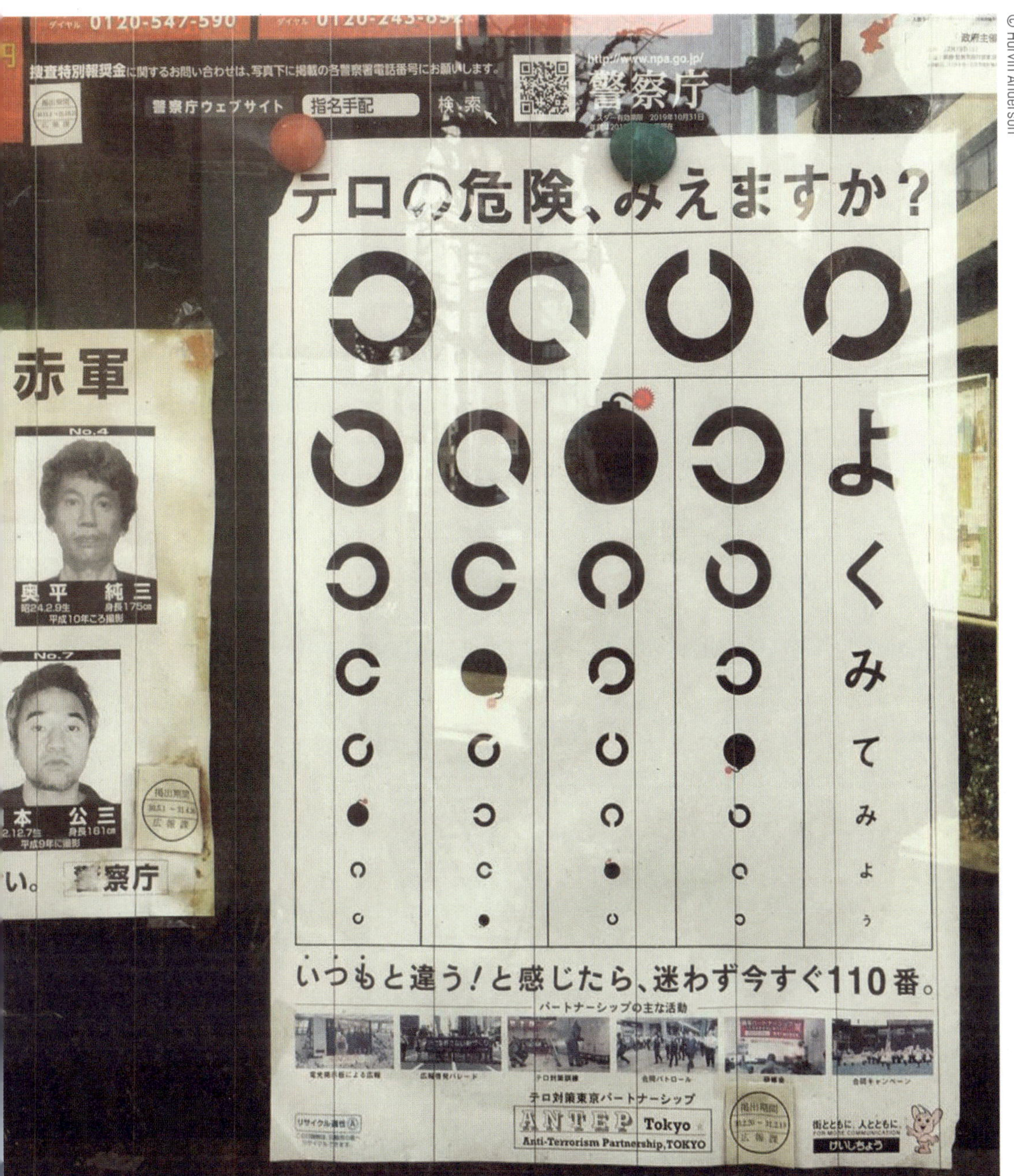

Hurvin Anderson: Terrorism vigilance poster, Tokyo.

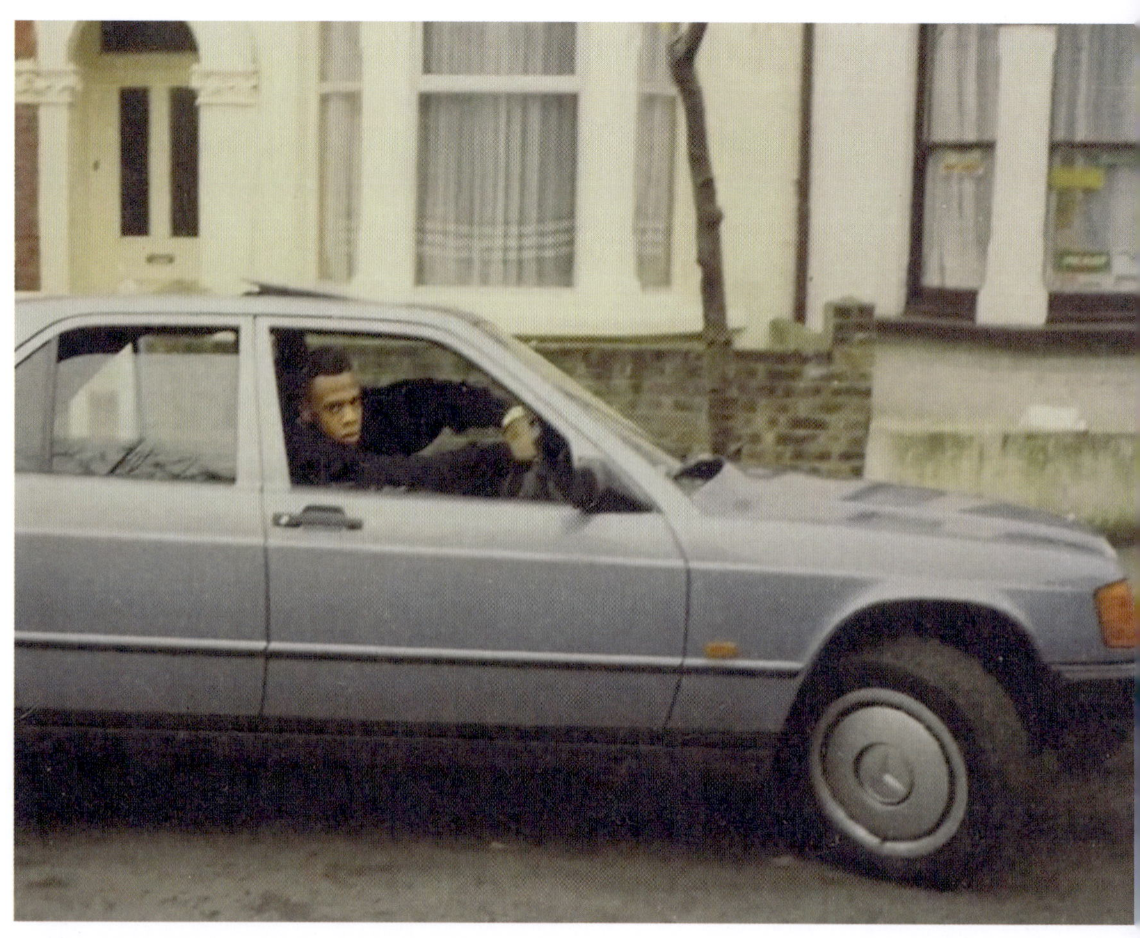

Ekow Eshun: Jay-Z in Willesden, London, 1989. (Unknown photographer.)

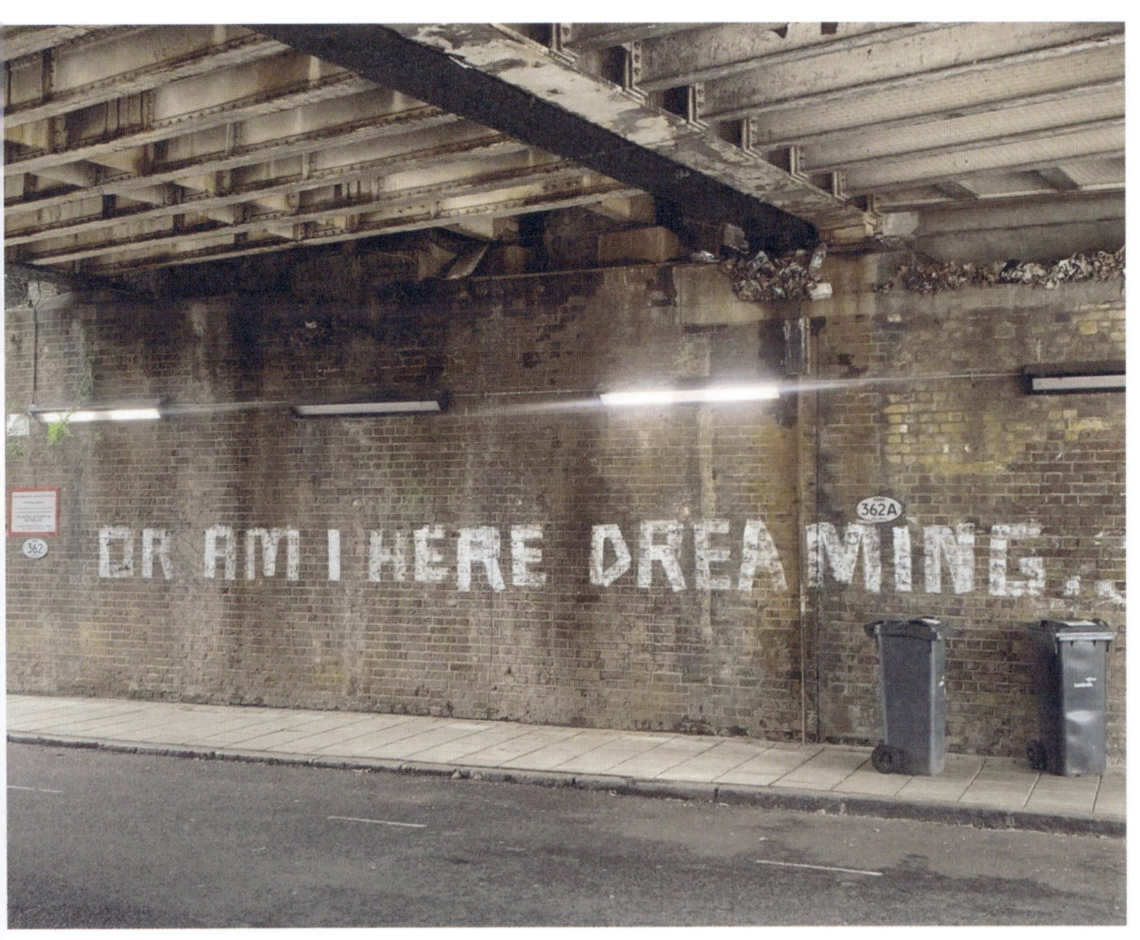

Jools Holland.

Whereas until the 1990s one could (provided that one profited from it) associate the horizon of modernization with the notions of progress, emancipation, wealth, comfort, even luxury, and above all rationality, the rage to deregulate, the explosion of inequalities, the abandonment of solidarities have gradually associated that horizon with the notion of an arbitrary decision out of nowhere in favour of the sole profit of the few. The best of worlds has become the worst.

Bruno Latour, *Down to Earth: Politics in the New Climatic Regime*, 2018.

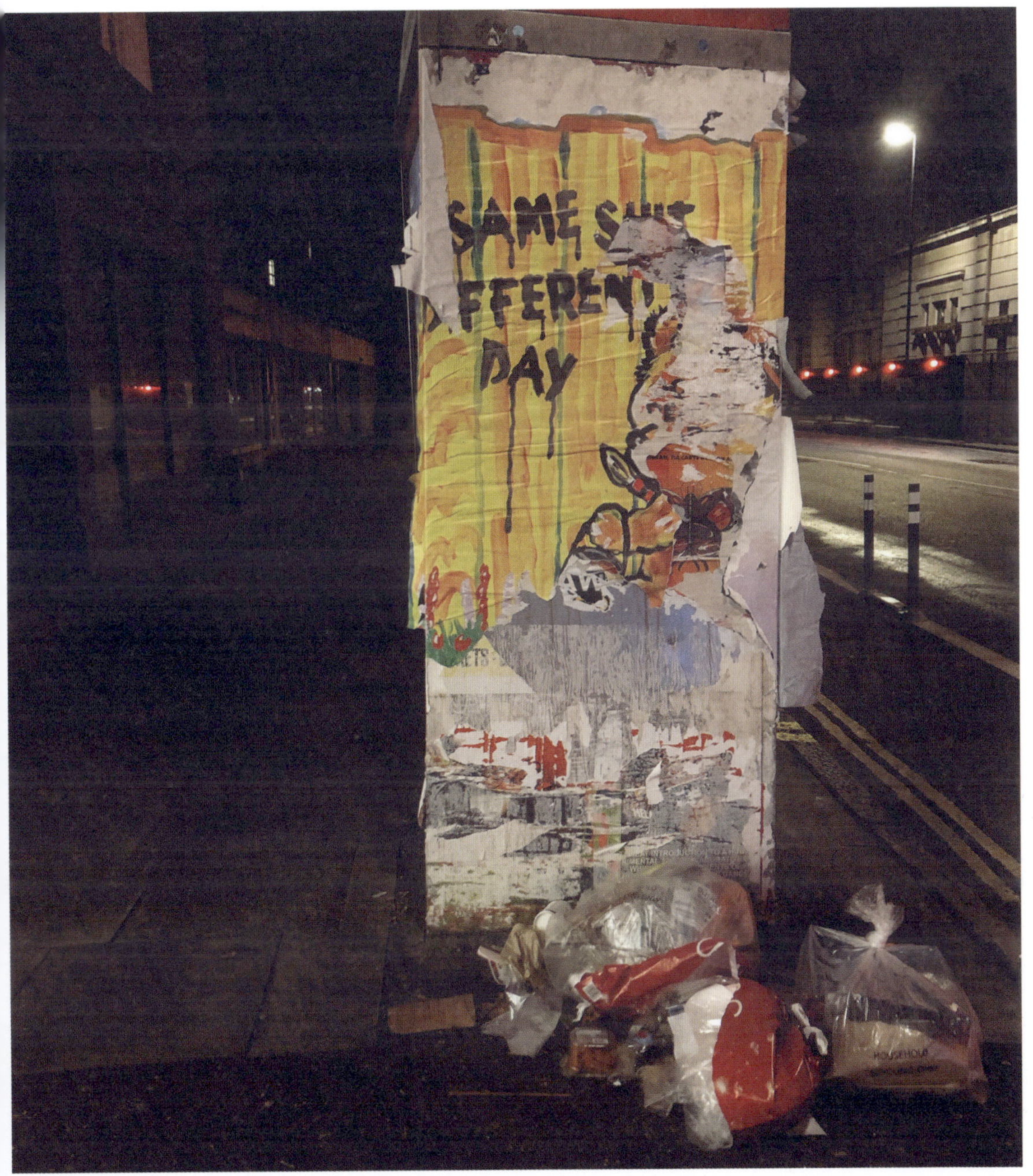
SAME SHIT
FFERENT
DAY

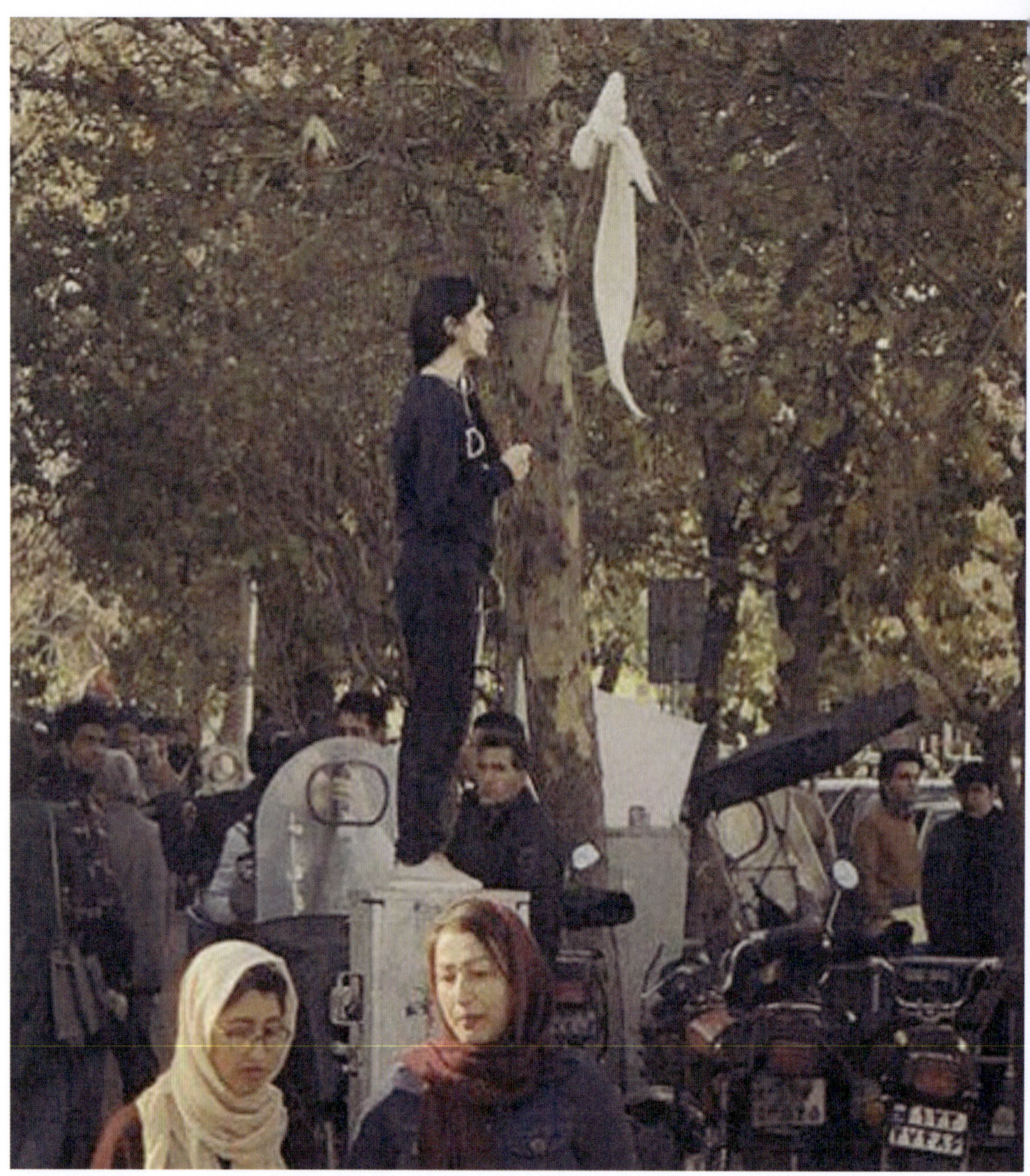

Shirin Neshat: Another fearless Iranian woman pushing the regime's tolerance by unveiling in public, her scarf hanging in the tree. Apparently she was later arrested. (Unknown photographer.)

I say all this because hope is not like a lottery ticket you can sit on the sofa and clutch, feeling lucky. I say it because hope is an axe you break down doors with in an emergency; because hope should shove you out the door, because it will take everything you have to steer the future away from endless war, from the annihilation of the earth's treasures and the grinding down of the poor and marginal. Hope just means another world might be possible, not promised, not guaranteed. Hope calls for action; action is impossible without hope. At the beginning of his massive 1930s treatise on hope, the German philosopher Ernst Bloch wrote, "The work of this emotion requires people who throw themselves actively into what is becoming, to which they themselves belong." To hope is to give yourself to the future, and that commitment to the future makes the present inhabitable.

Rebecca Solnit, *Hope in the Dark: Untold Histories, Wild Possibilities*, 2004.

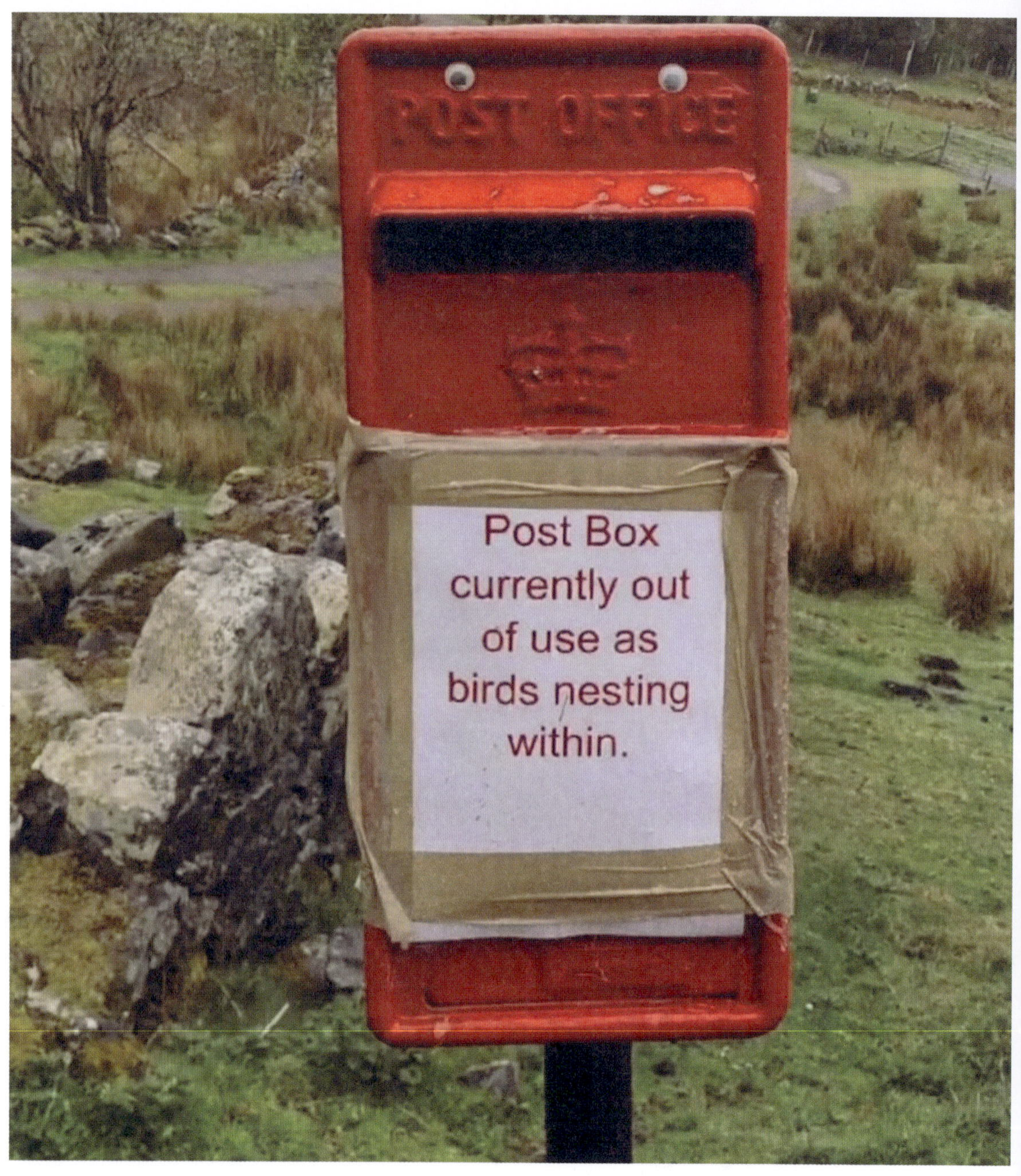

Nikki Renshaw. (Unknown photographer.)

4: GAZING

My mom and me, Newkirk Plaza, Brooklyn, 1958. Buy tokens at YOUR leisure.

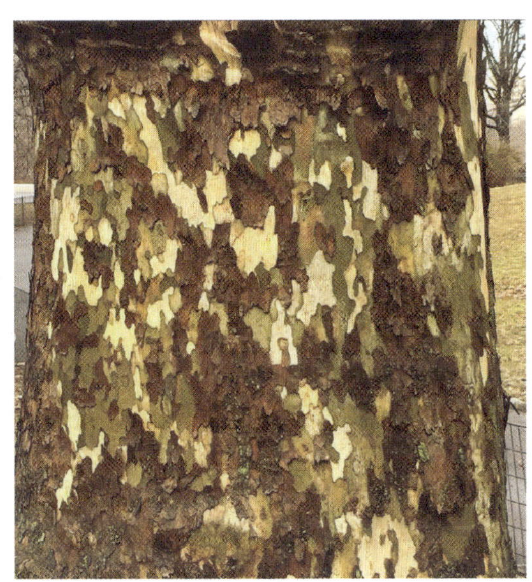

Two examples of tree camouflage in Central Park. Didn't work.

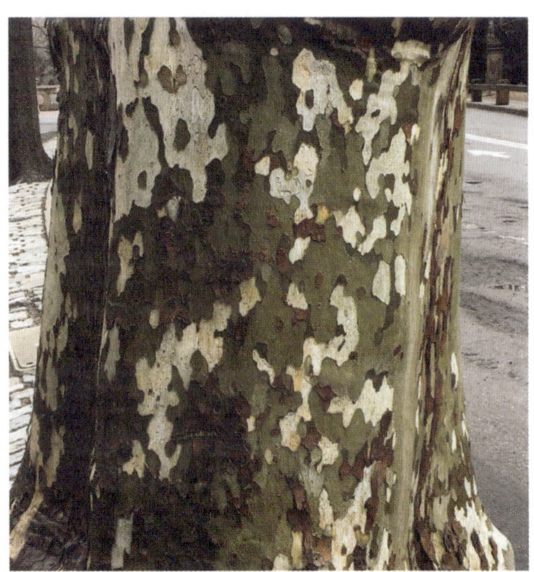

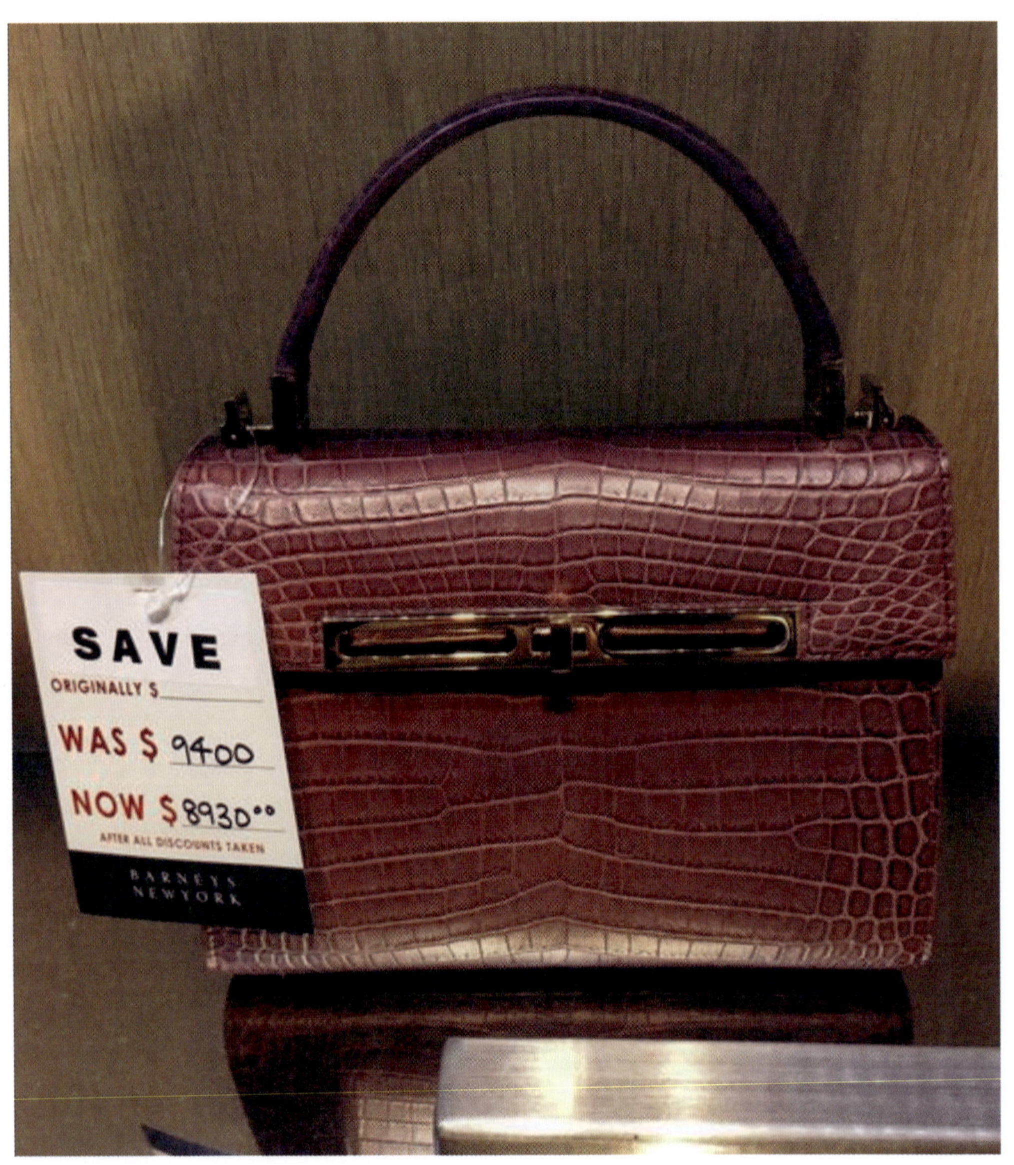

Now on sale at Barneys Mad Ave. Hurry!

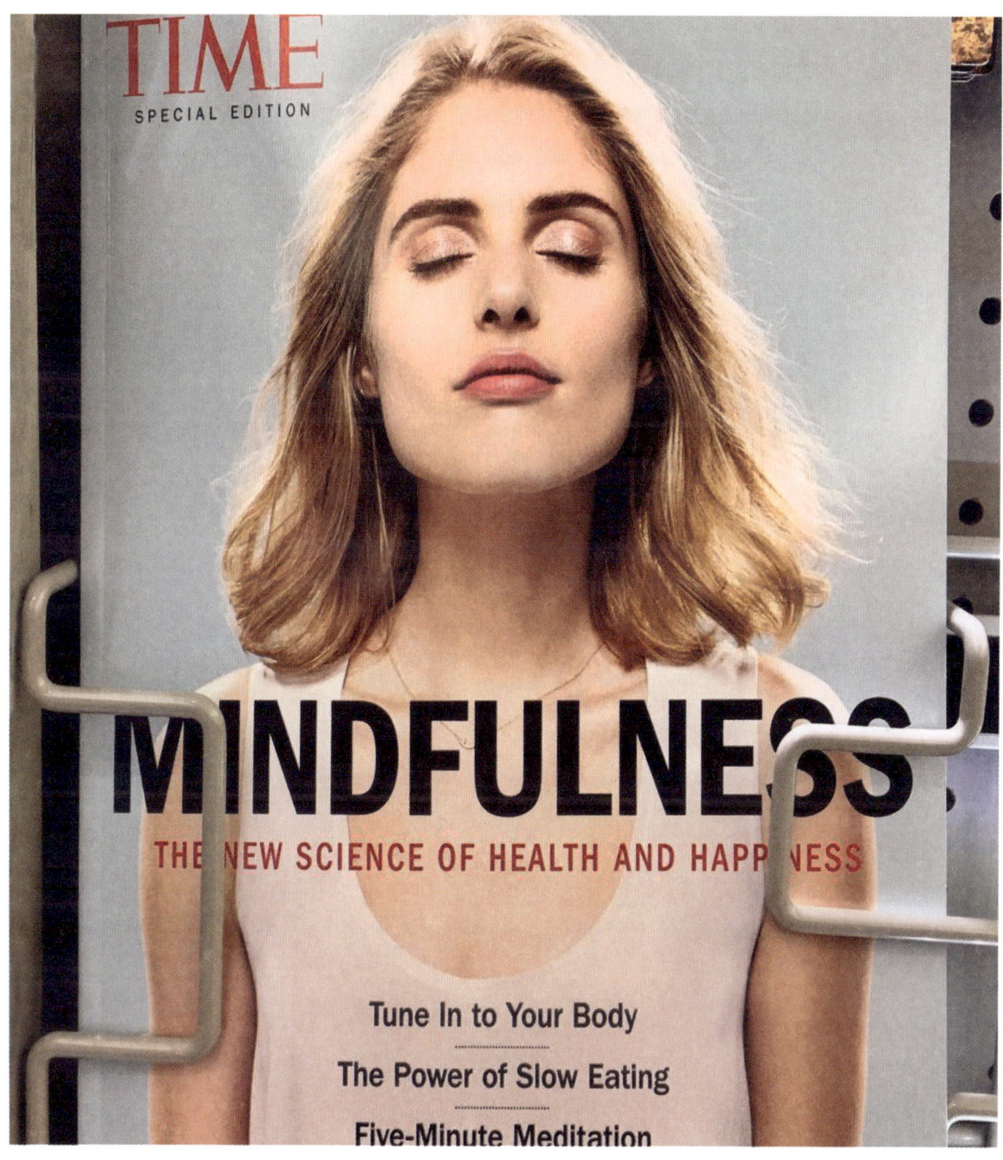
TIME
SPECIAL EDITION
MINDFULNESS
THE NEW SCIENCE OF HEALTH AND HAPPINESS
Tune In to Your Body
The Power of Slow Eating
Five-Minute Meditation

No.

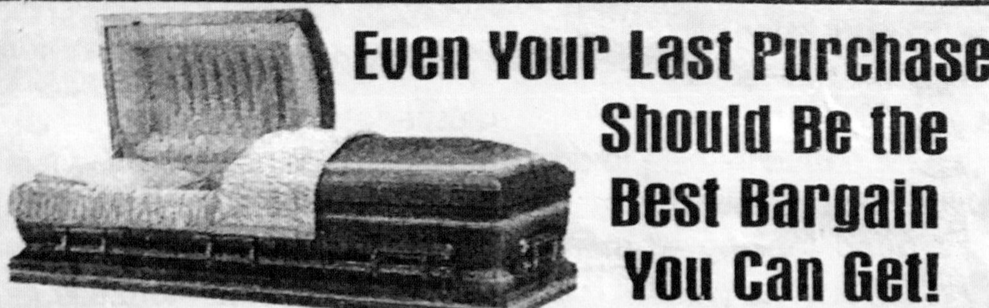

From my archives.

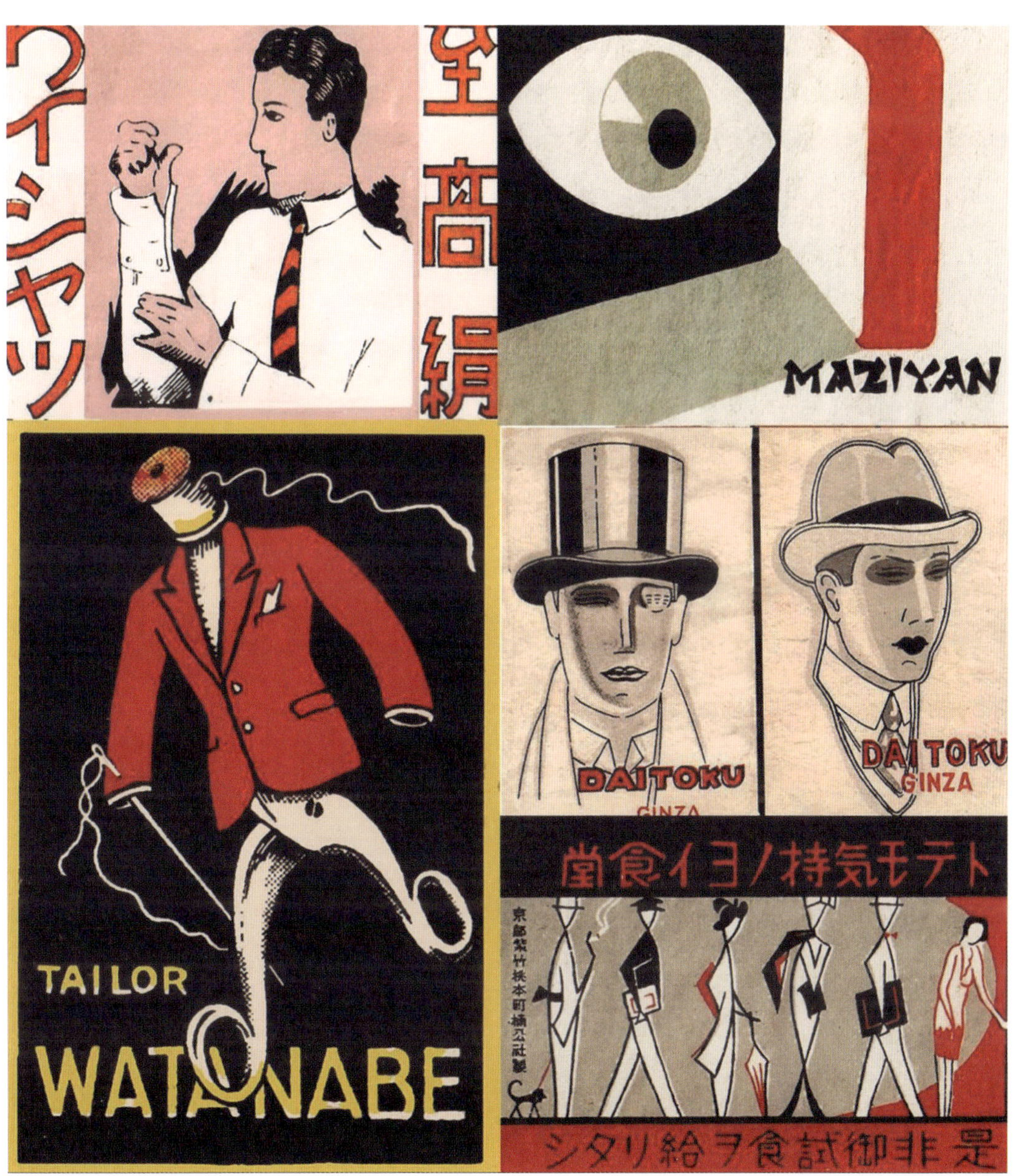

Japanese matchbox labels.

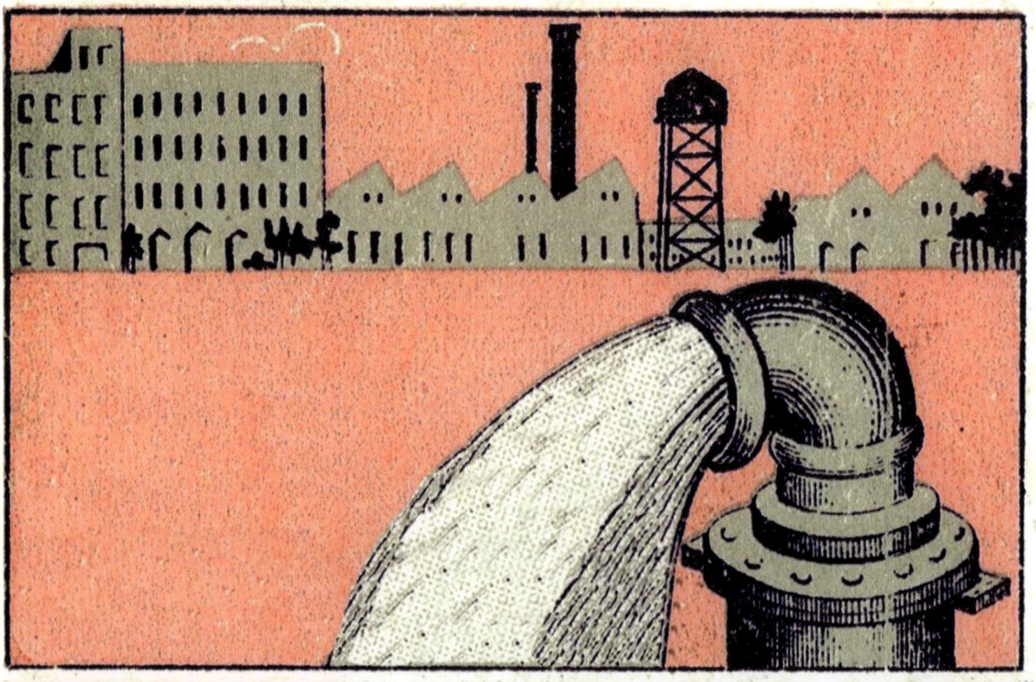

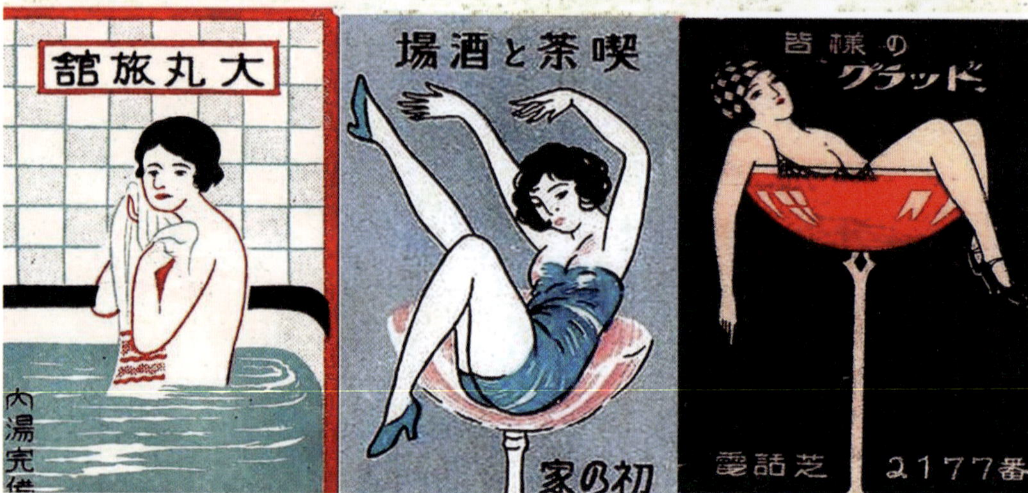

For the love of God, keep cool and don't forget to hydrate.

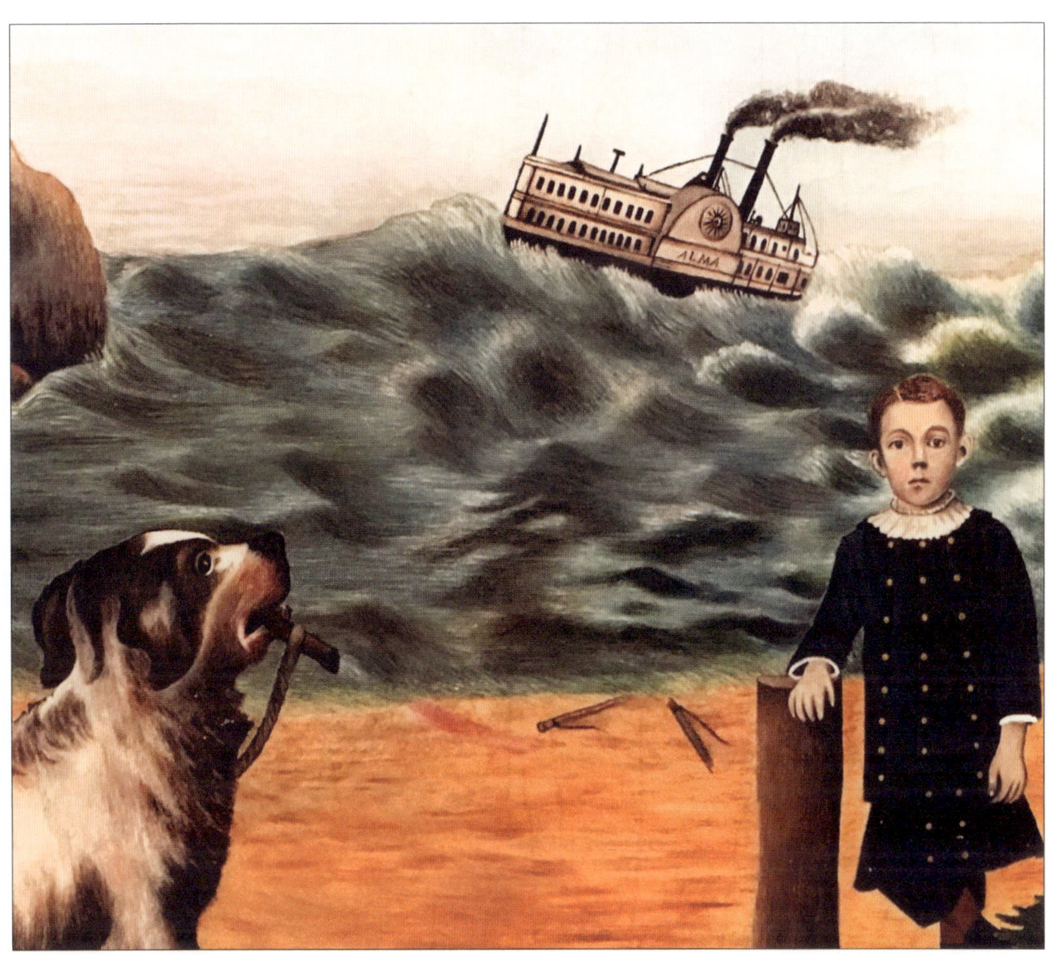

It's hard to paint water.

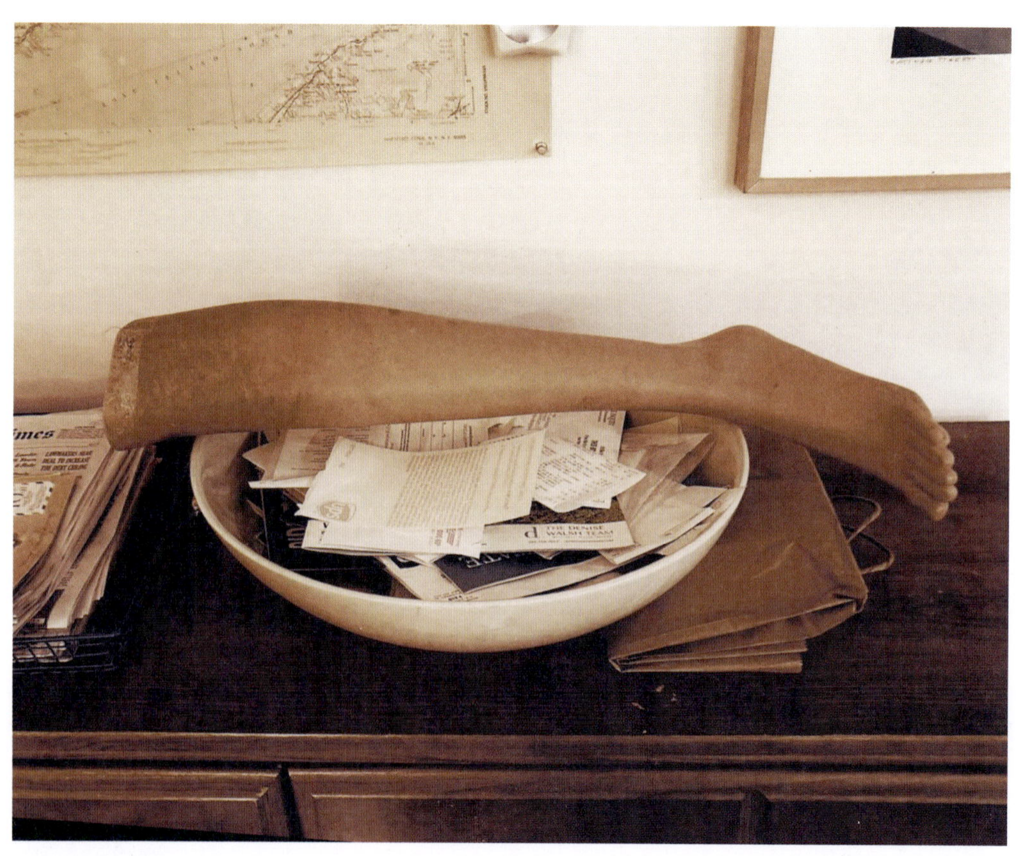

Mail bowl tonight.

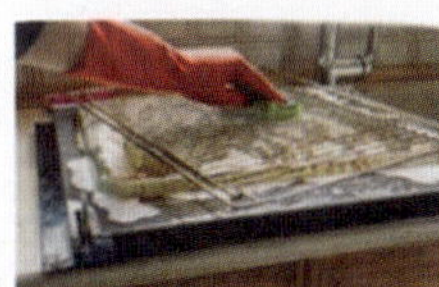

How To Clean Dirty Oven Racks So They'll Look Brand New

WHY BOTHER

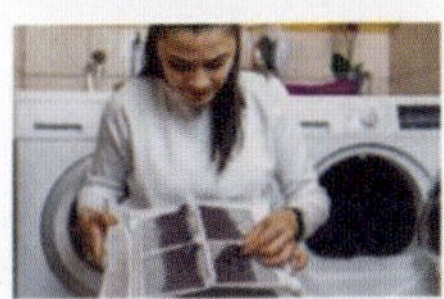

A Pipe Leak Made Me Realize I Really Should Be Cleaning My Dryer

...AND THEN I REALIZED SOME OTHER THINGS.

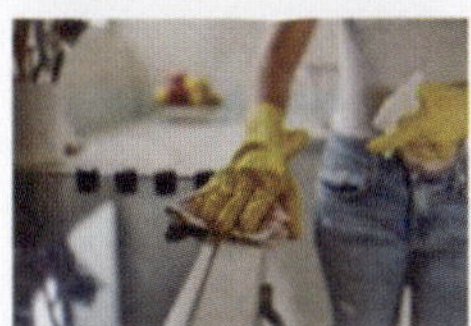

9 Cleaning Mistakes That Make Your Home Dirtier

OH, GOD!!! ...

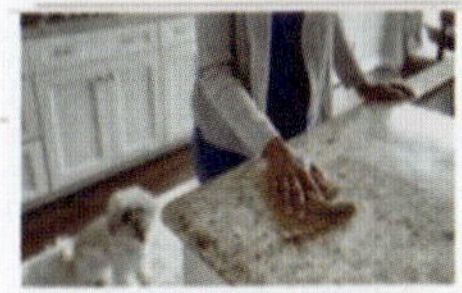

Here's How Often To Clean Every Surface In Your Kitchen

ONCE EVERY SEVEN YEARS?

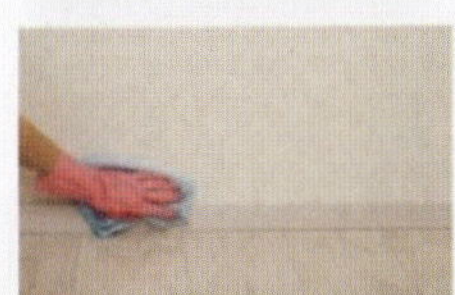

How To Deep Clean Baseboards

BITE ME.

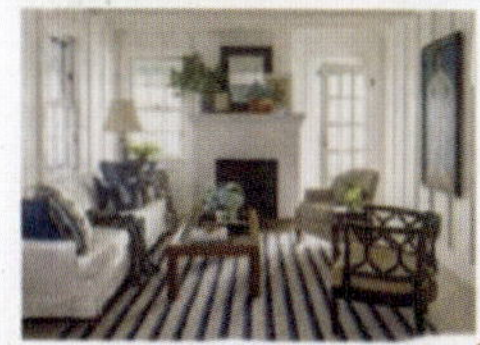

How To Clean Your Walls and Why You Should Do It Now

YOU CAN'T MAKE ME.

No you can't eat off my floors.

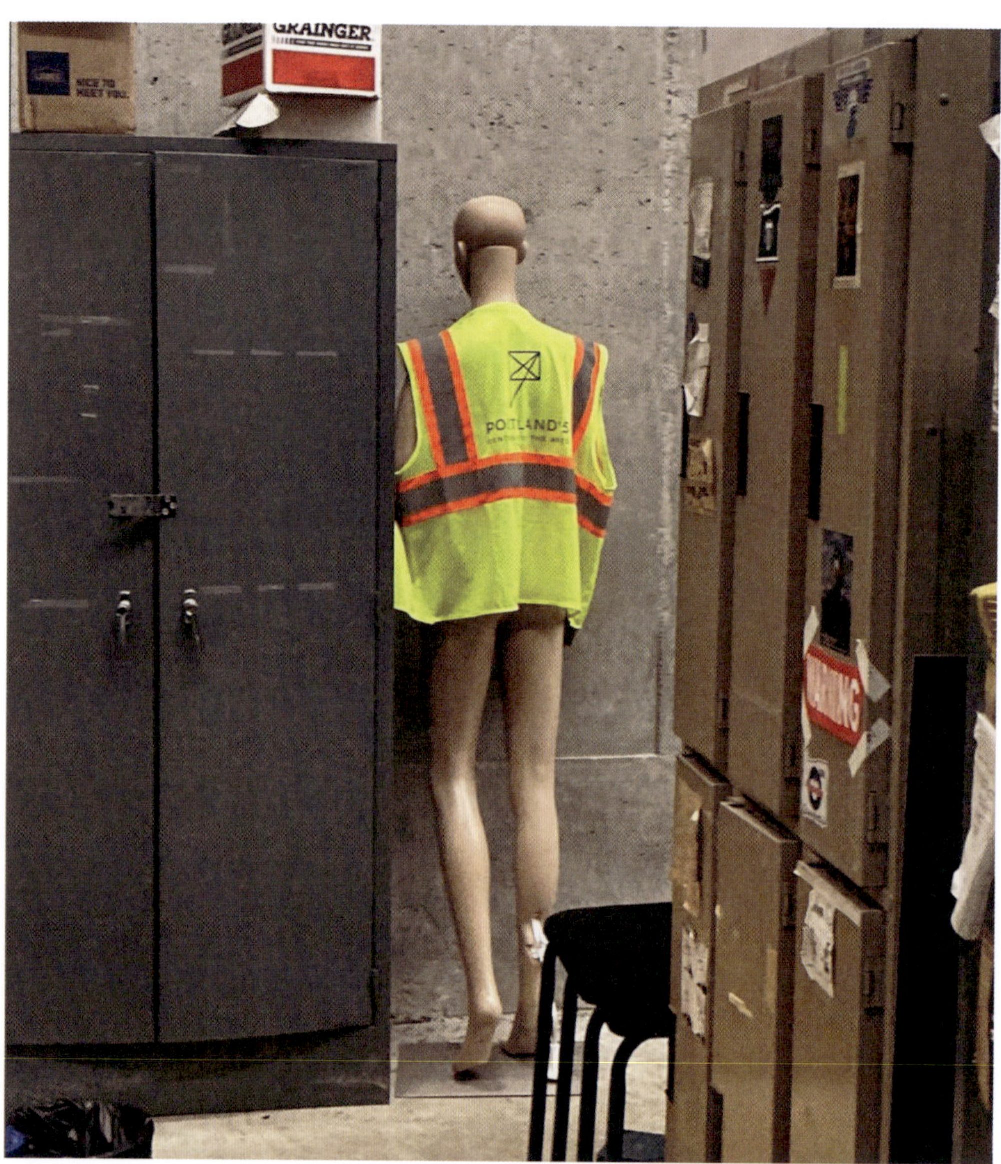

I don't know what this guy did but I'm sure it was very bad.

5: WATCHING

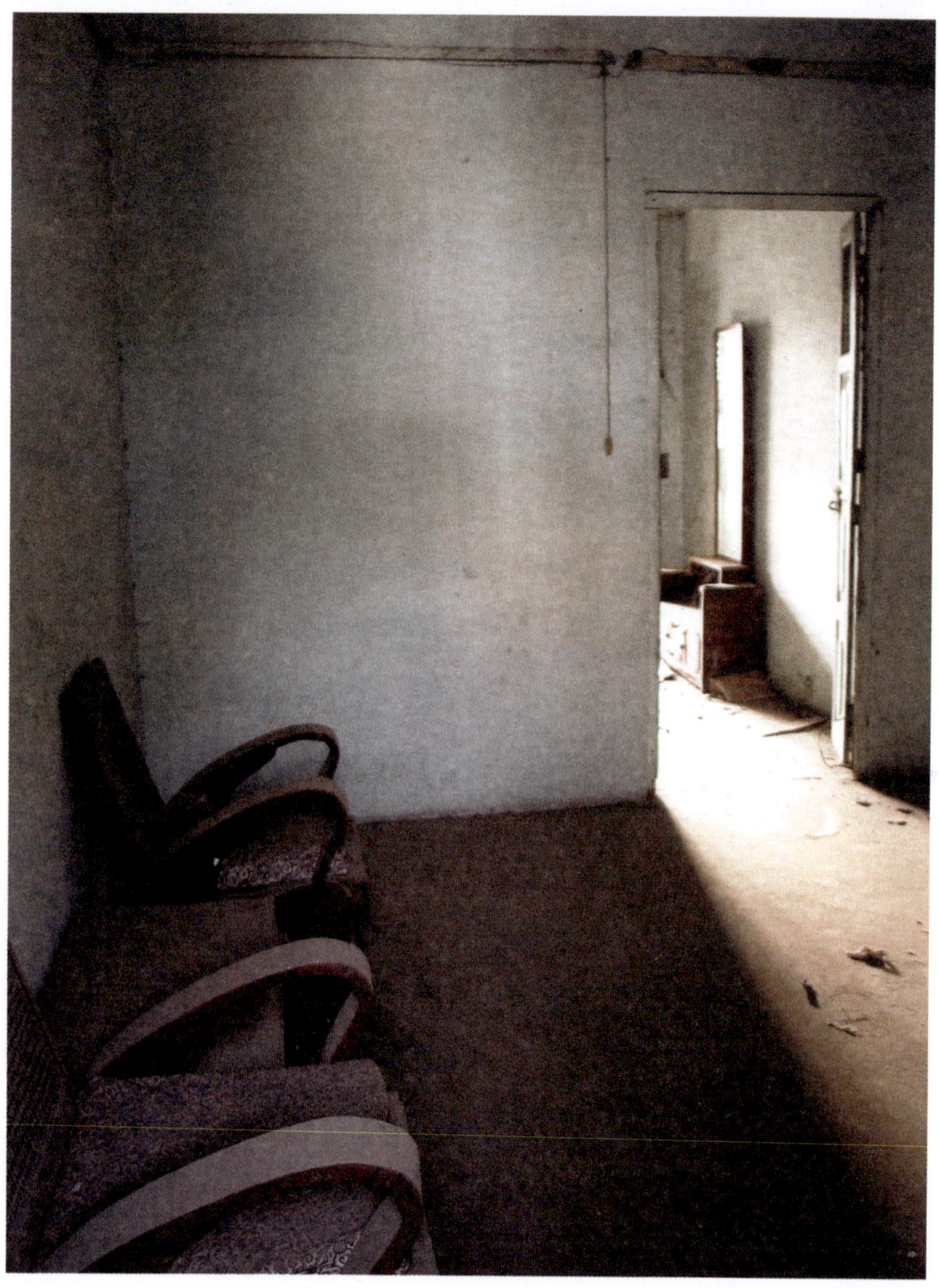

Aradhana Seth, *The Waiting Room*, Goa, 2005.   126

Ships at a distance have every man's wish on board. For some they come in with the tide. For others they sail forever on the horizon, never out of sight, never landing until the Watcher turns his eyes away in resignation, his dreams mocked to death by Time. That is the life of men.

Zora Neale Hurston, *Their Eyes Were Watching God*, 1937.

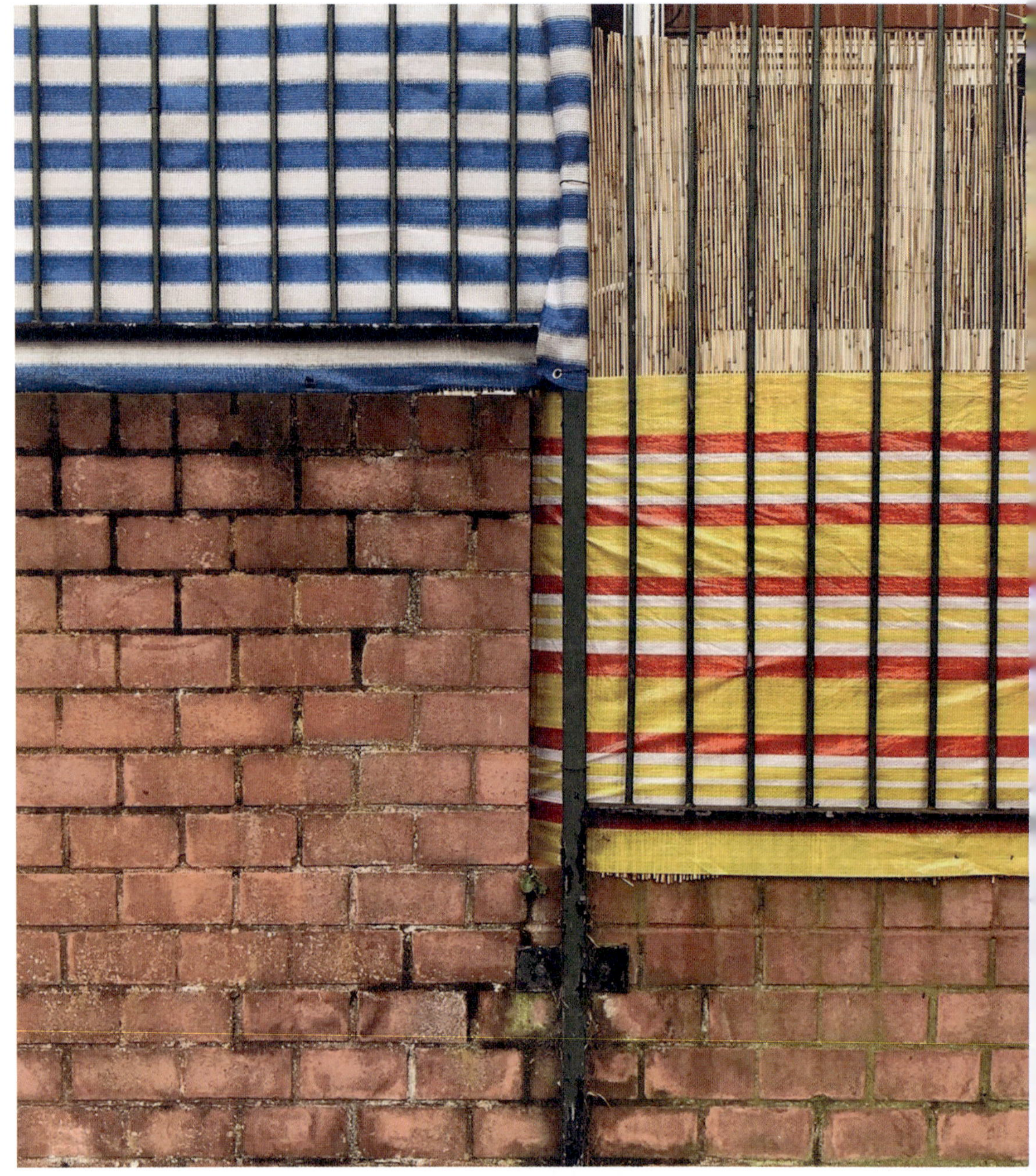

Nicky Hirst.

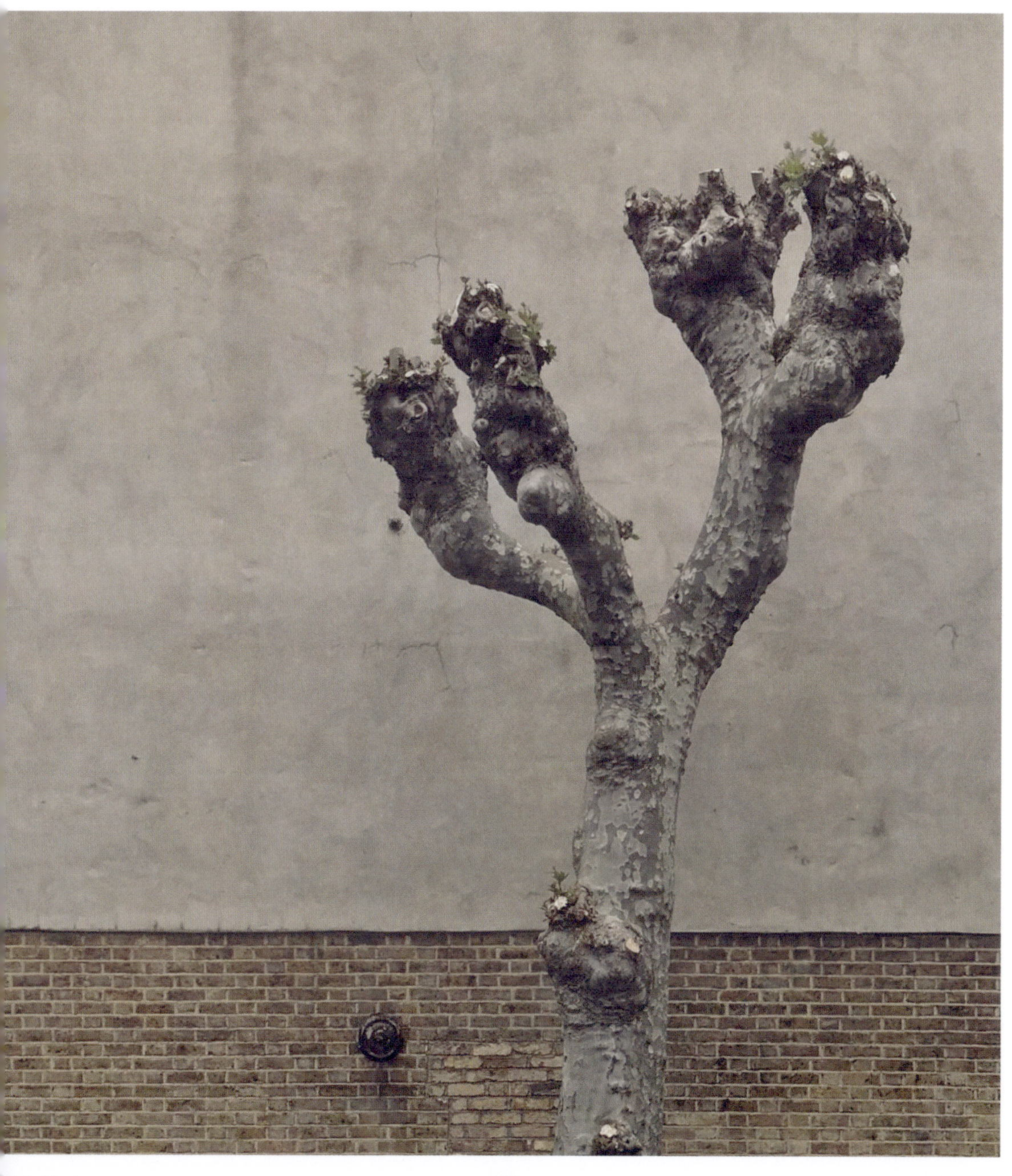

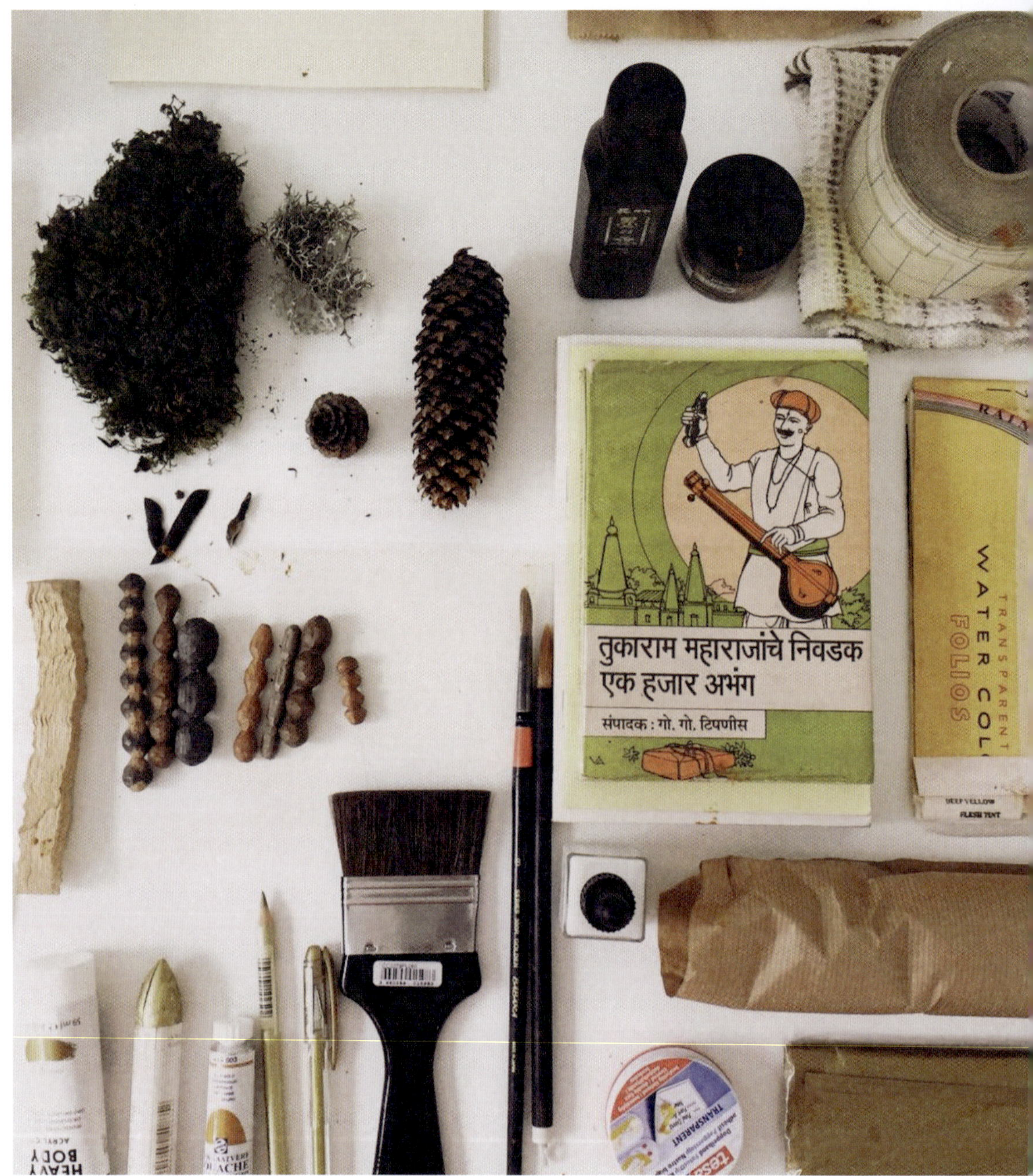

Hemali Bhuta.

The more I looked at the objects on my desk next to my notebook — rusty keys, candy boxes, pliers and lighters — the more I felt as if they were communicating with one another. Their ending up in this place having been uprooted from the places they used to belong to and separated from the lives of the people whose lives they were once part of — their loneliness in a word — aroused in me the shamanic belief that objects too have spirits.

Orhan Pamuk, *The Innocence of Objects*, translated by Ekin Oklap, 2012.

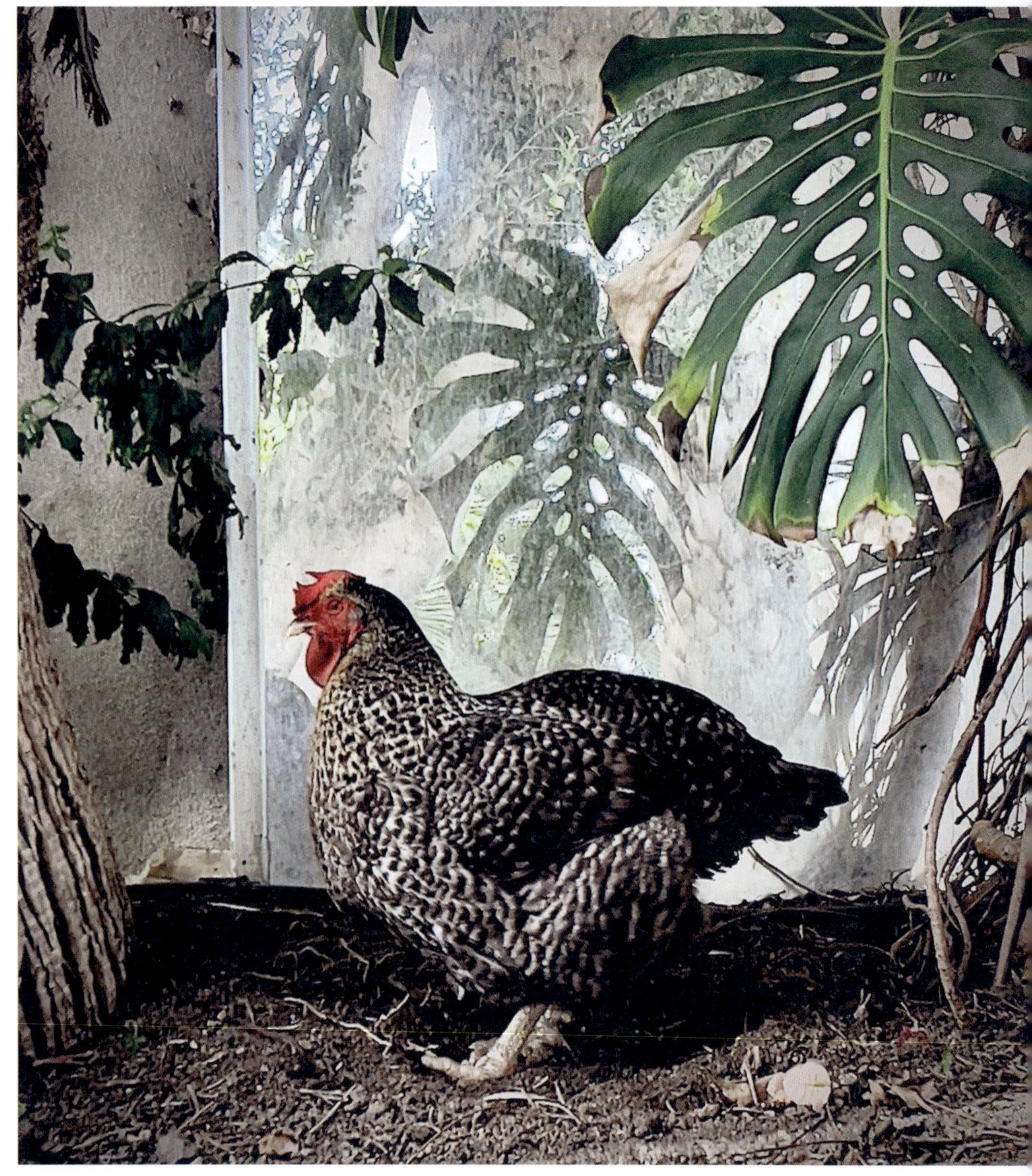

Zak Ové: My dear chicken Clementine busy checking herself out in the mirror.

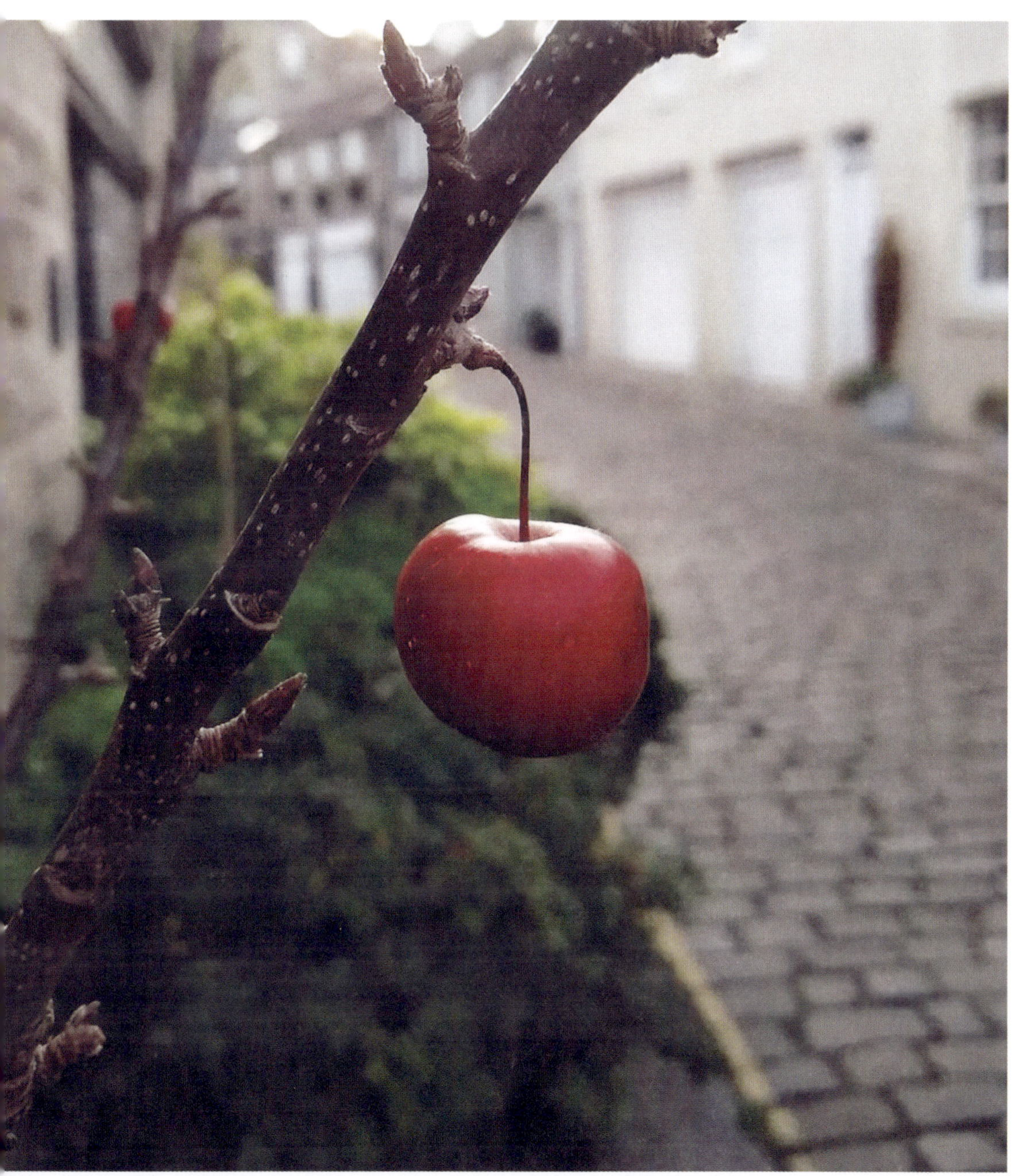

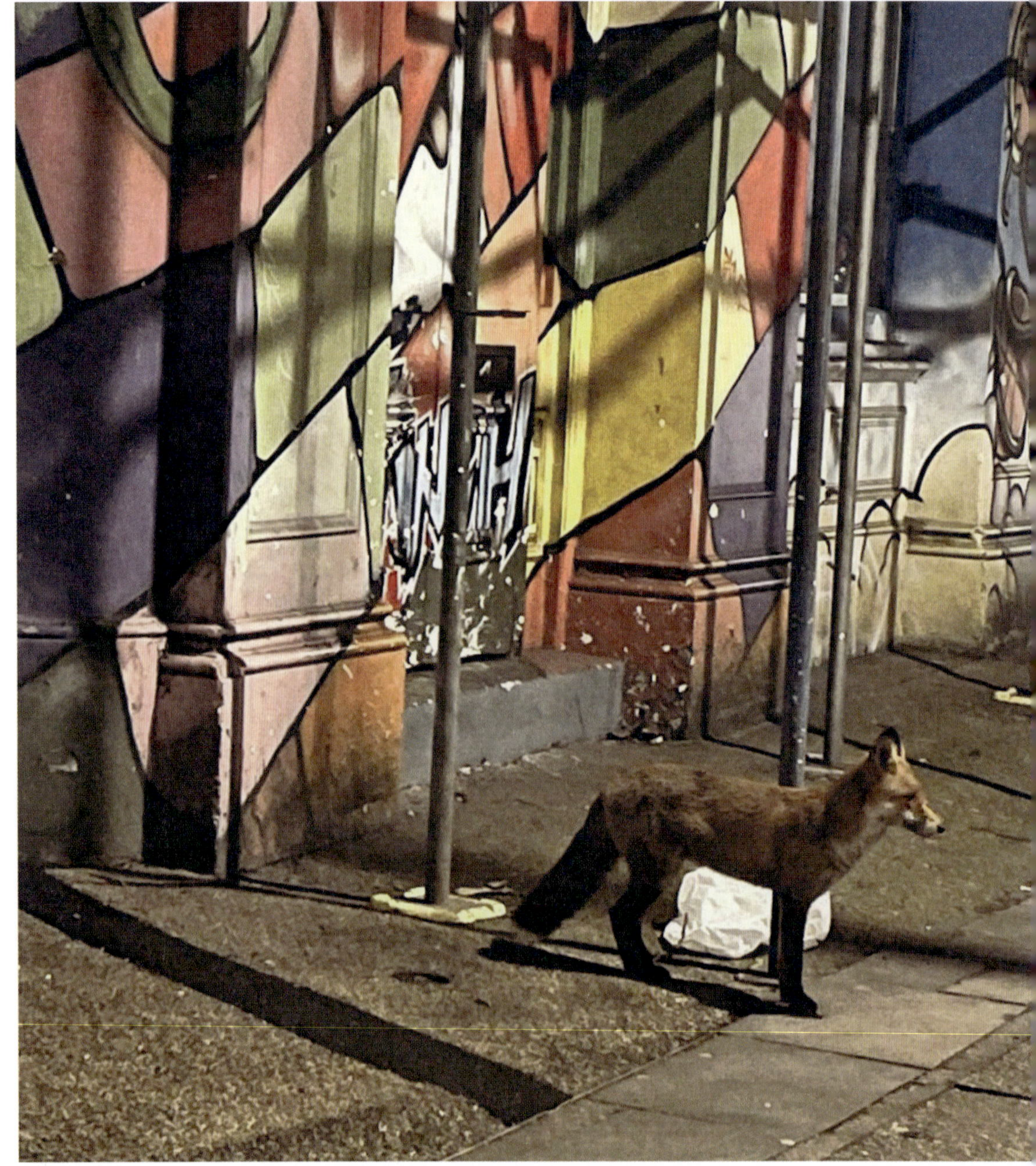

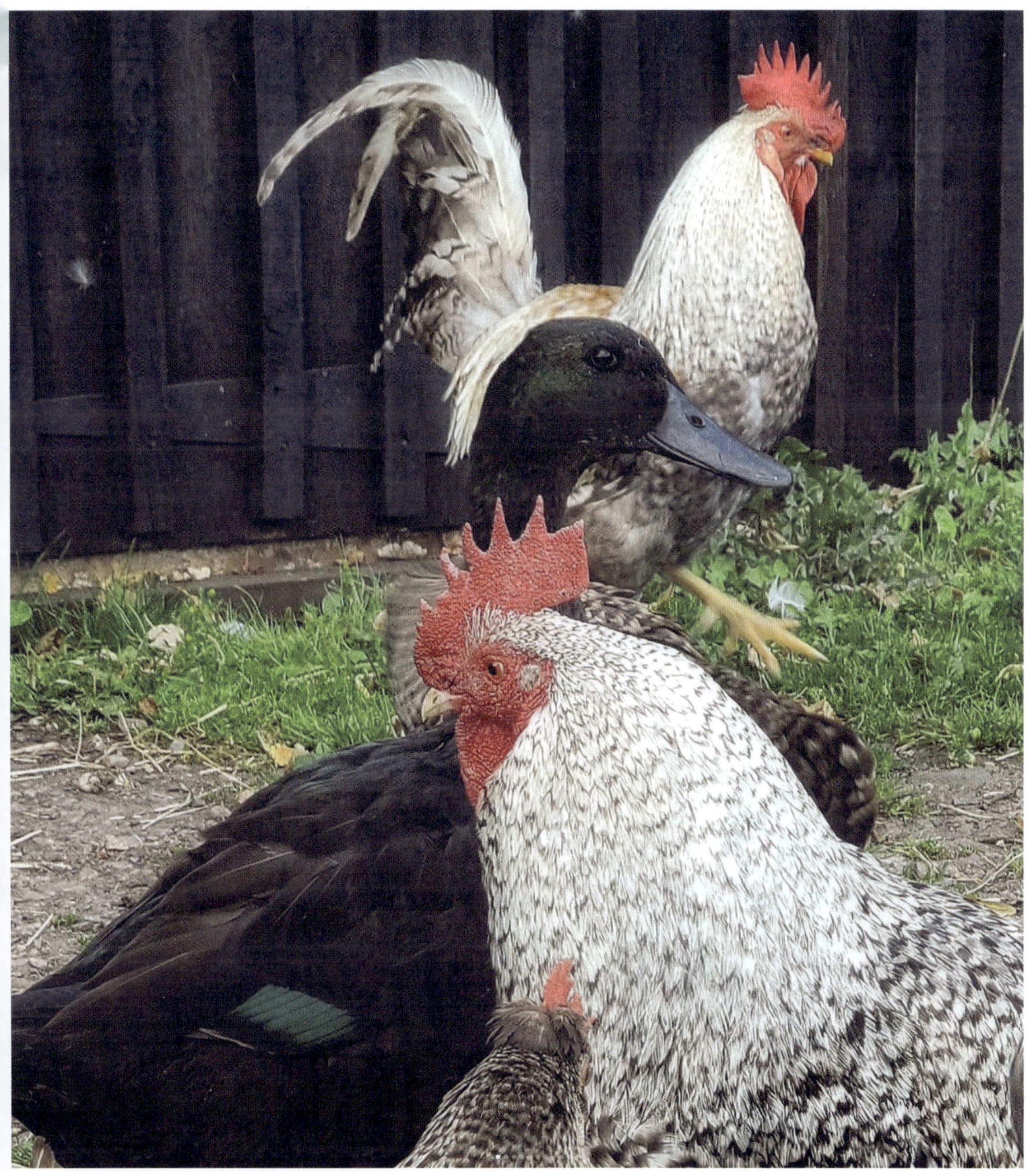

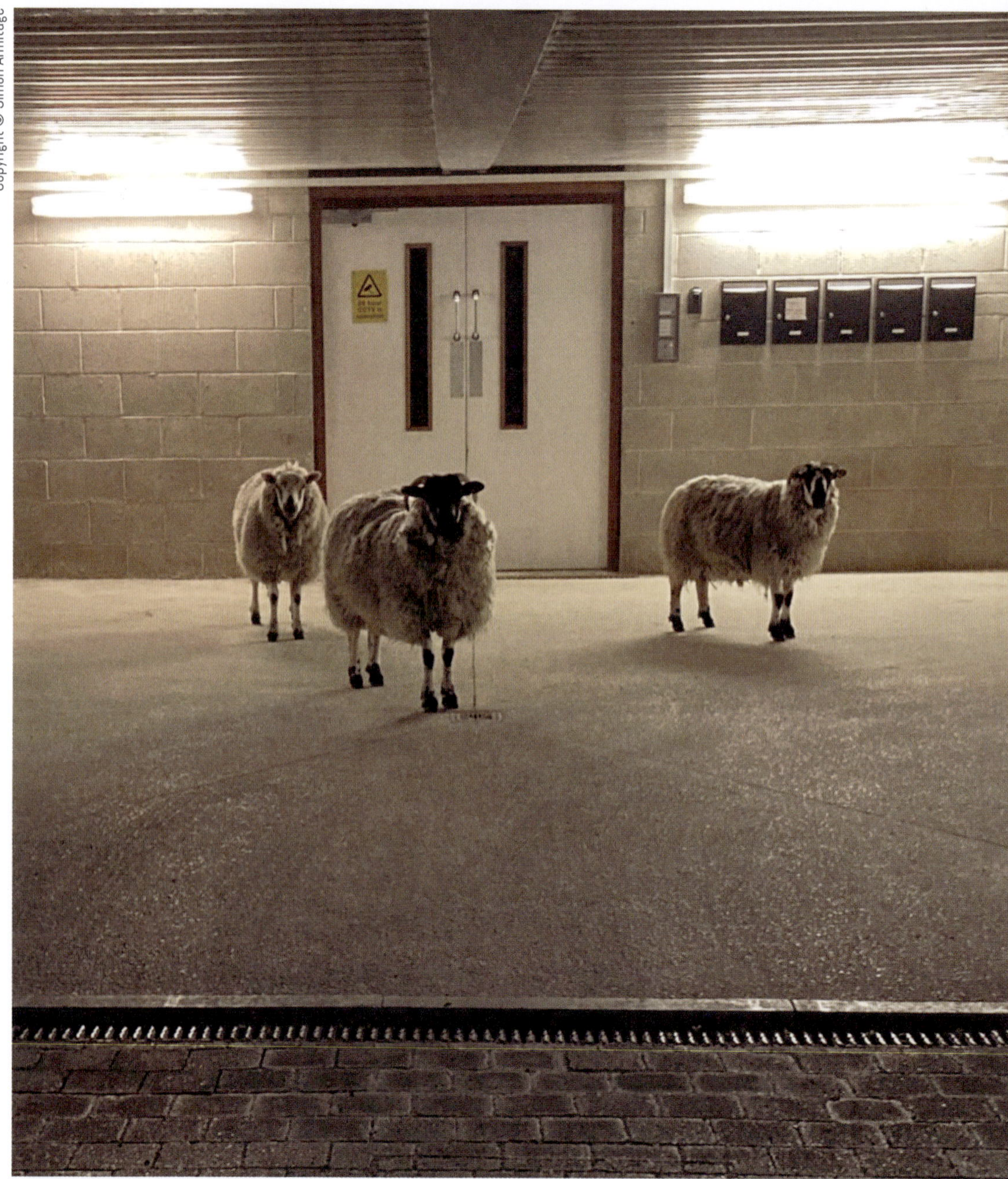

Simon Armitage: Midnight in Maaaaarsden.

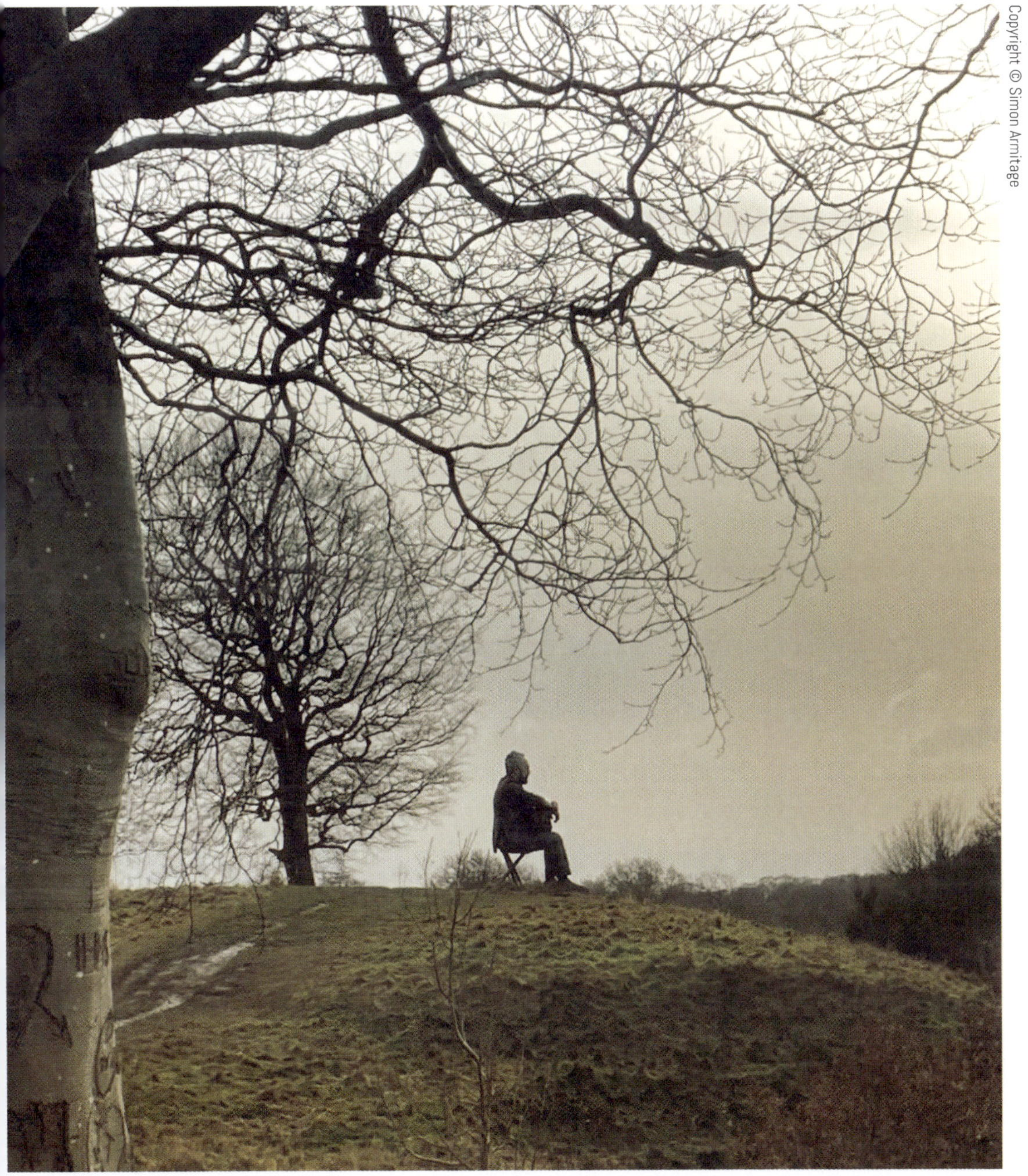

Simon Armitage.

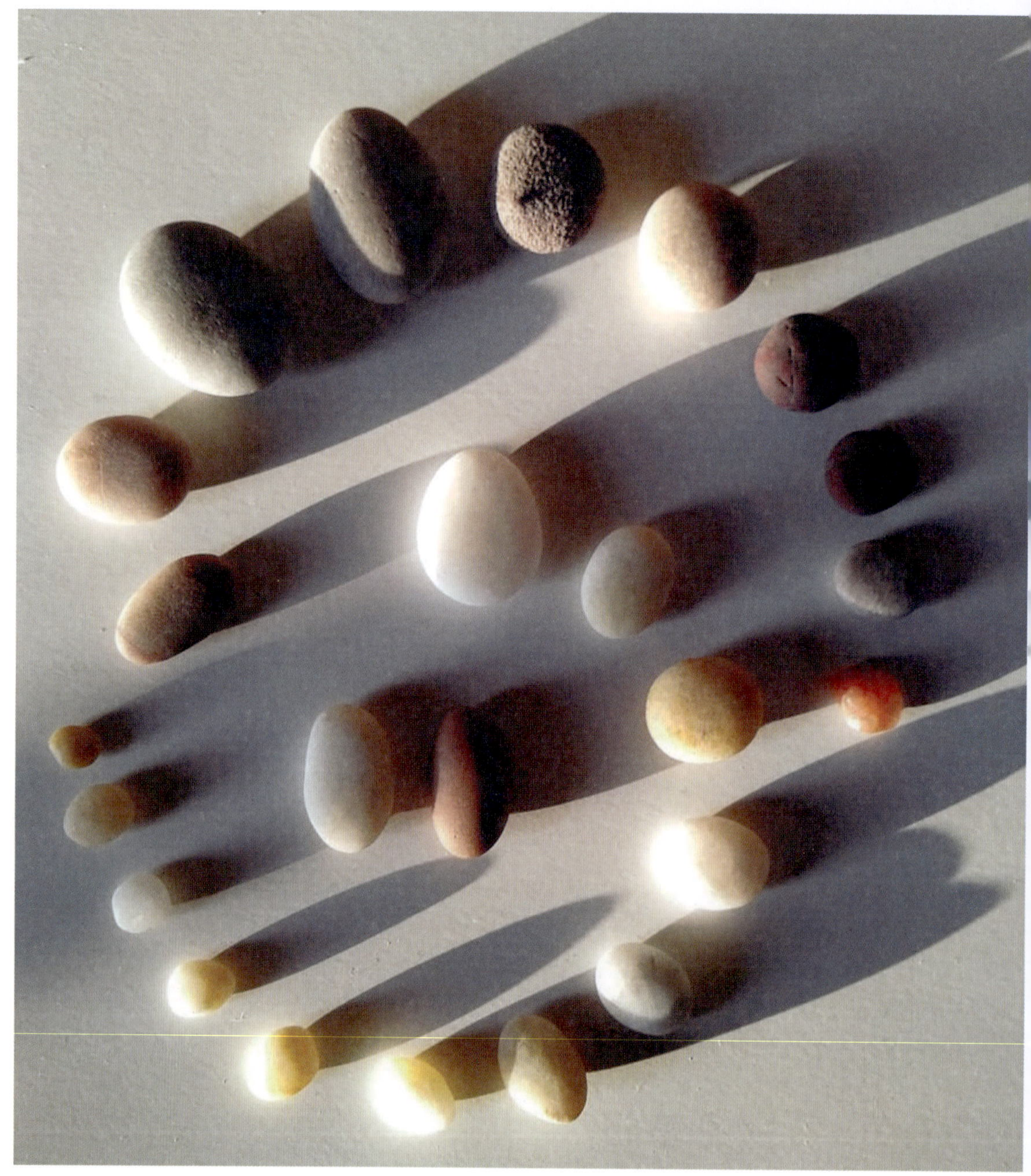

Henry Noltie.

To collect is to create. Collectors do not so much arrange or even possess
objects as transform them. In a collection, each object becomes an artefact,
something entirely different from what it was before, and an object's meaning
changes when it finds a new home in a new place among other objects and
in the possession of a person who desires it. Its value shifts, and so does its
context. It is no longer just a "thing": it is a metaphor, a material embodiment
of something important to the collector – a childhood memory, perhaps, or, as
is often the case, a particular chapter of history that the collector wishes to
restore.

James McAuley, *The House of Fragile Things: Jewish Art Collectors and the Fall of France*, 2021.

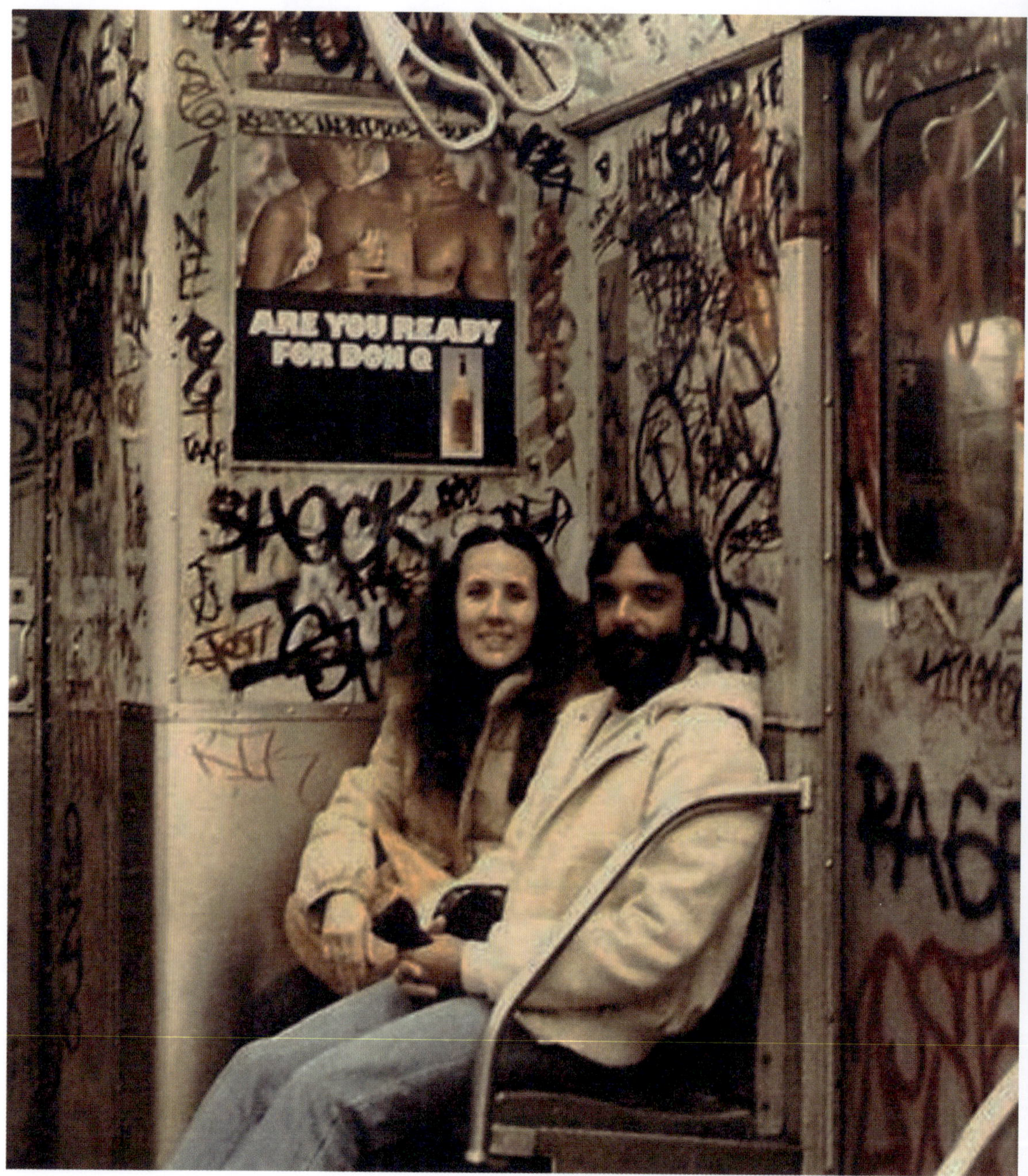

Andrew Eliopoulos: NYC subway, 1980s.

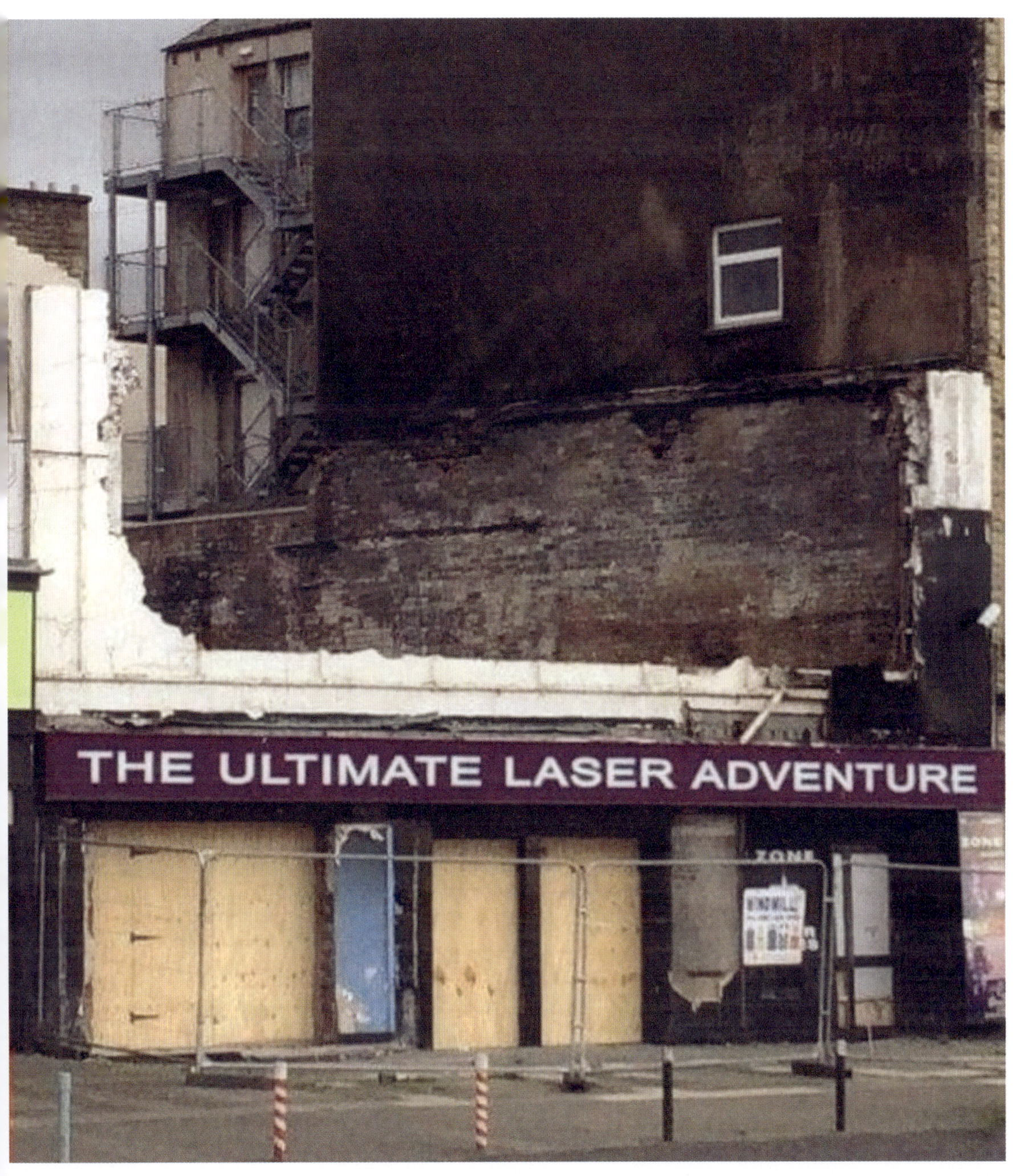

Shane Reiner-Roth.

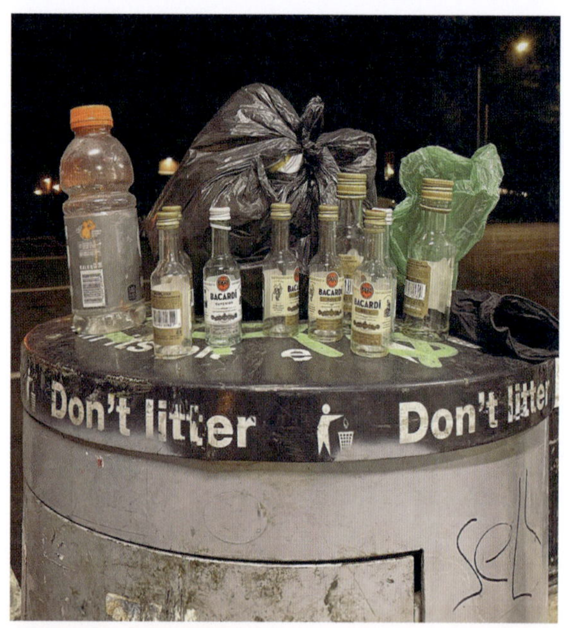

Matthew Higgs: *Nature Morte* (midnight dog walk).

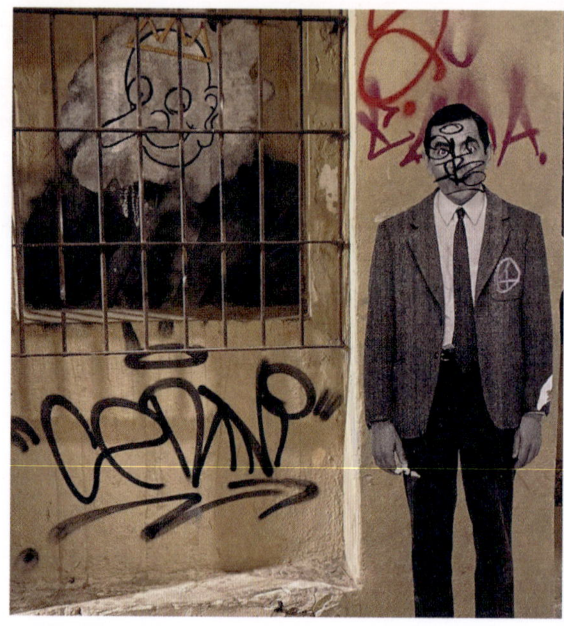

Janet Cardiff: Lots of great graffiti in both Palma and Barcelona.

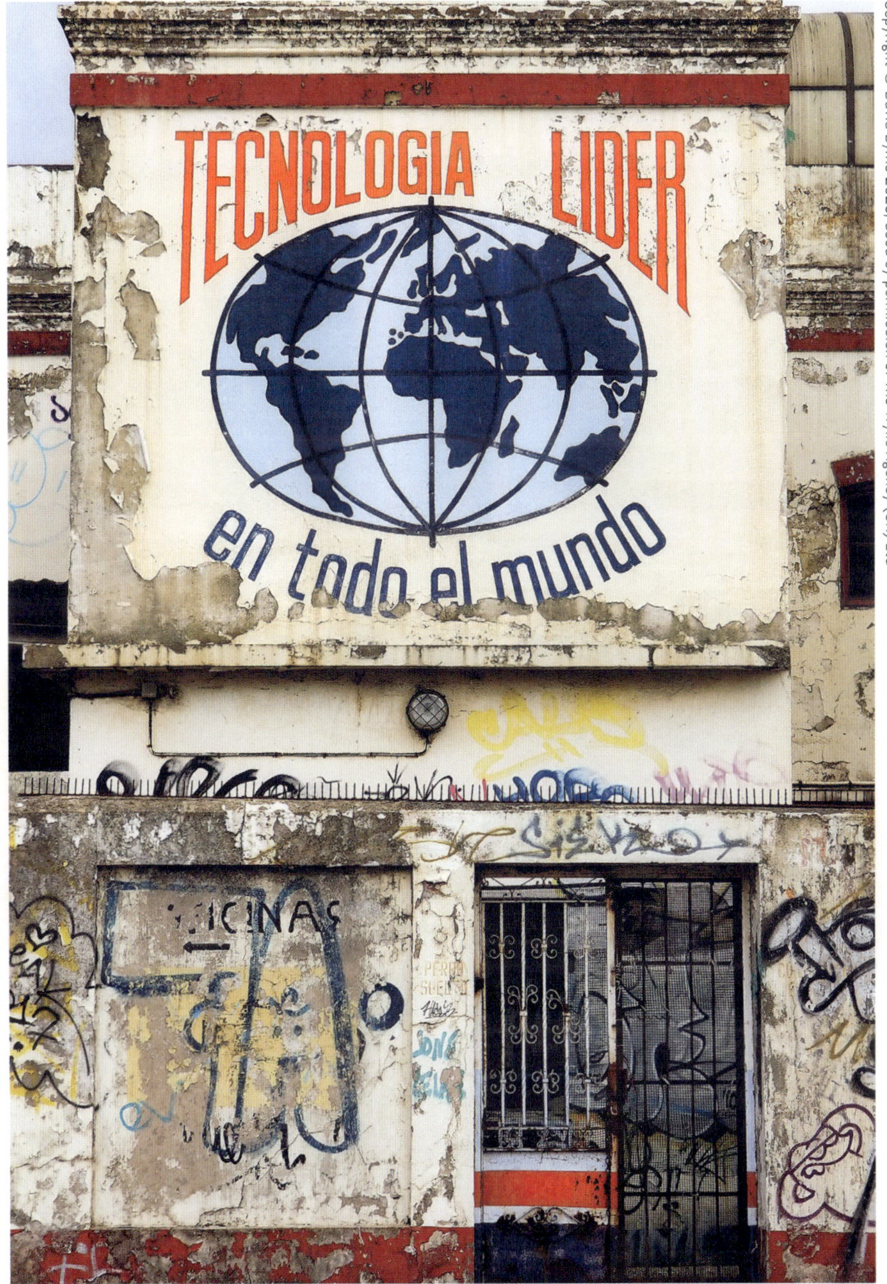

David Byrne: World Technology Leader, Bilbao.   143

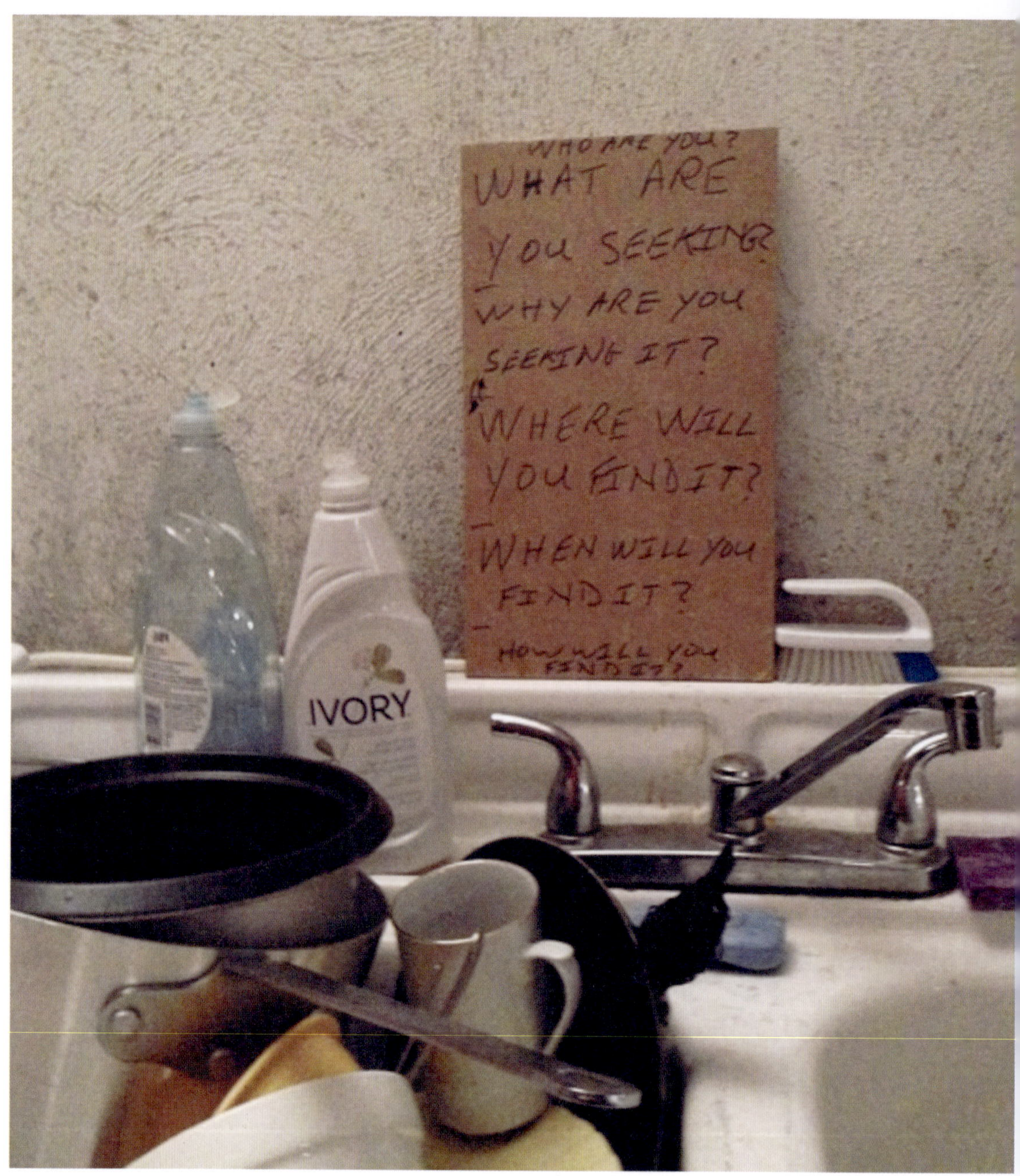

WHO ARE YOU?
WHAT ARE
YOU SEEKING?
WHY ARE YOU
SEEKING IT?
WHERE WILL
YOU FIND IT?
WHEN WILL YOU
FIND IT?
HOW WILL YOU
FIND IT?

IVORY

Liz Brown.

Your New Door Explained

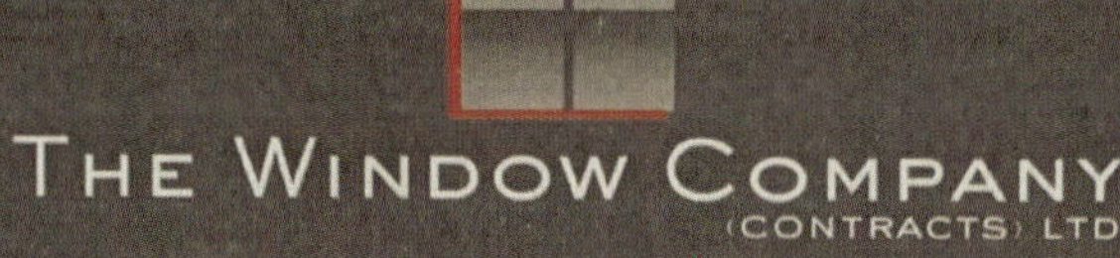

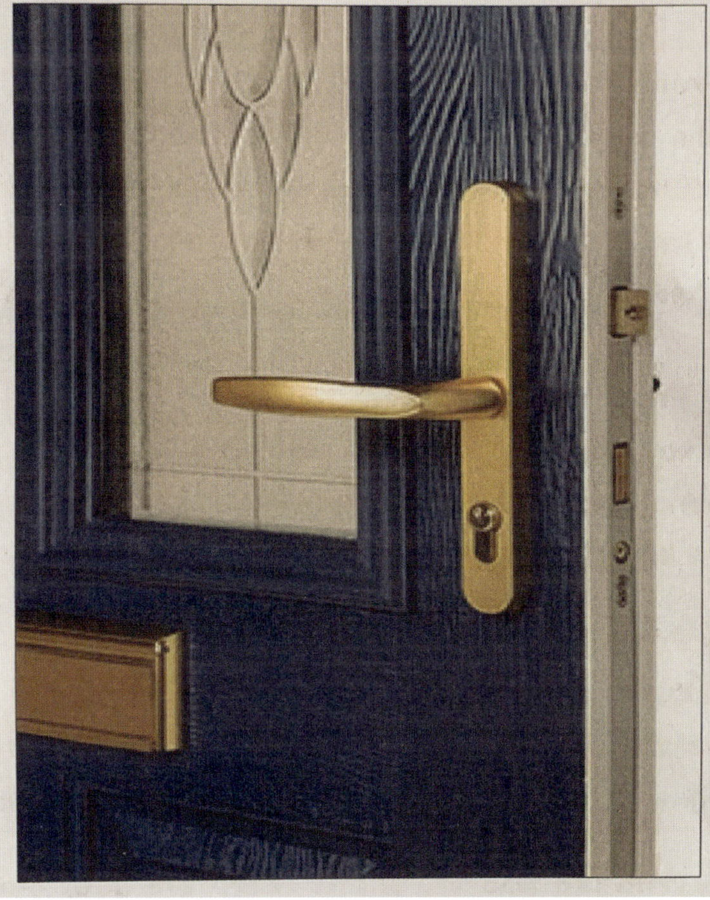

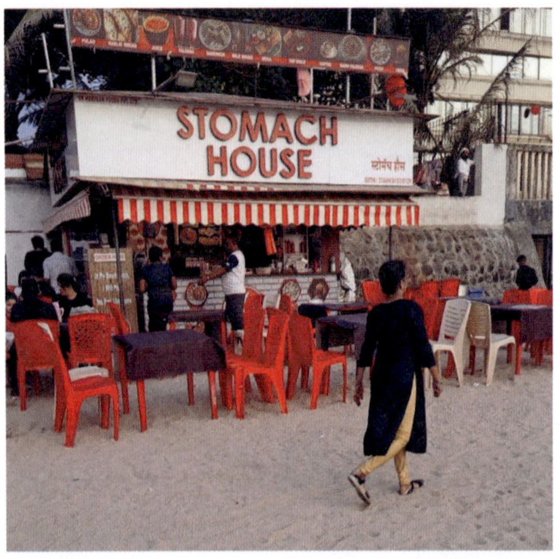

Sam Miller.

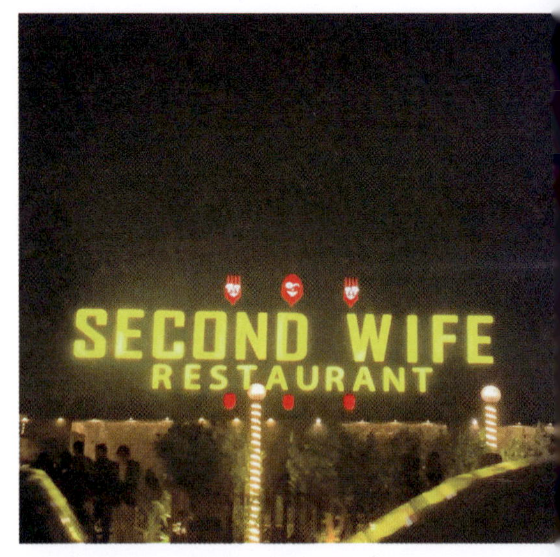

Kamila Shamsie.

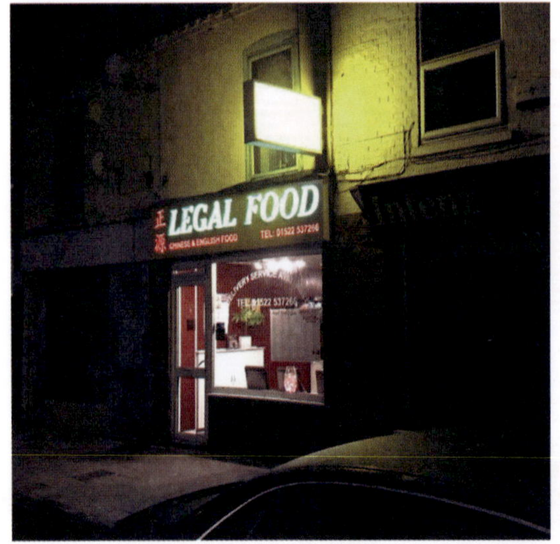

Will Hobson.

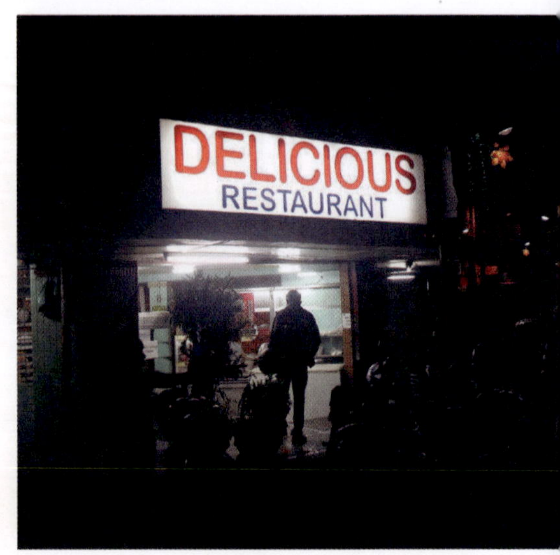

Mark Salvatus.

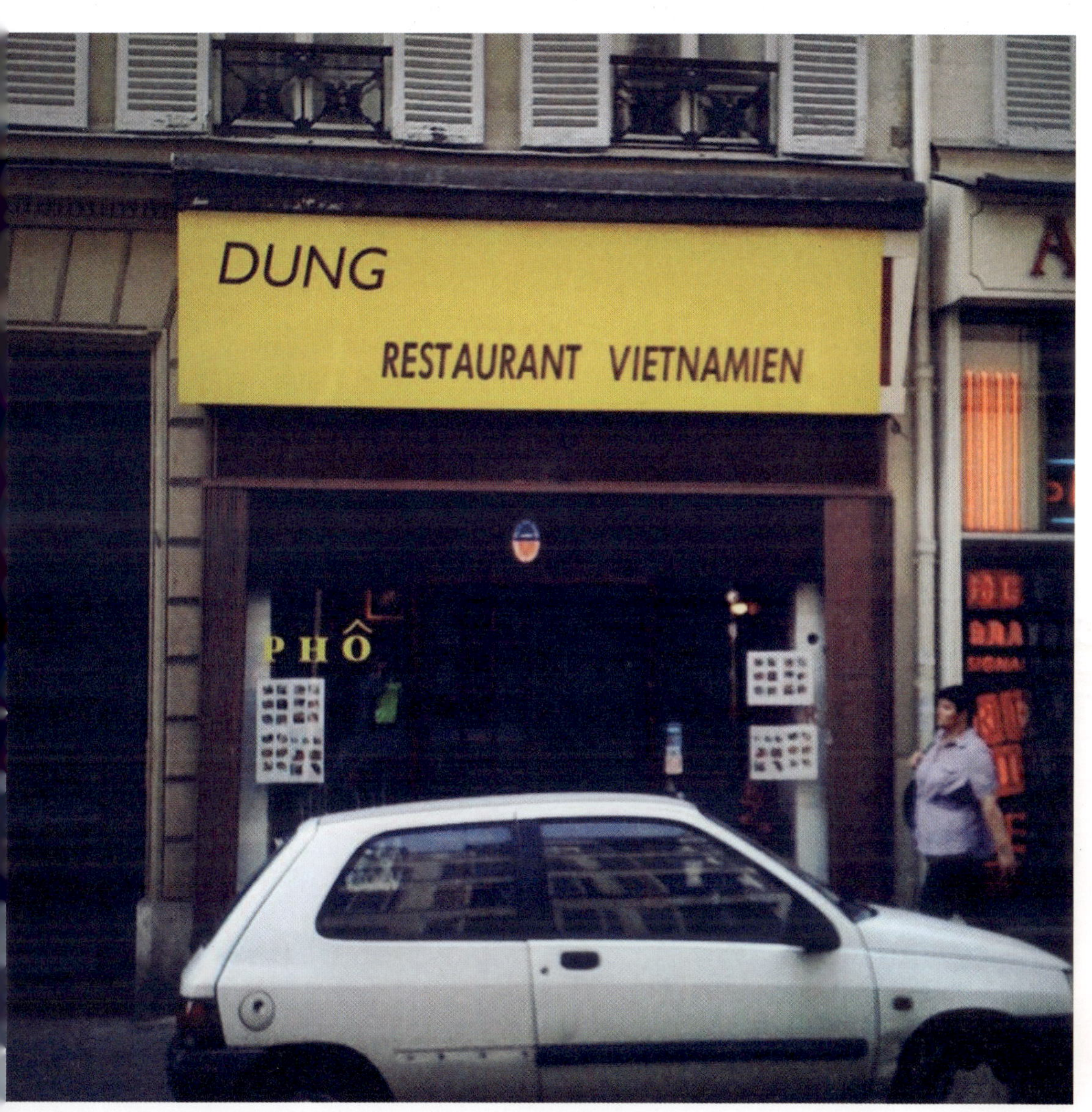

Jarvis Cocker: This is an old picture: the restaurant closed down a while ago. I wonder why?

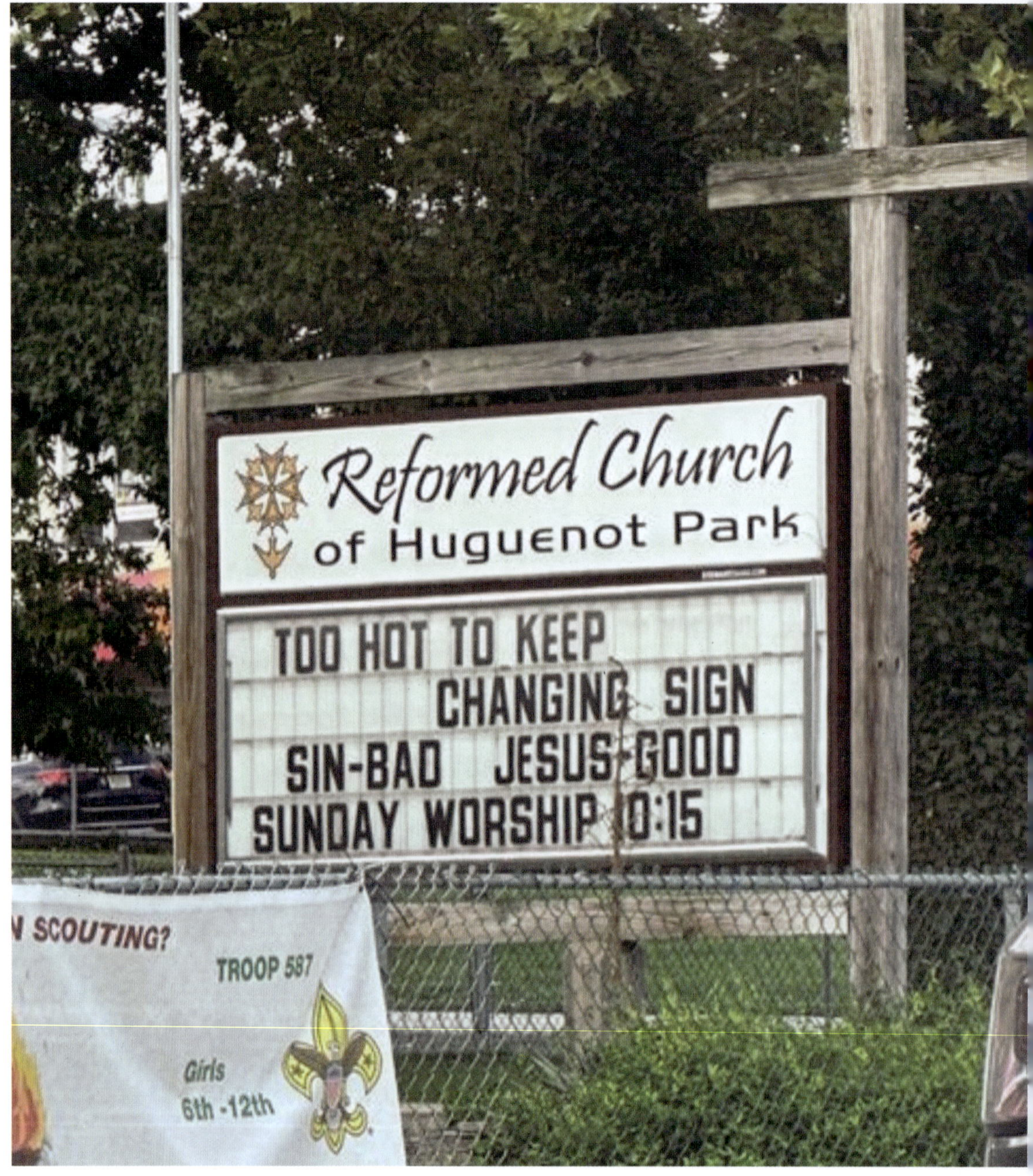
Reformed Church
of Huguenot Park
TOO HOT TO KEEP
CHANGING SIGN
SIN-BAD JESUS-GOOD
SUNDAY WORSHIP 10:15
SCOUTING?
TROOP 587
Girls
6th -12th

6: SURVEYING

FROM HANS ULRICH OBRIST'S INSTAGRAM

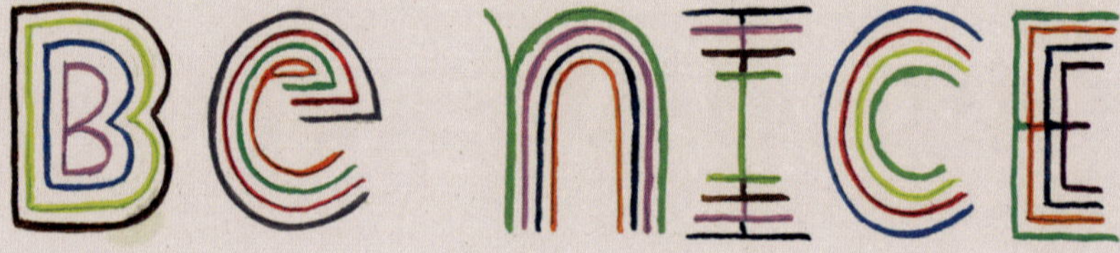

Joseph Grigely.

I say that if you have to choose between life and happiness or art, remember always to choose life and happiness. Art solves nothing, either for the artist himself or for those who receive his art. Art shouldn't be overrated. It started to be in the latter eighteenth century, and definitely was in the nineteenth. The Germans started the business of assessing the worth of society by the quality of the art it produced. But the quality of art produced in a society does not necessarily — or maybe seldom — reflect the degree of well-being enjoyed by most of its members. And well-being comes first. I deplore the tendency to over-value art.

Clement Greenberg, quoted in "Clement Greenberg", Tim Hilton, *The New Criterion*, September 2000.

Otobong Nkanga.

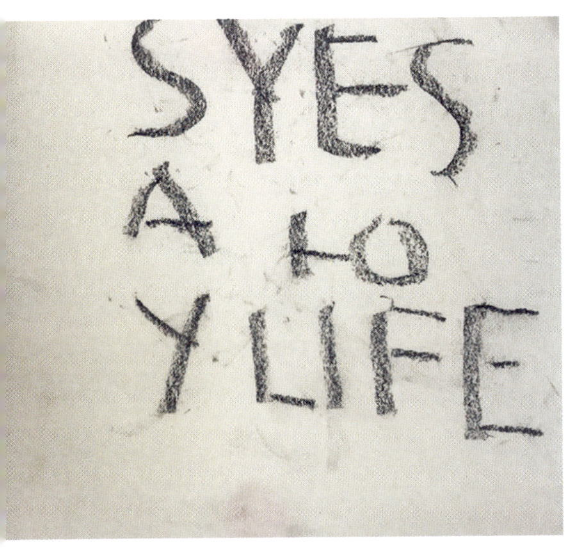

Luchita Hurtado: SAY YES TO LIFE.

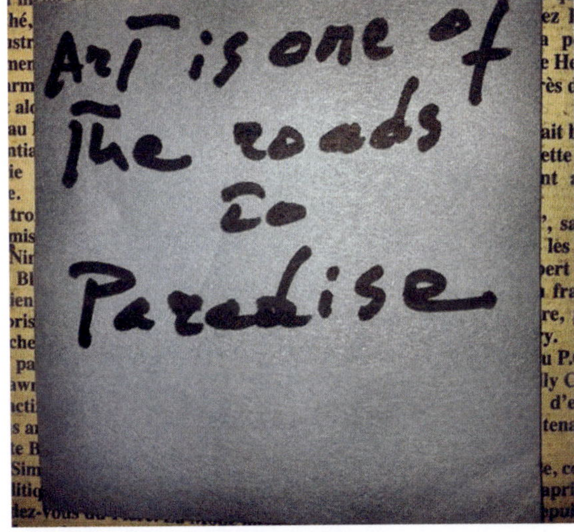

Etel Adnan: Art is one of the roads to Paradise.

ILLEGAL IMMIGRANT CLAIMS TO BE DIRECT DESCENDANT OF THE FIRST HUMAN BEING

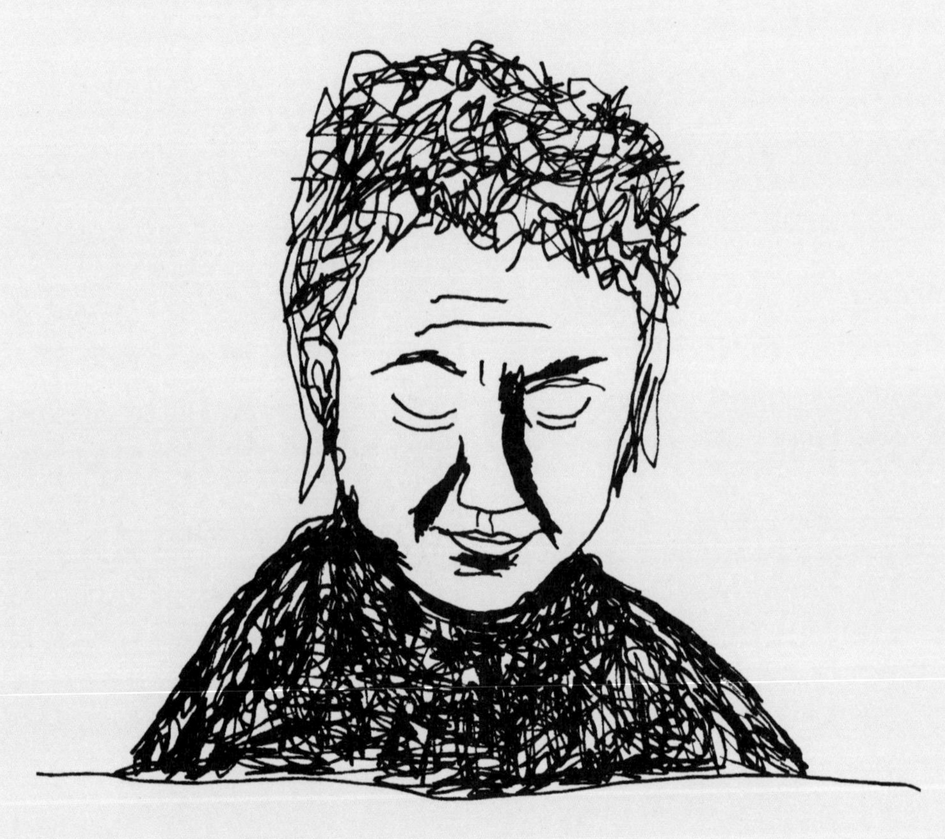

Jimmie Durham.

I see more in
radio than TV
because the
IMAGINATION HAS
A LARGER colour
palette.
Lemn SISSAY

Lemn Sissay.

Jonas Mekas.

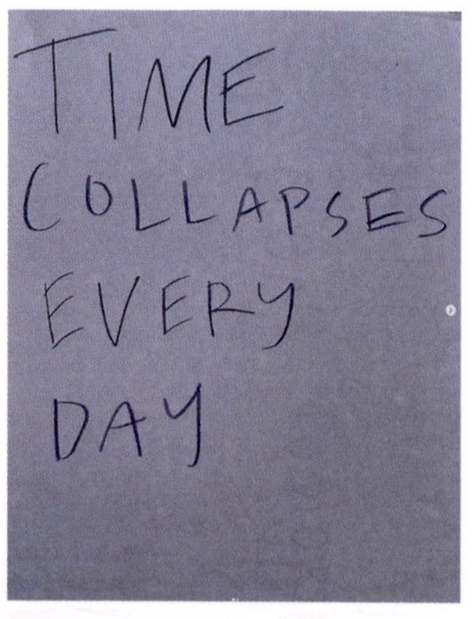

Emily Segal.

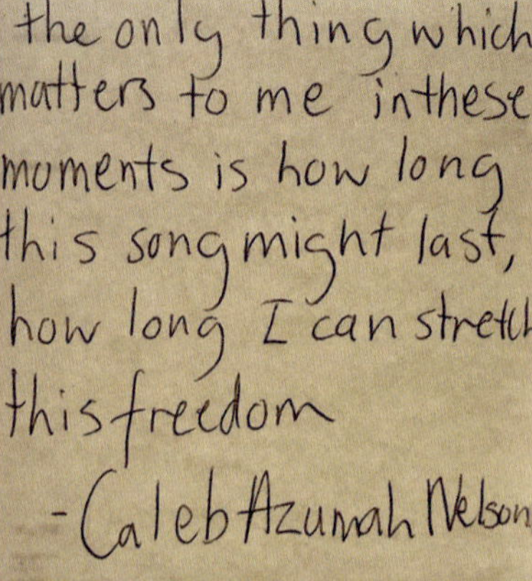

Caleb Azumah Nelson.

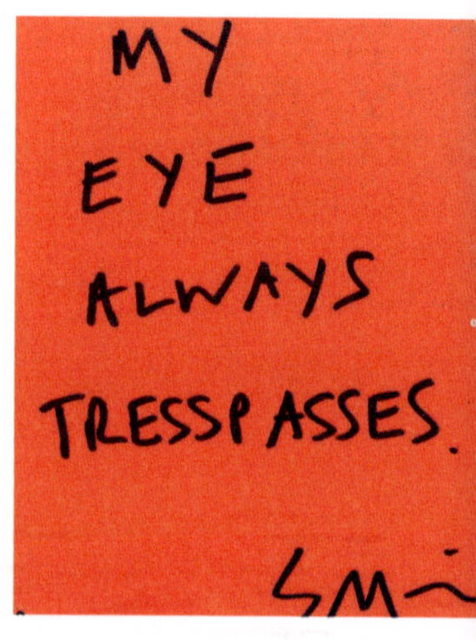

Sarah Morris.

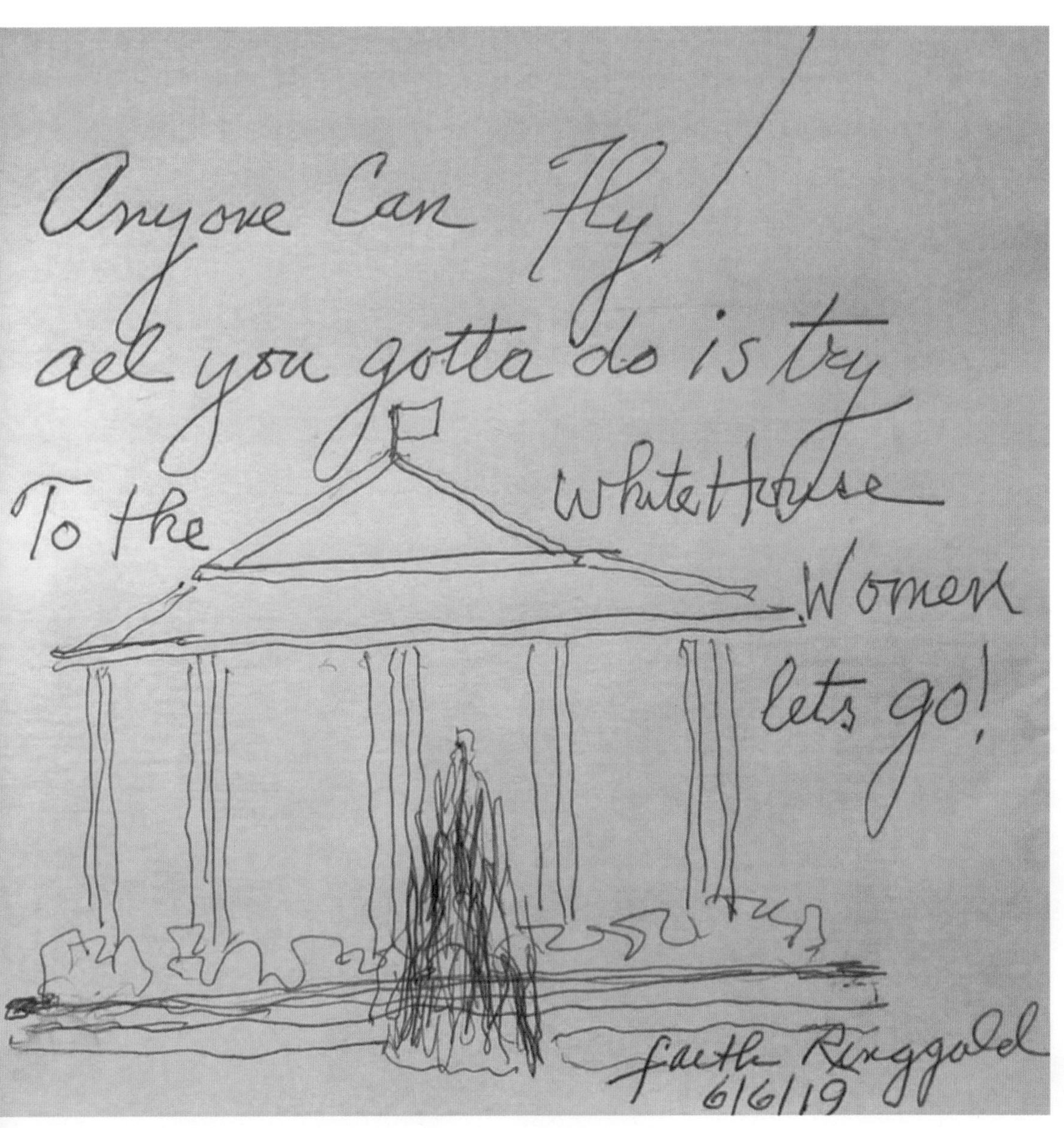

Faith Ringgold: Anyone can fly, all you gotta do is try. To the White House Women let's go!

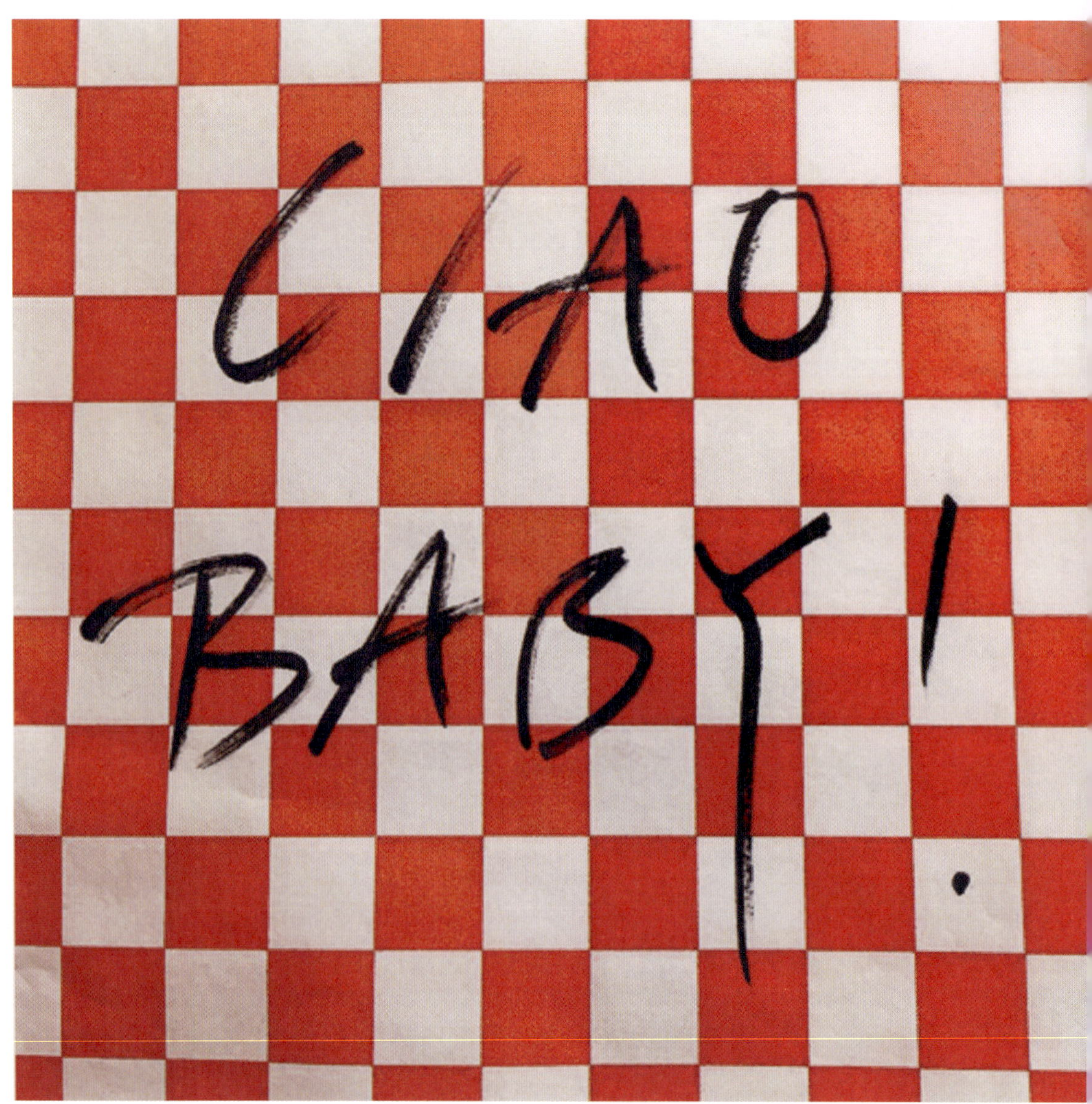

Sarah Ortmeyer.

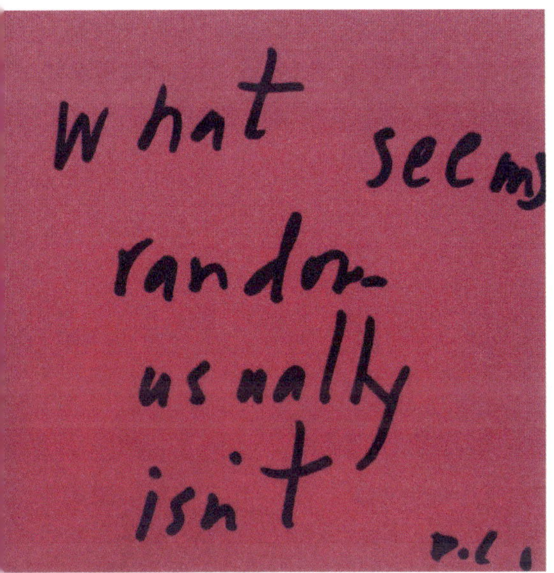

Douglas Coupland.

FKA twigs.

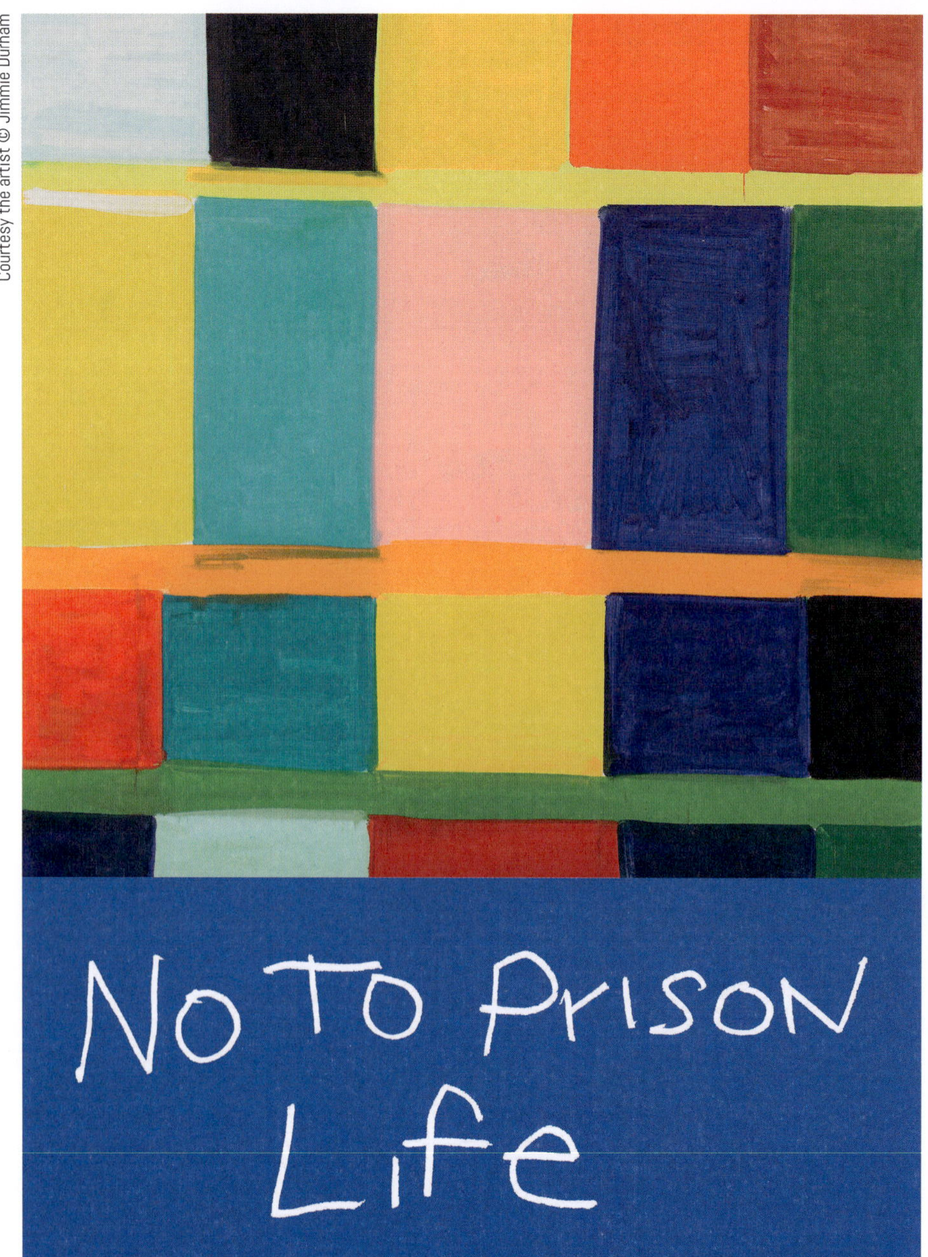

Jimmie Durham.

7: OBSERVING

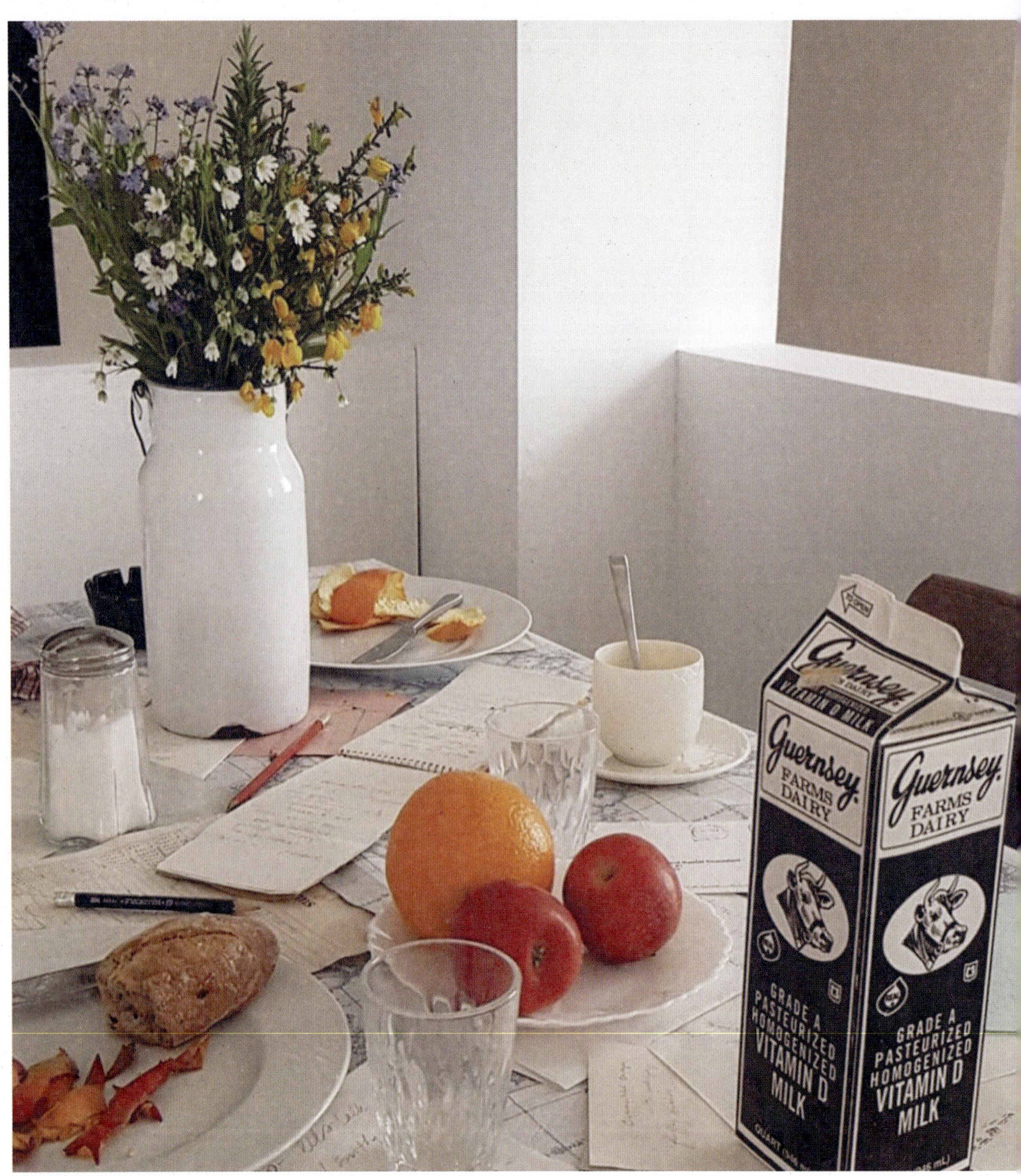

Joseph Grigely, *Kitchen Conversations* (detail), 1996.

Looking is not commonly understood as a complex matter. Generally, vision is treated as autonomous, free and pure. However, looking is not a simple matter, and seeing is related both to what is known and to what counts as available to be observed. What is seen depends on who is looking, at what, in which site...to recognise something it is necessary to have prior knowledge of it – thus observation depends on already knowing that for which one is searching.

Eilean Hooper-Greenhill, *Museums and the Shaping of Knowledge*, 1992.

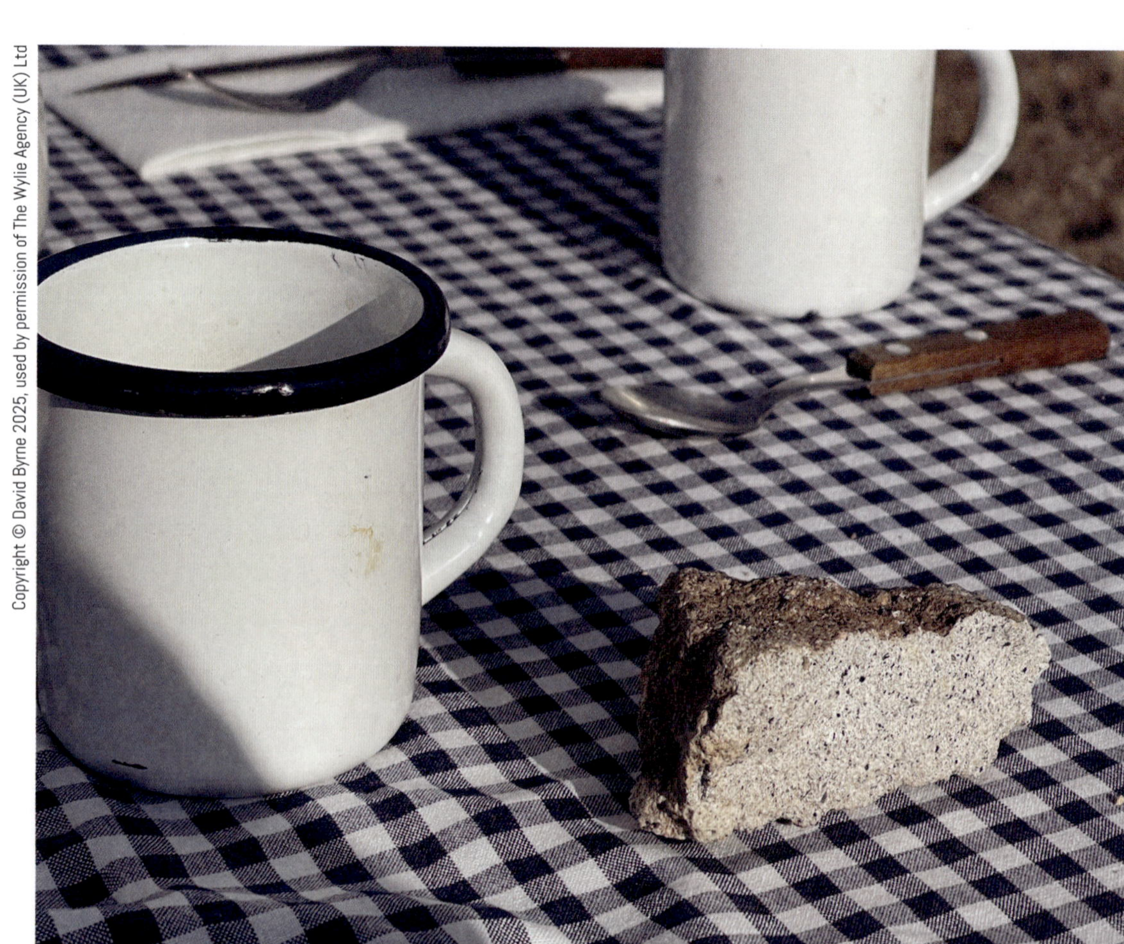

David Byrne.

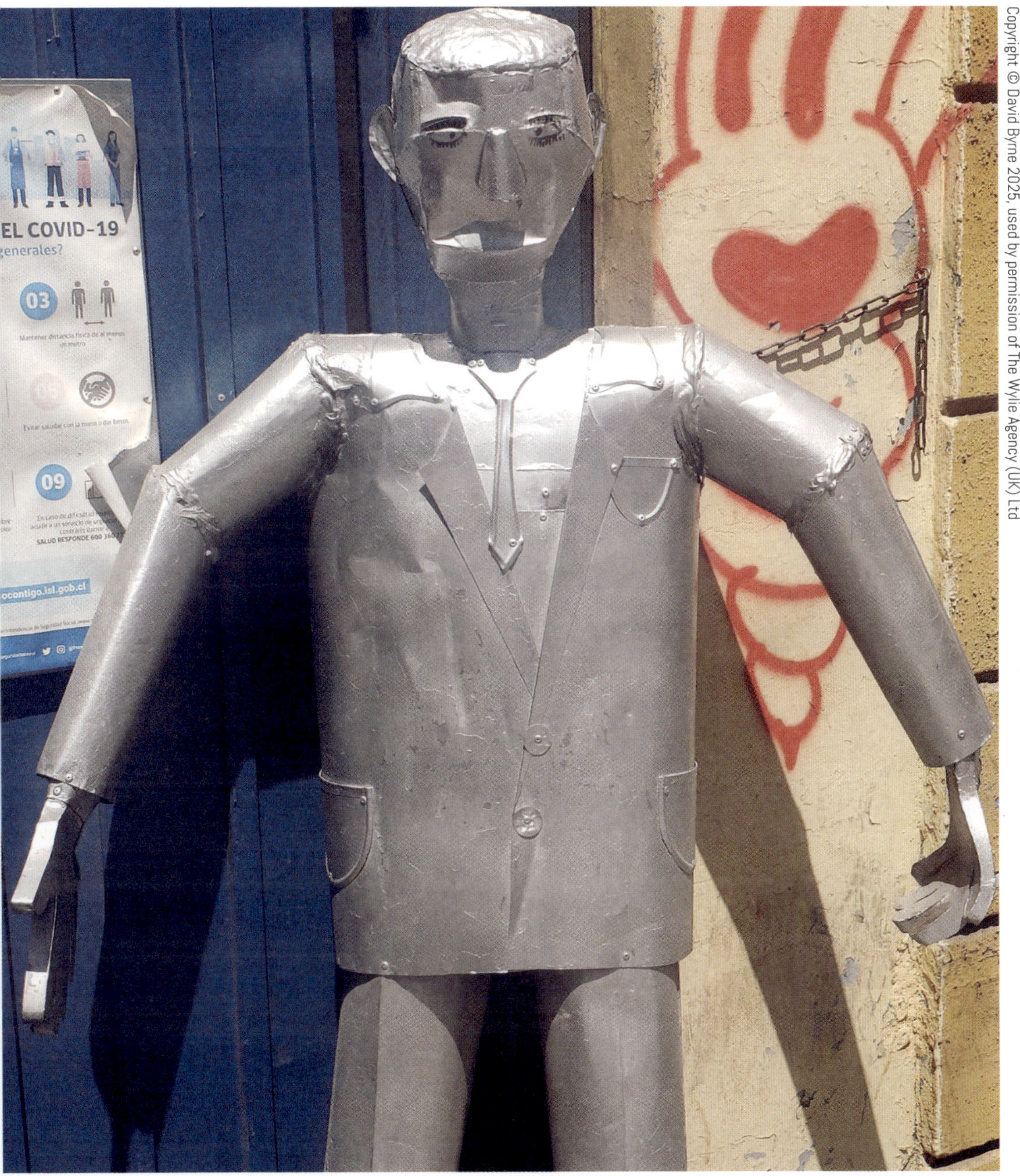

David Byrne: The man of steel.

I used to go to Bob's Big Boy restaurant just about every day from the mid-seventies until the early eighties. I'd have a milk shake and sit and think. There's a safety in thinking in a diner. You can have your coffee or your milk shake, and you can go off into strange dark areas, and always come back to the safety of the diner.

David Lynch, *Catching the Big Fish: Meditation, Consciousness, and Creativity*, 2006.

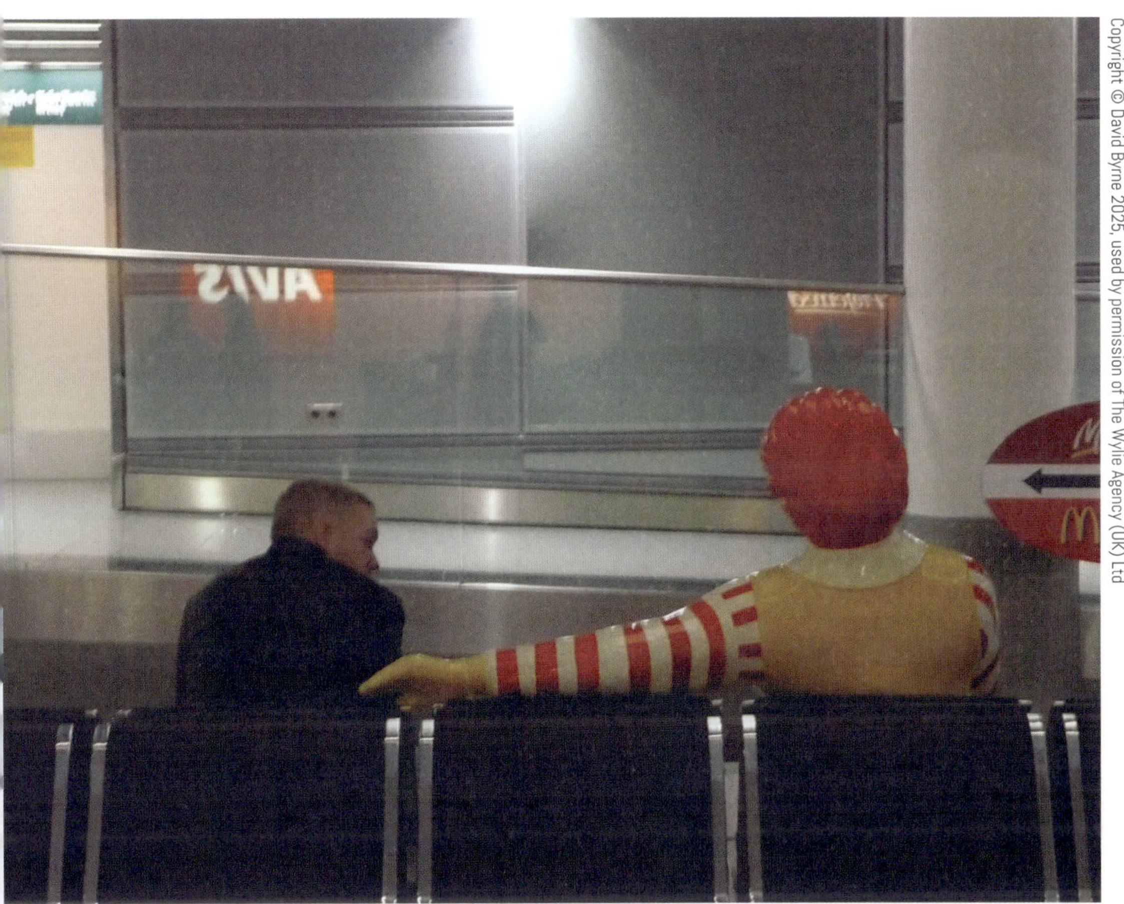

David Byrne: An intimate chat with Ronald.

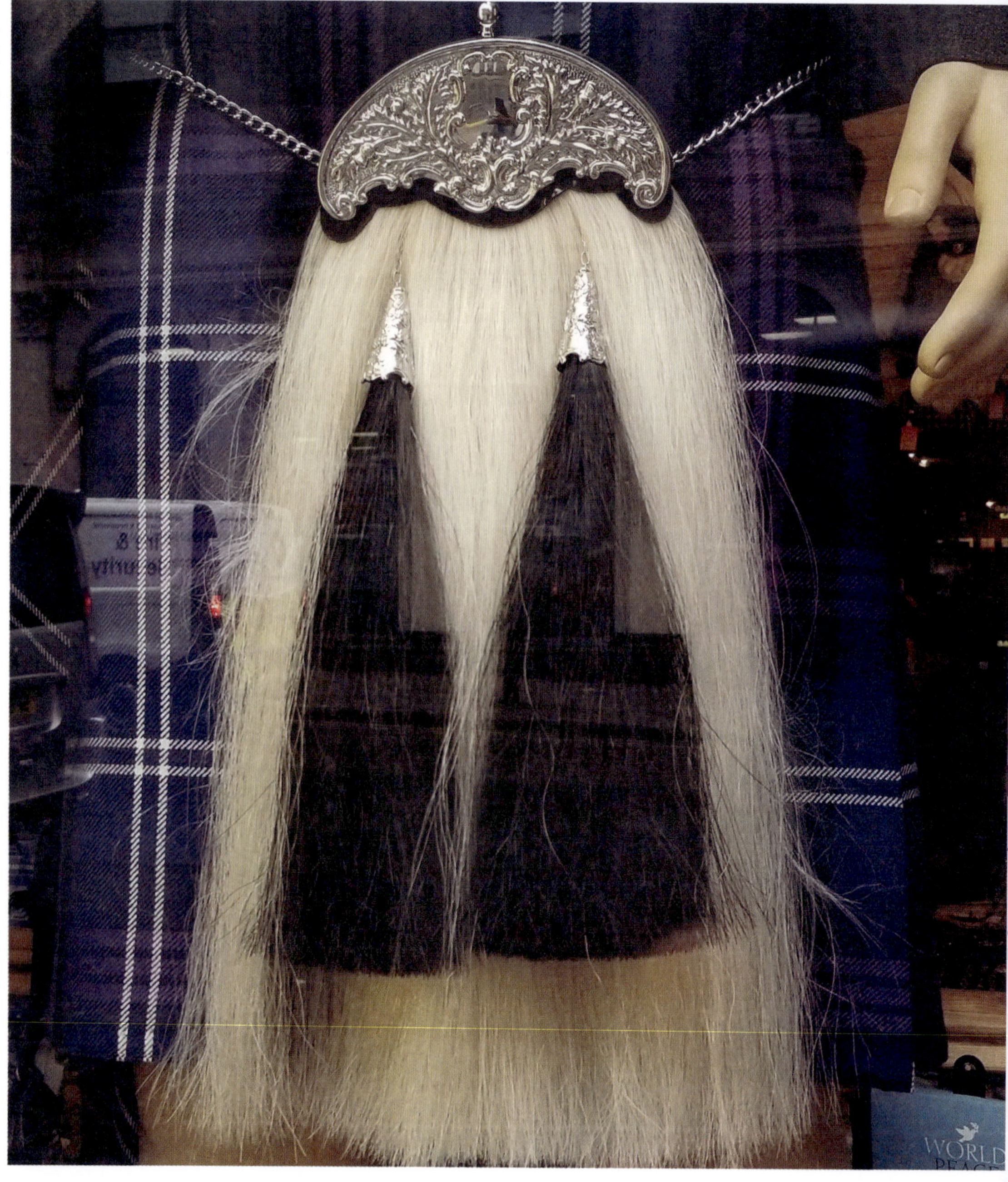

David Byrne: Sporran, Glasgow.

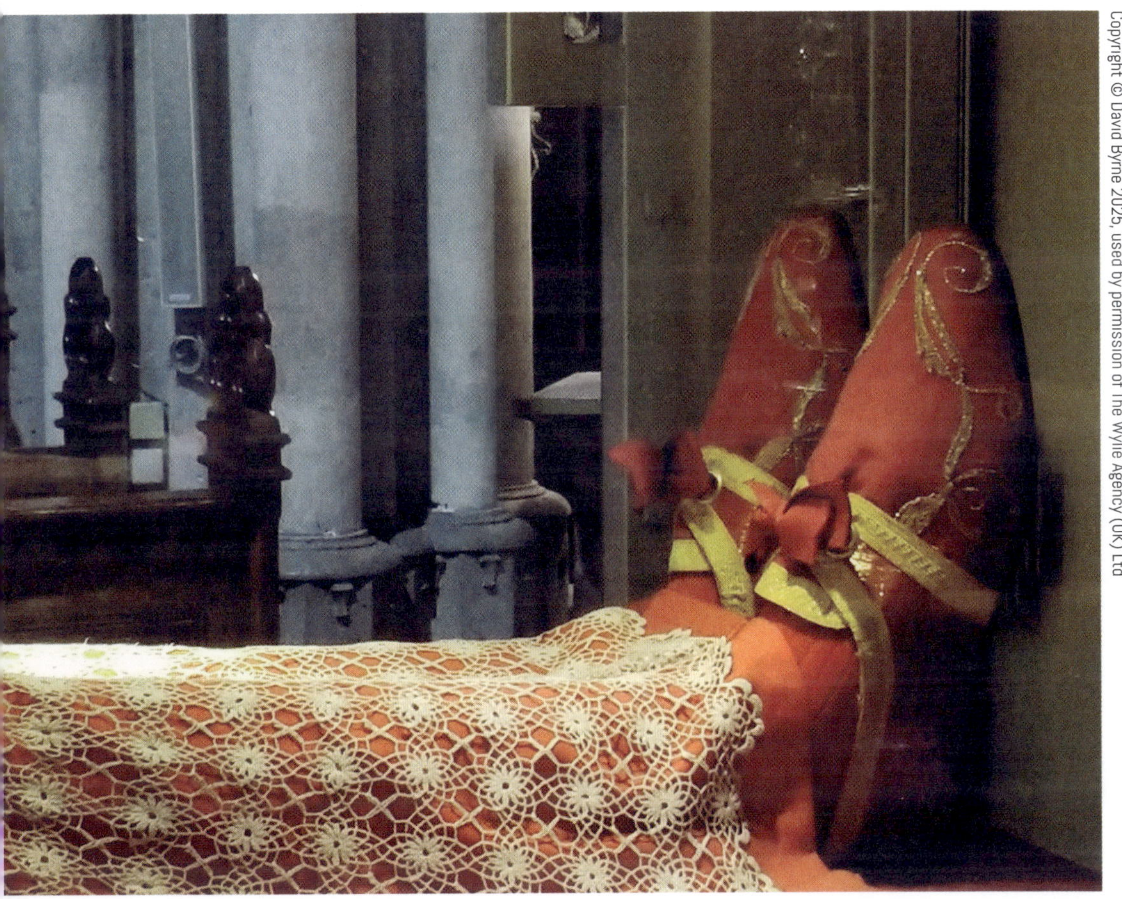

David Byrne: Spiritual footwear, Zagreb.

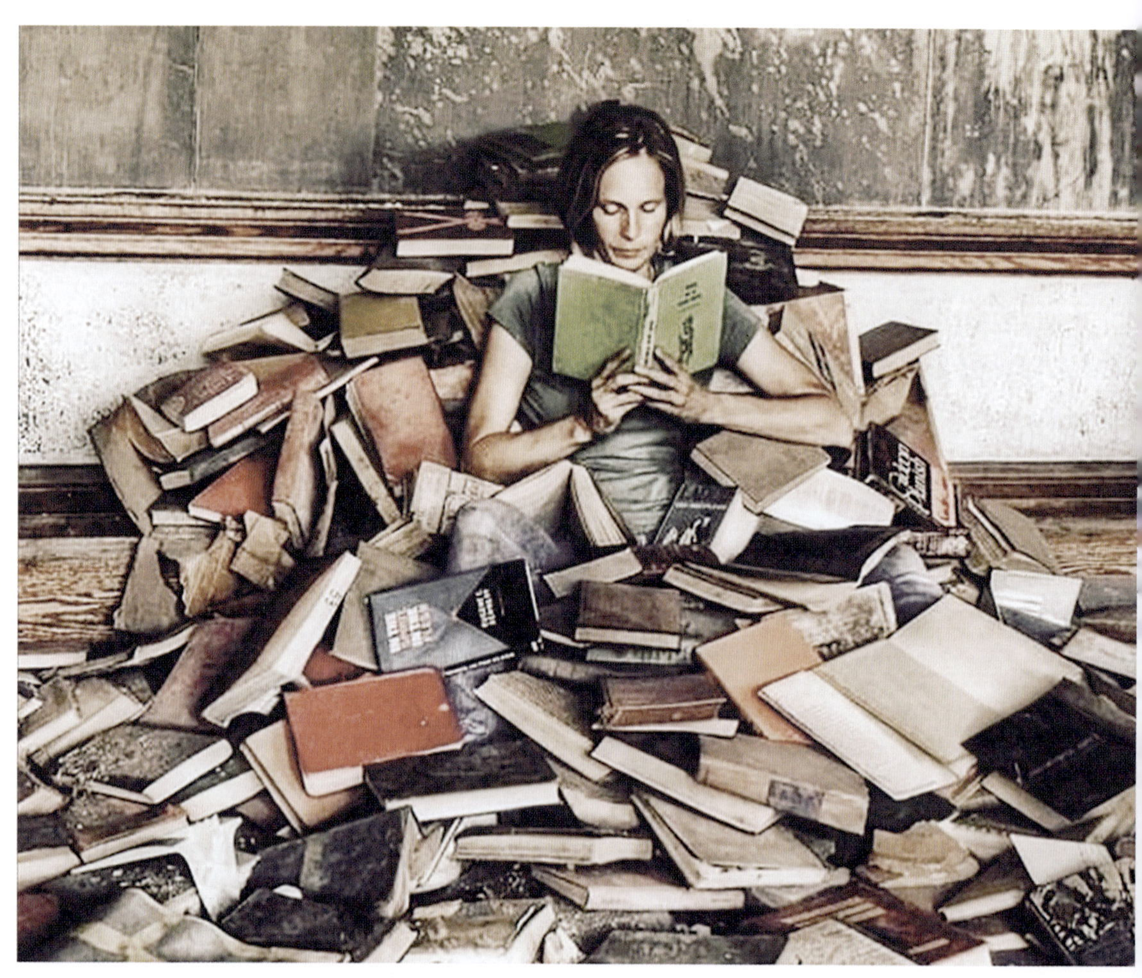

Elif Shafak: Surround yourself with books. (Unknown photographer)

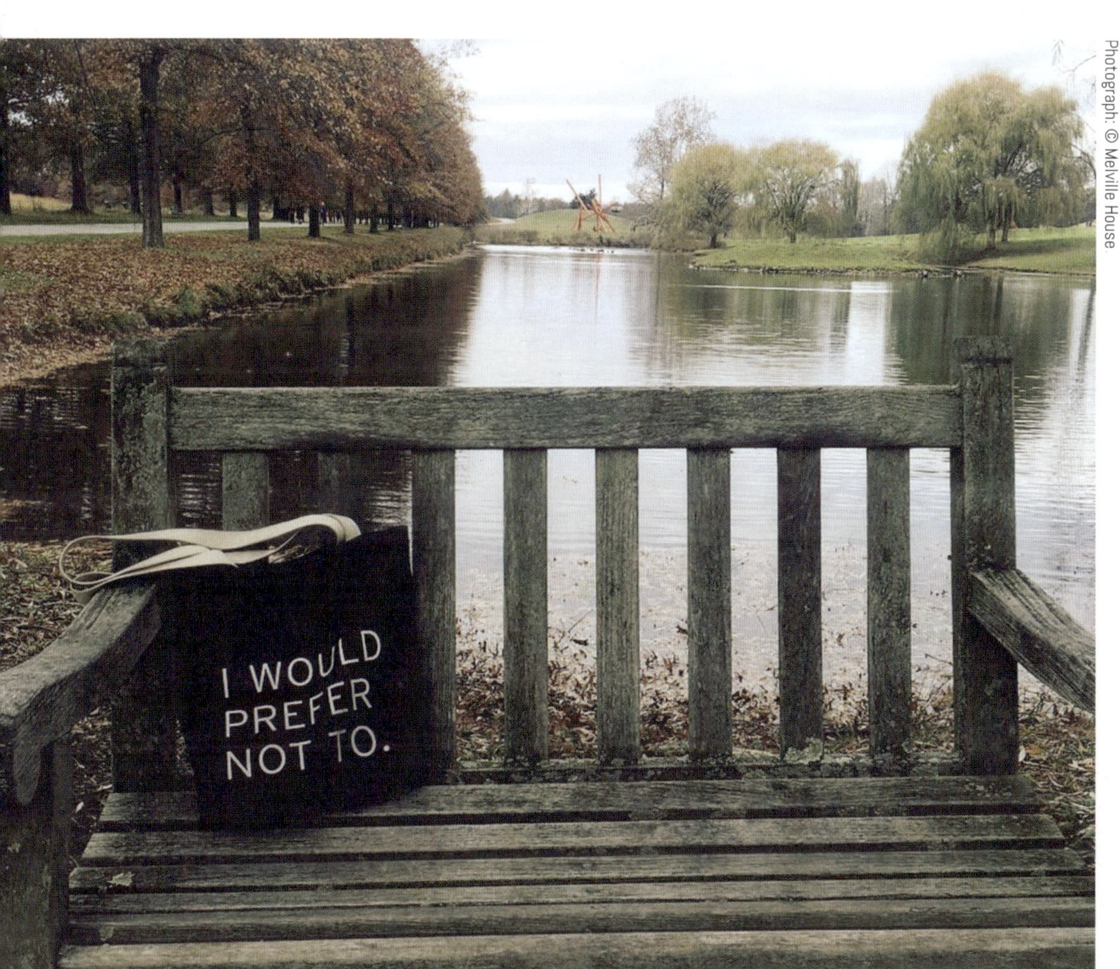

Photograph: © Melville House.

Ayanna Lloyd Banwo: Me, basically.

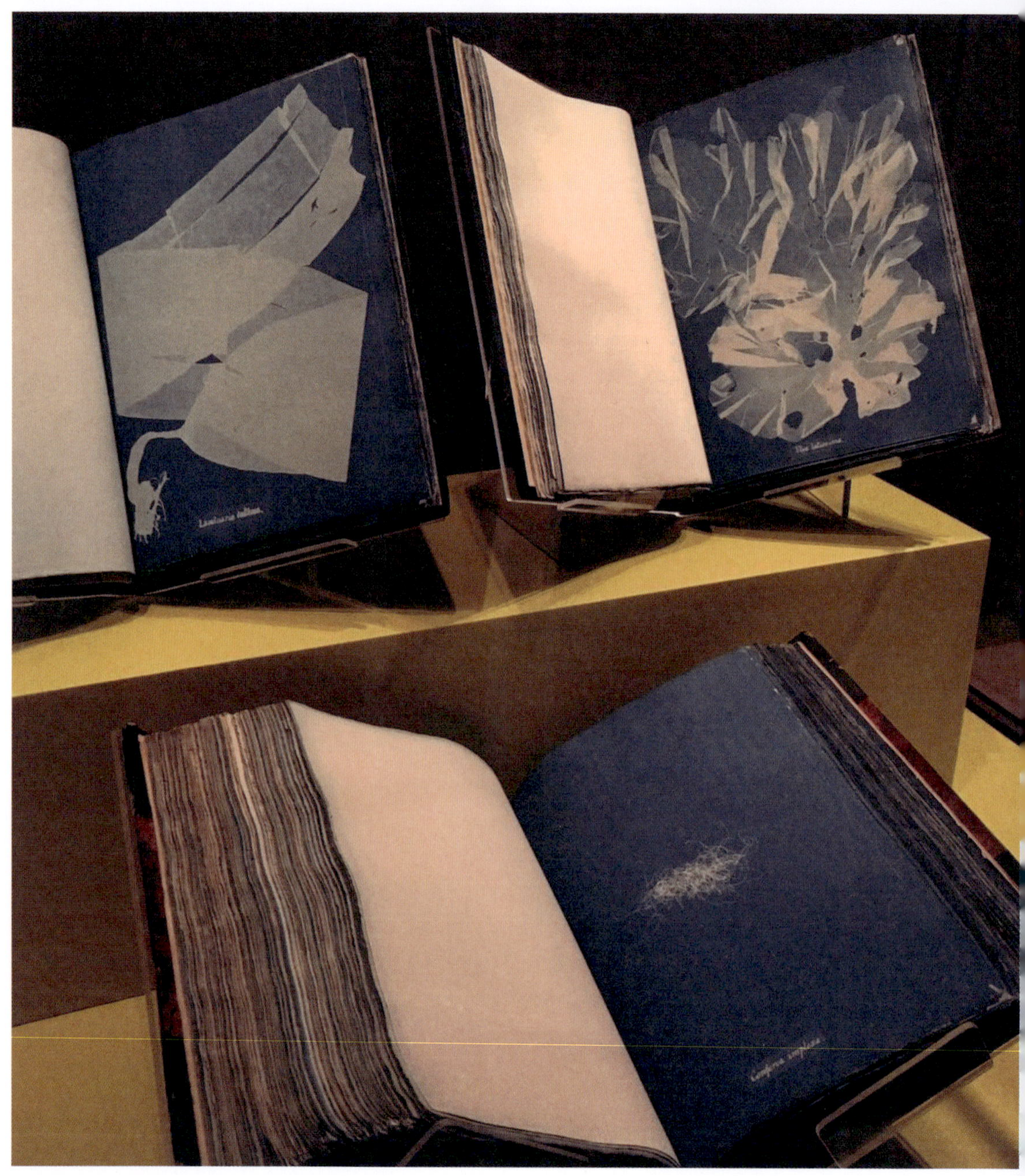

Moyra Davey: Anna Atkins on her last day at the NYPL.

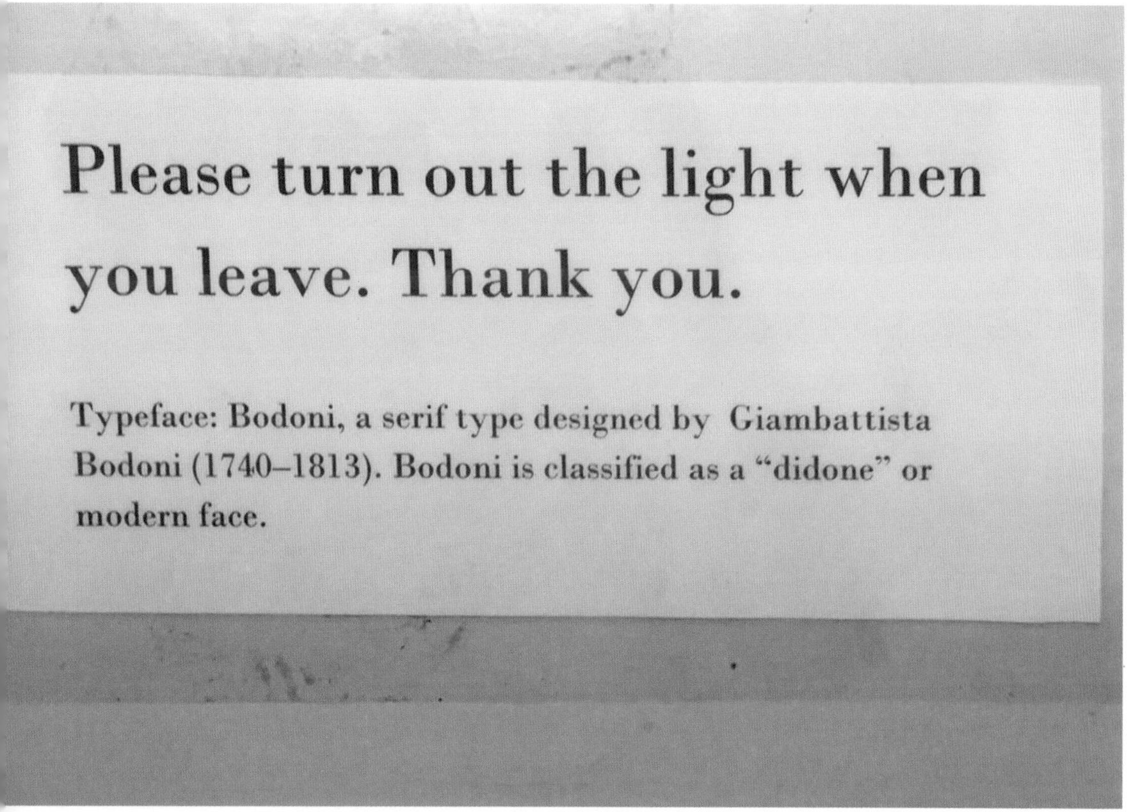

Please turn out the light when you leave. Thank you.

Typeface: Bodoni, a serif type designed by Giambattista Bodoni (1740–1813). Bodoni is classified as a "didone" or modern face.

Liz Brown: Restroom at the American Bookbinders Museum.

W-L
1-1
0-1
2-1
3-0
0-2
0-2

0-3
2-1
7   1-1
12   0-3
2   1-0
4   2-0
23   11   2-1
23   5   2-1
23   12   1-1
22   7   1-2

Last 3 Outs
IP   ER   W-L
0   0-0
12   0-2
ord

MIGHTY QUINN

E-mail from Nicky Letterese.

"Let's face it, English is a crazy language. There is no egg in eggplant nor ham in hamburger; neither apple nor pine in pineapple. English muffins weren't invented in England or French fries in France.

"We take English for granted. But if we explore its paradoxes, we find that quicksand can work slowly, boxing rings are square, and a guinea pig is neither from Guinea nor is it a pig. And why is it that writers write but fingers don't fing, grocers don't groce, and hammers don't ham? If the plural of tooth is teeth, why isn't the plural of booth beeth? One goose, 2 geese. So one moose, 2 meese? One index, 2 indices?

"If you have a bunch of odds and ends and get rid of all but one of them, what do you call it? If teachers taught, why didn't preachers praught? If a vegetarian eats vegetables, what does a humanitarian eat?

"Sometimes I think all the English speakers should be committed to an asylum for the verbally insane. In what language do people recite at a play and play at a recital? Ship by truck and send cargo by ship? Have noses that run and feet that smell? How can a slim chance and a fat chance be the same, while a wise man and a wise guy are opposites?"

Mighty likes the Yankees today. No play yesterday. Deficit is 410 sirignanos.

James Rosenquist.

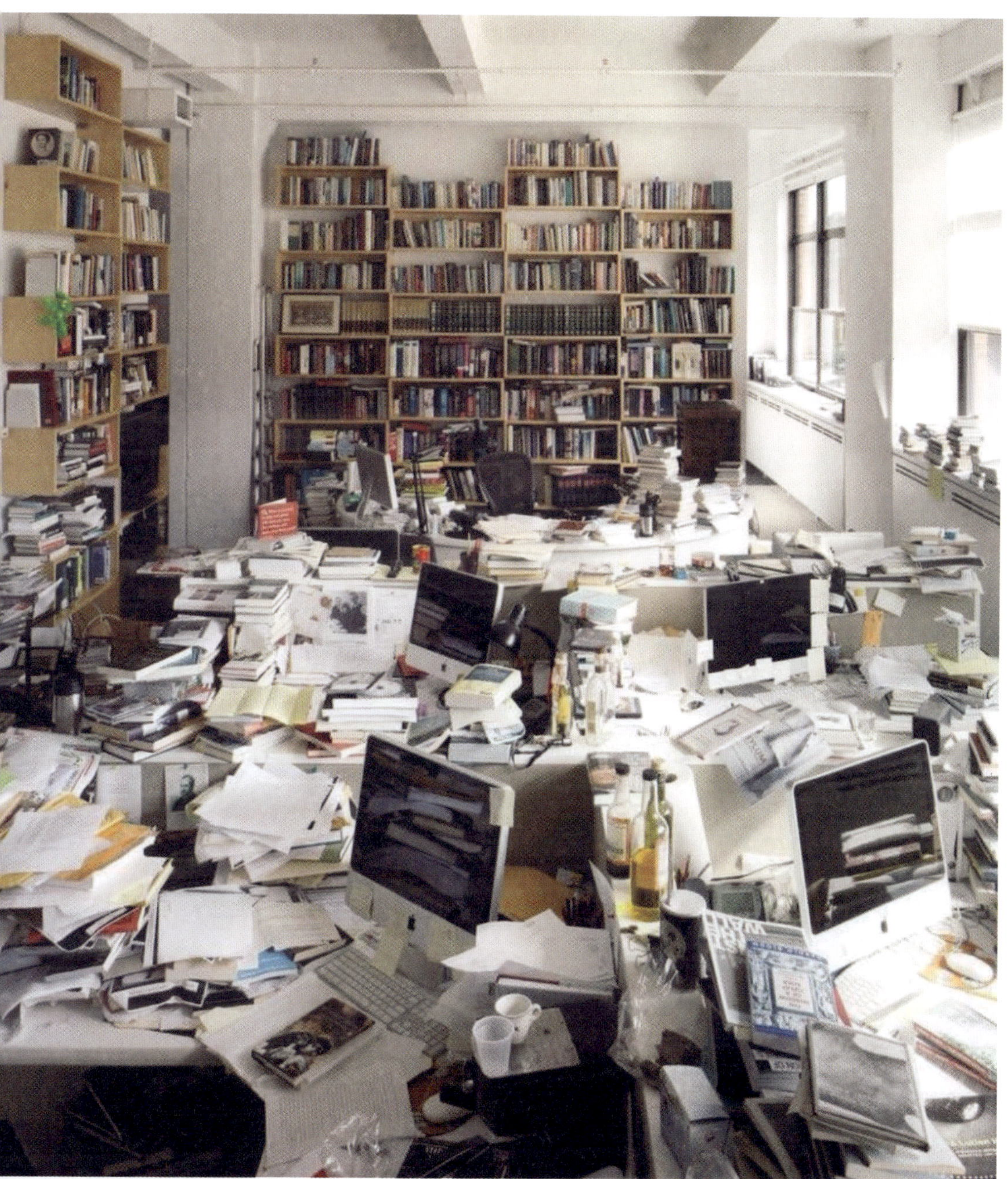

Nijay Gupta: The *New York Review of Books* office.

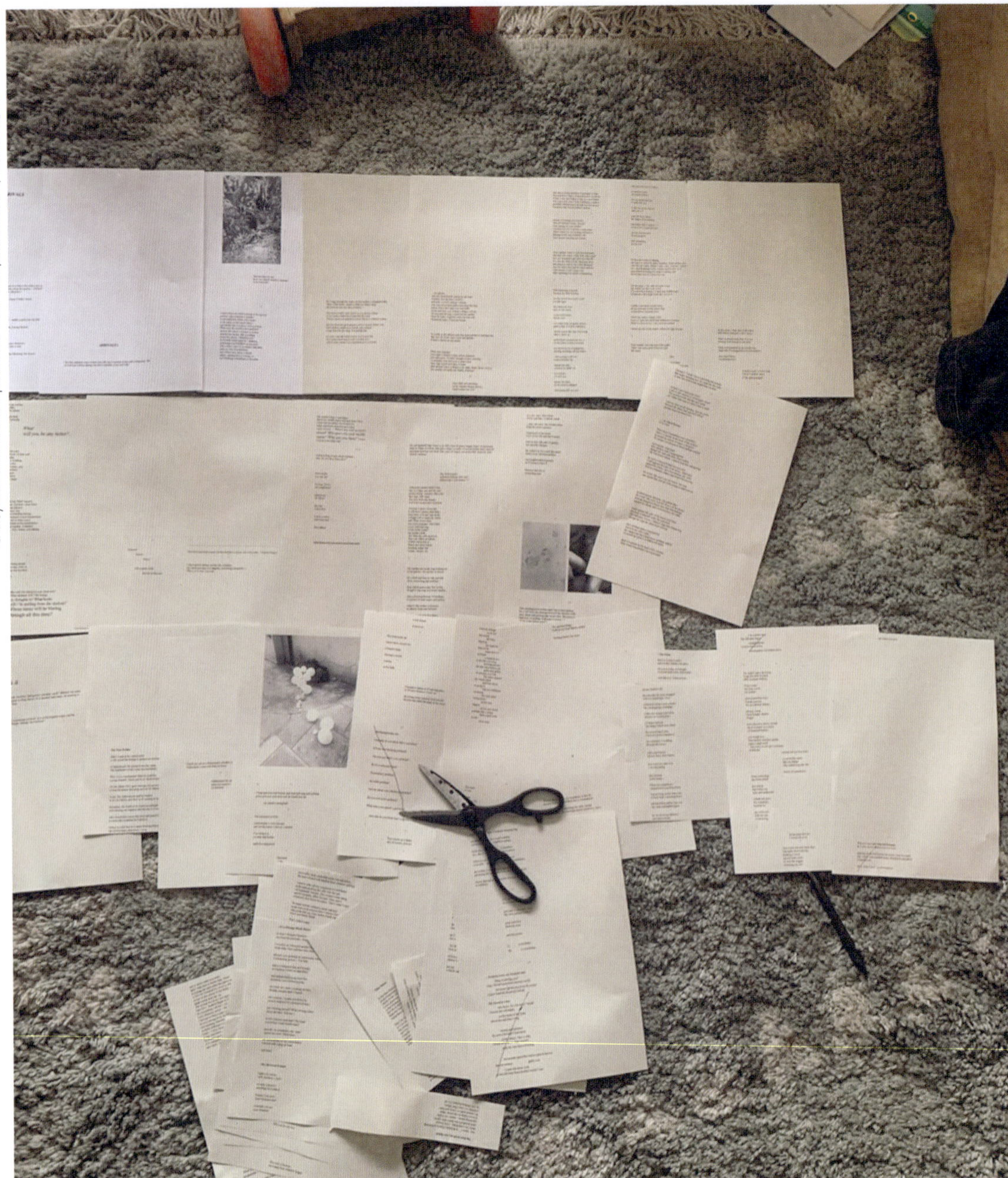

Raymond Antrobus, Writing / editing is hard so sometimes I just need the space to play.

I still thought that to get something you had to go straight for your goal whereas it is only distractions, uncertainty, distance that bring us closer to our targets, and then it is the targets which strike us.

Fleur Jaeggy, *Sweet Days of Discipline*, translated by Tim Parks, 1989.

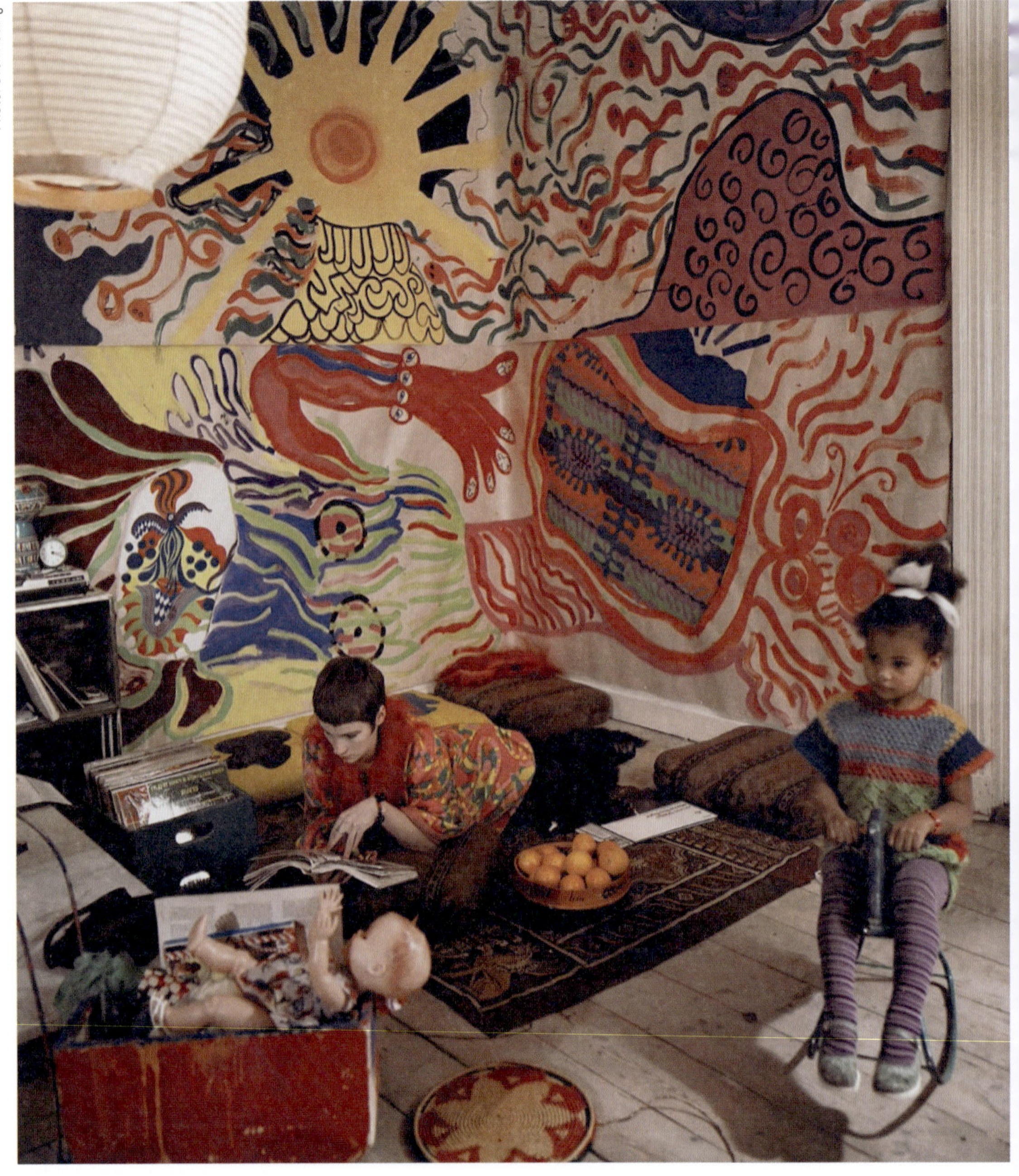

Cindy Greene: Neneh Cherry at home with her mom Moki, a Swedish painter and textile artist, in 1967.

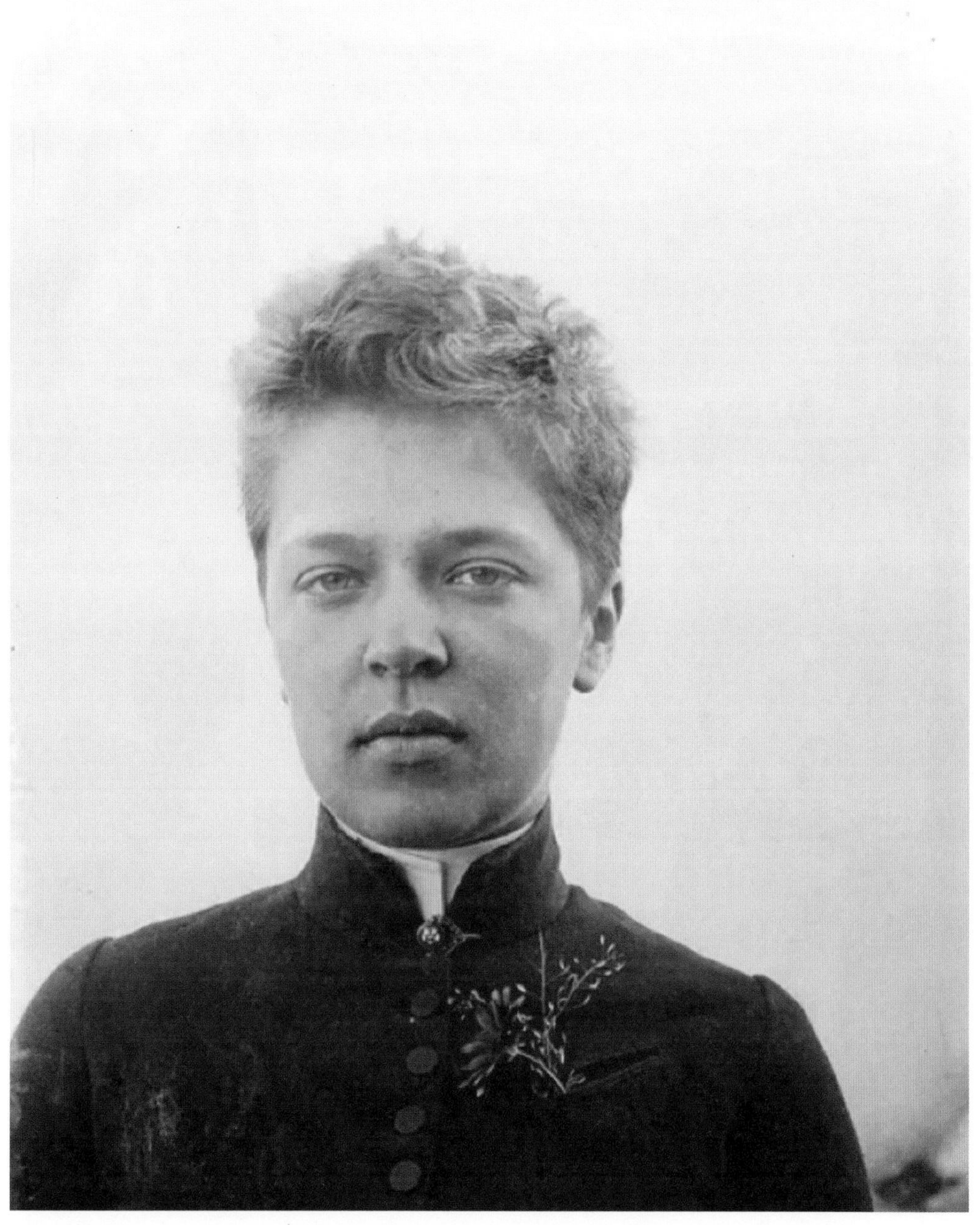

Jennifer Higgie: An extraordinary portrait from the 1890s that could have been taken today, of the Finnish painter Ellen Thesleff.

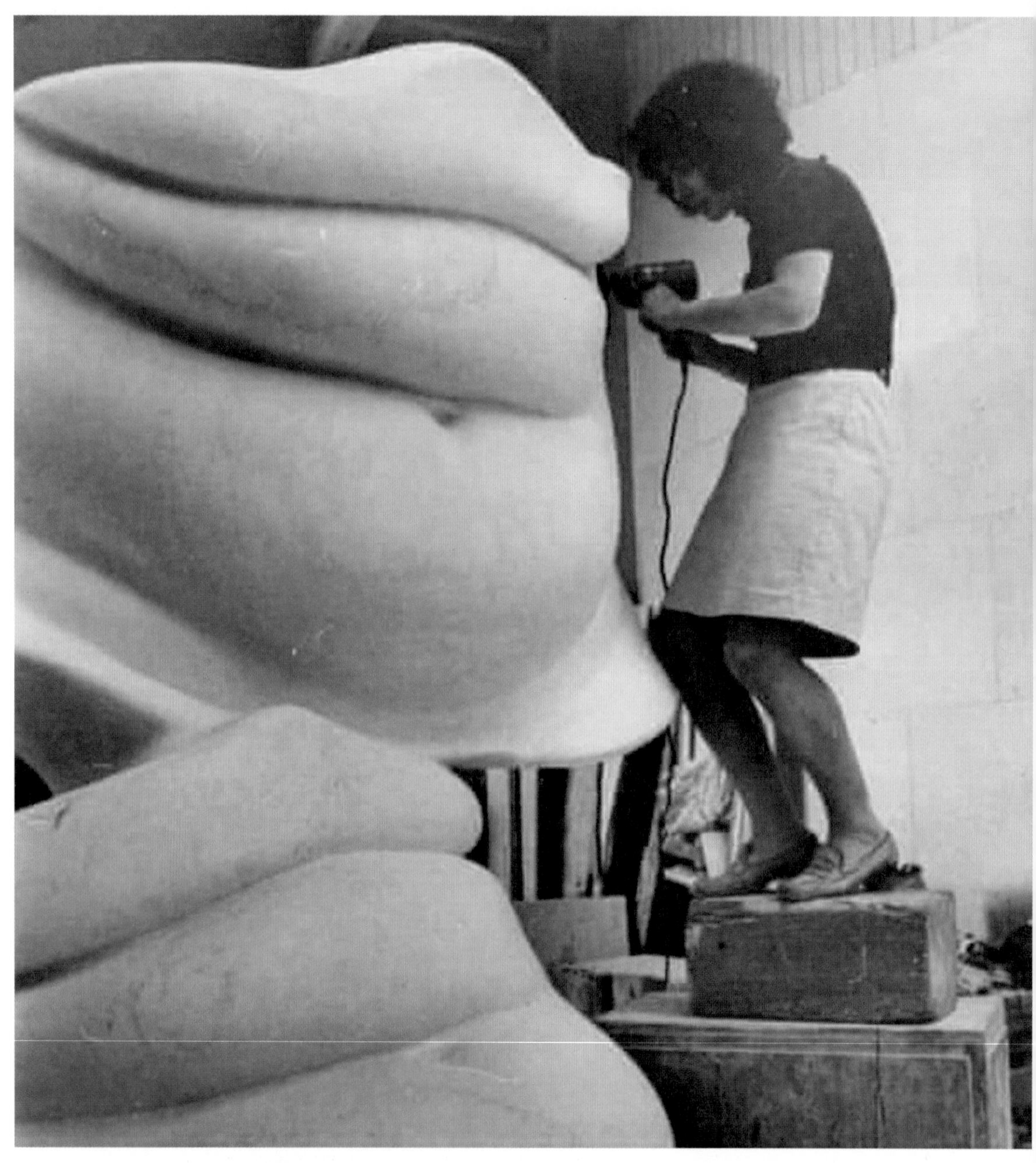

Jennifer HIggie: The great Polish sculptor and Holocaust survivor Alina Szapocznikow was born 16 May 1926 in Kalisz. In 1972, she wrote that "through casts of the body, I try to fix the fleeting moments of life, its paradoxes and absurdity."

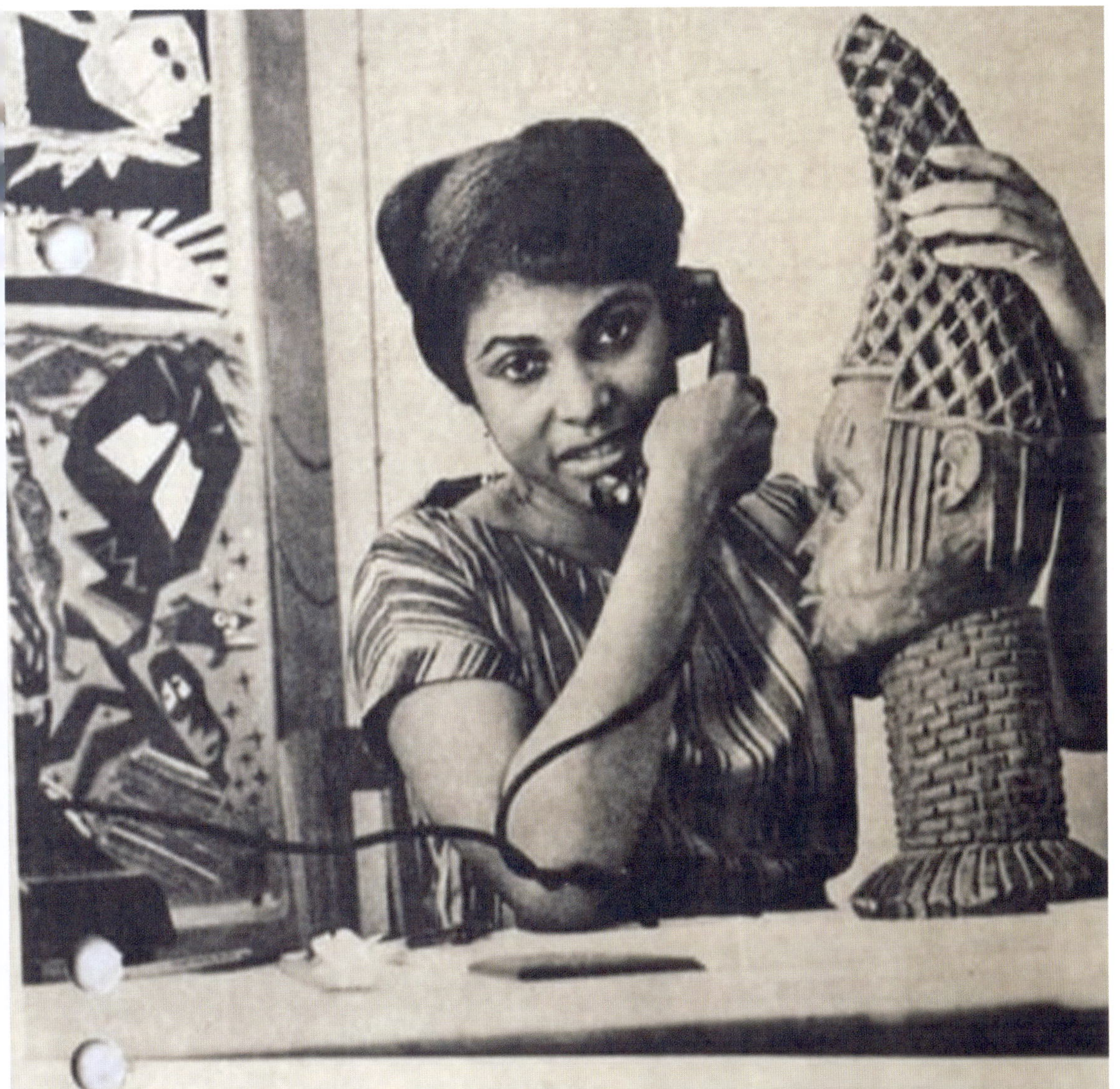

Jennifer Higgie: The Nigerian artist, designer, art collector, art promoter and humanitarian Constance Afiong "Afi" Ekong.

The condition of being alienated and "othered" reflects the ways in which navigating Western societies as a Black person is an endlessly unsettling experience, something that might be ripped whole from the pages of a speculative novel. Because of this, the search for lost cultural touchstones is a gesture towards survival: it is an Afrofuturistic act. At its heart it is the creation of a possible future based on a reconstructed, or reimagined past. In this way, a war is waged against erasure.

Esi Edugyan, *Out of the Sun: On Race and Storytelling,* 2021.

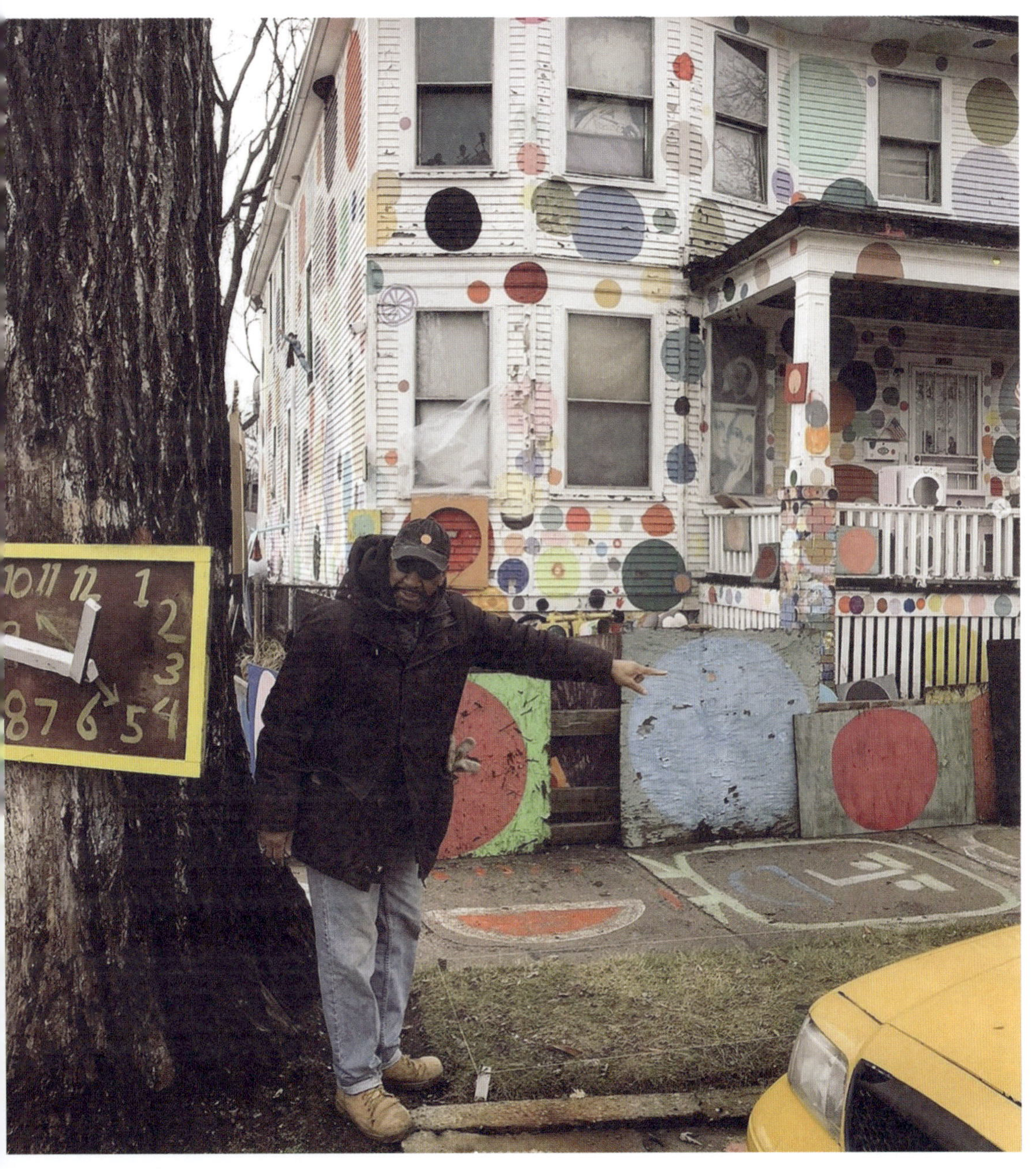

Matthew Higgs: February 2018, A visit to Detroit to meet Tyree Guyton, artist and founder-creator of the Heidelberg project, among the greatest of the samizdat works of public art ever created!

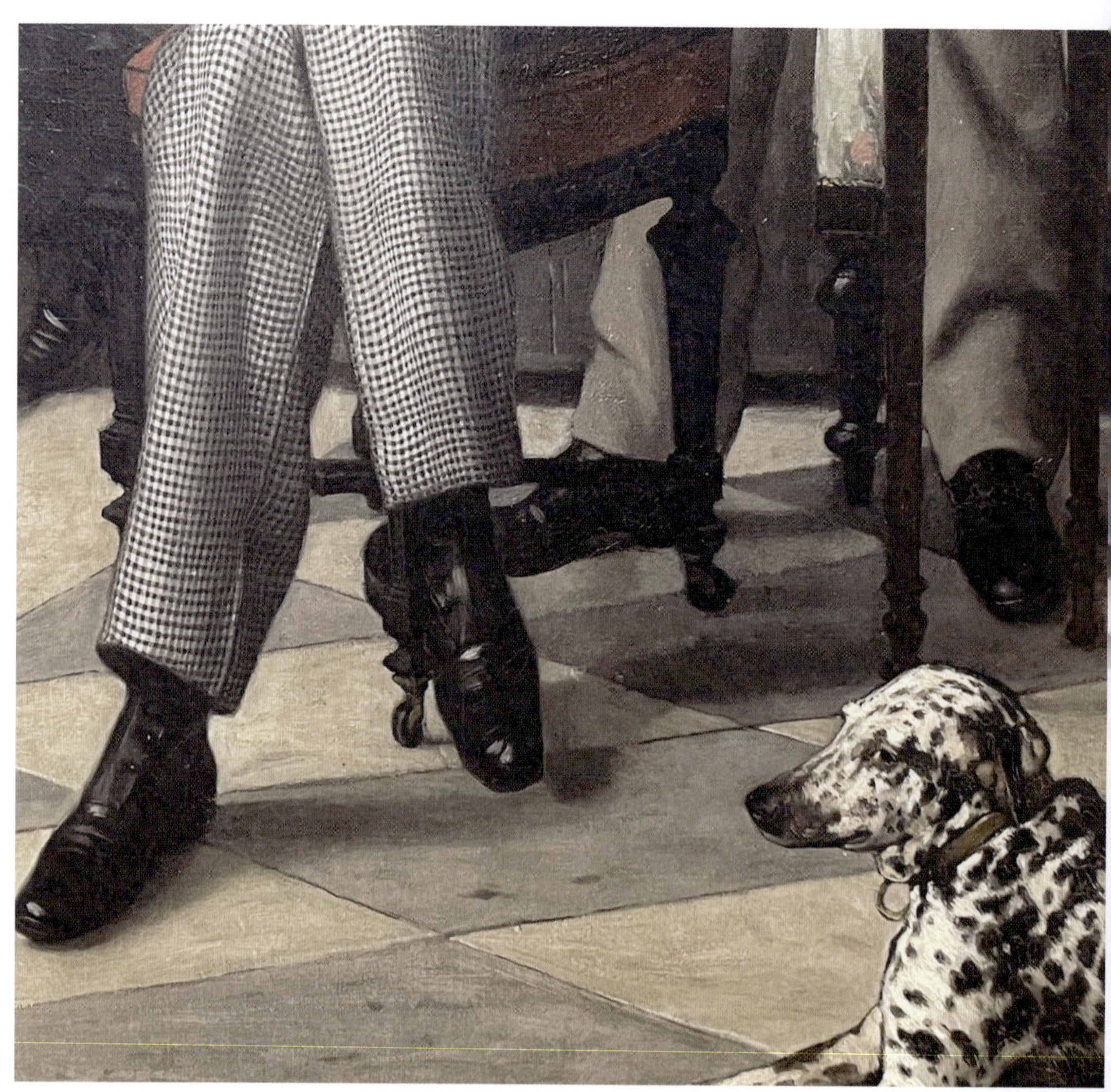

Peter Doig: Musée d'Orsay.

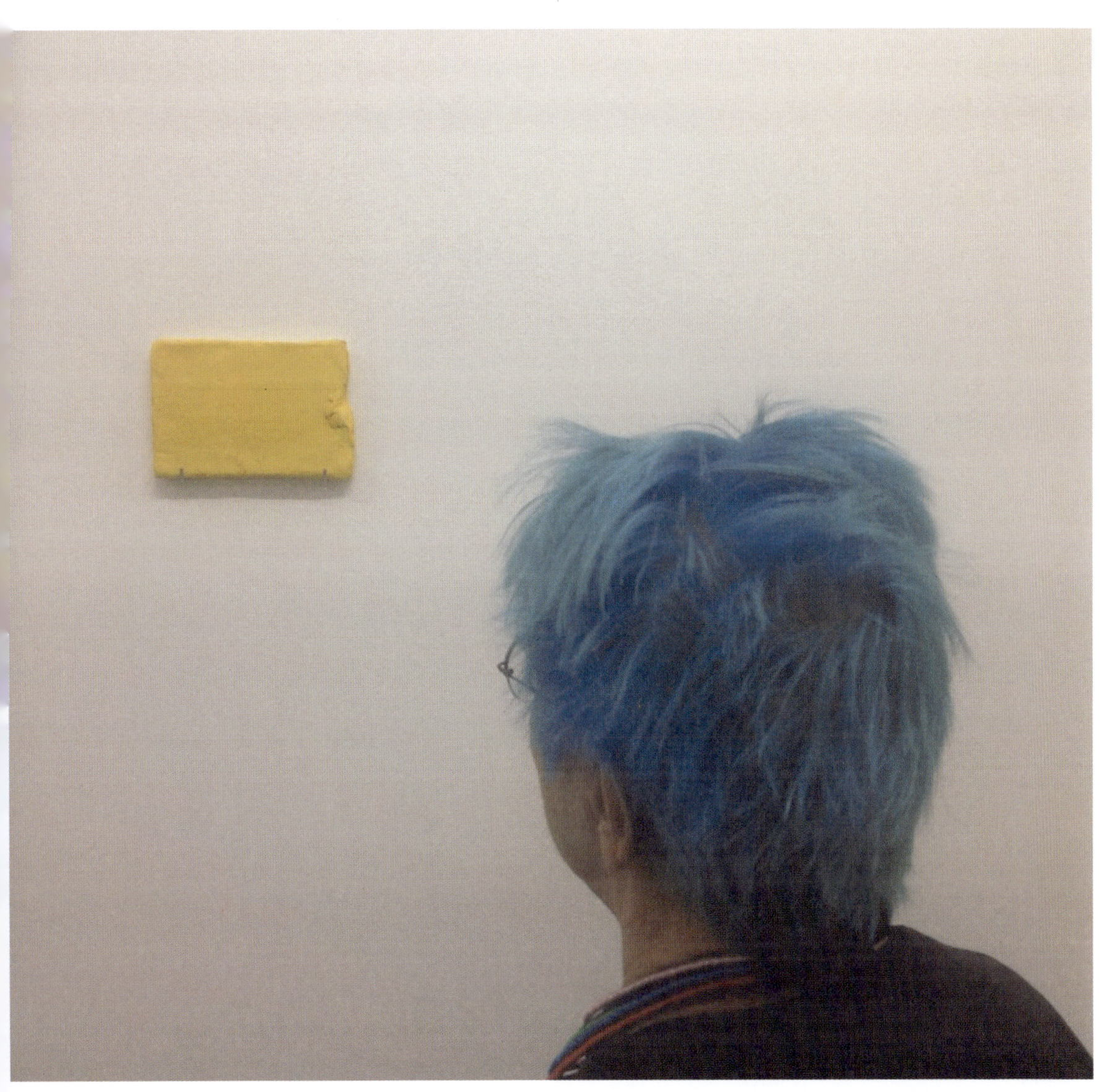

Jimena Kato: Solid Colour.

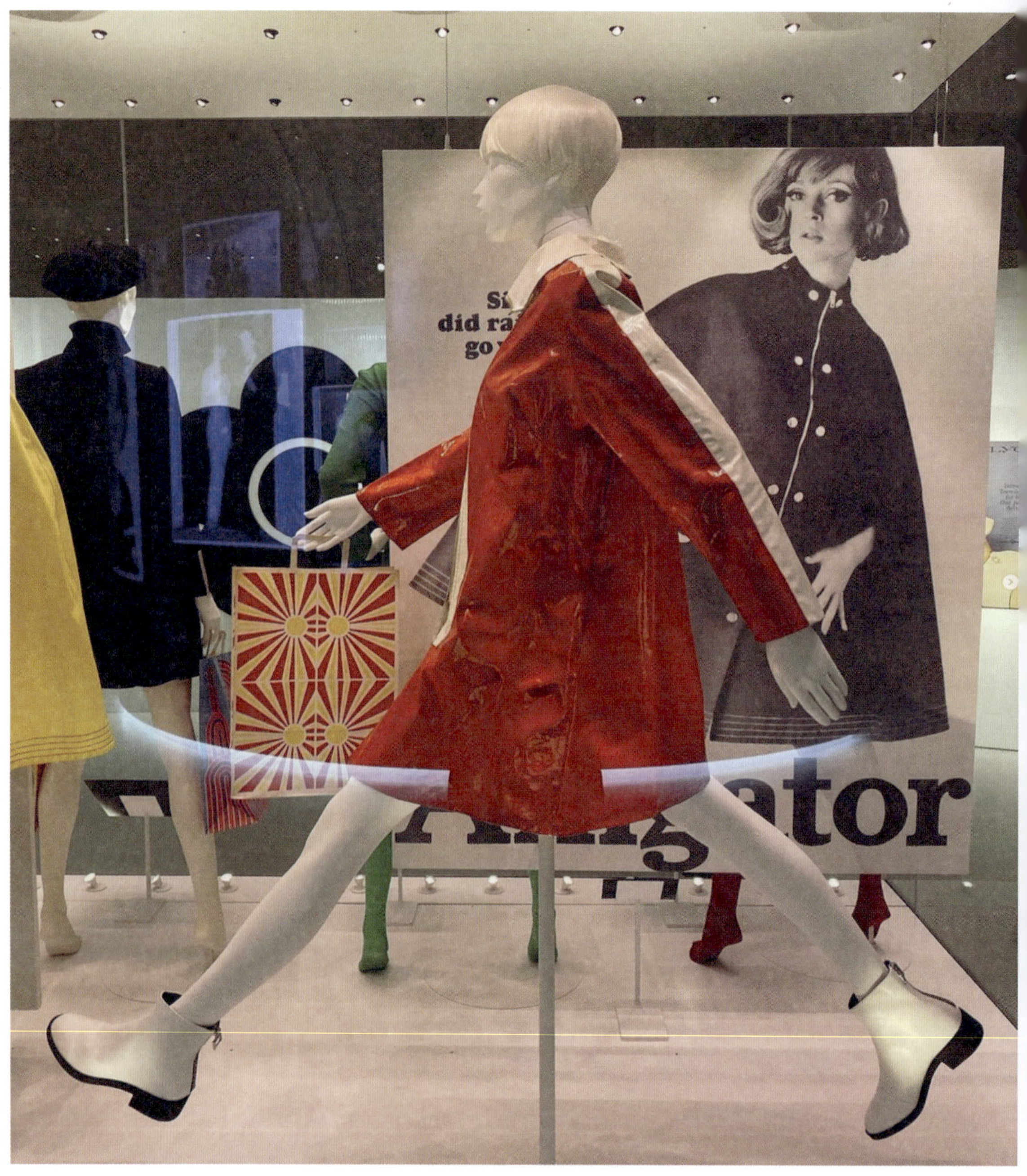

Simon Wallis: Mary Quant exhibition at the Victoria and Albert Museum, 2019.

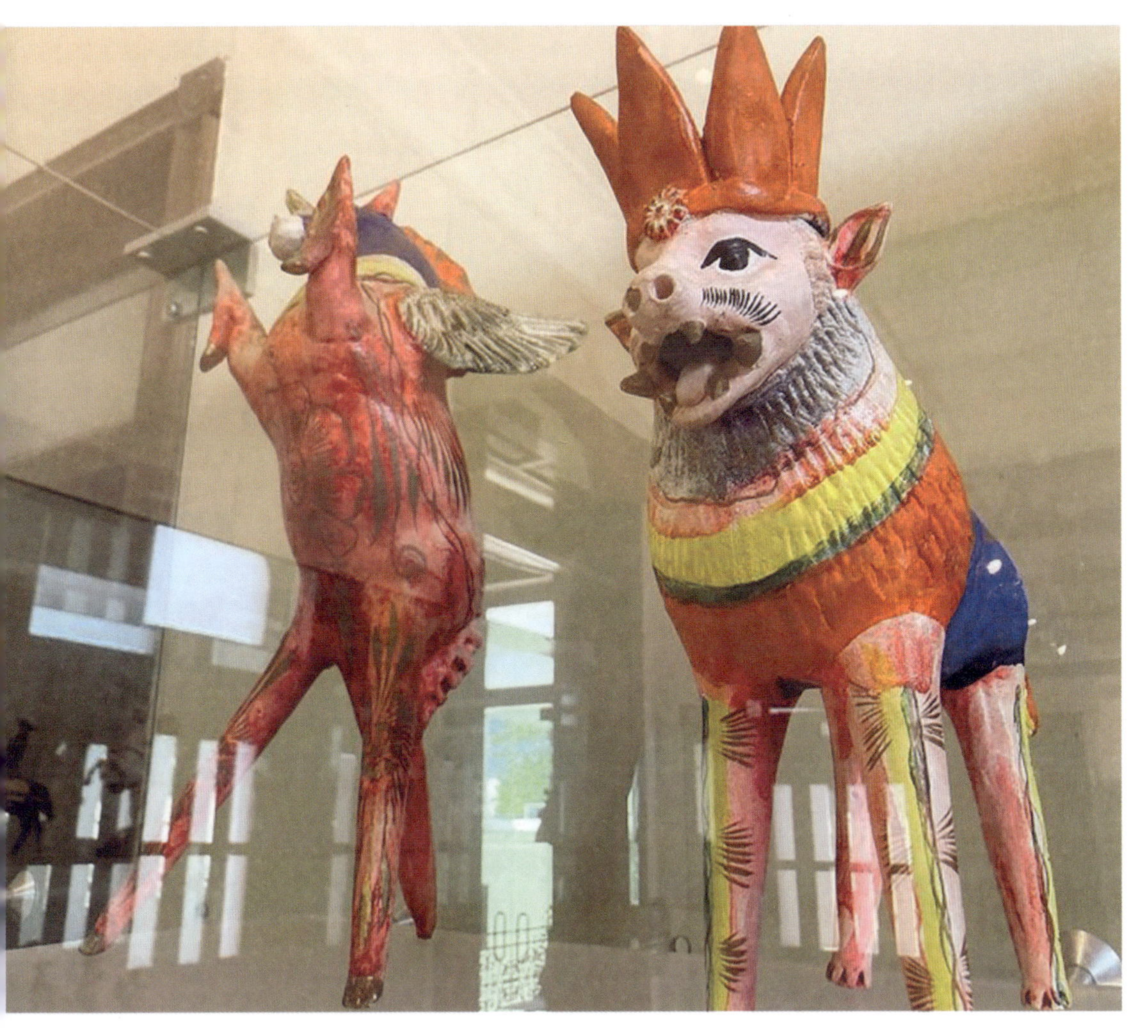

Joanna Ebenstein: The Museum of Popular Arts, Mérida, Mexico.

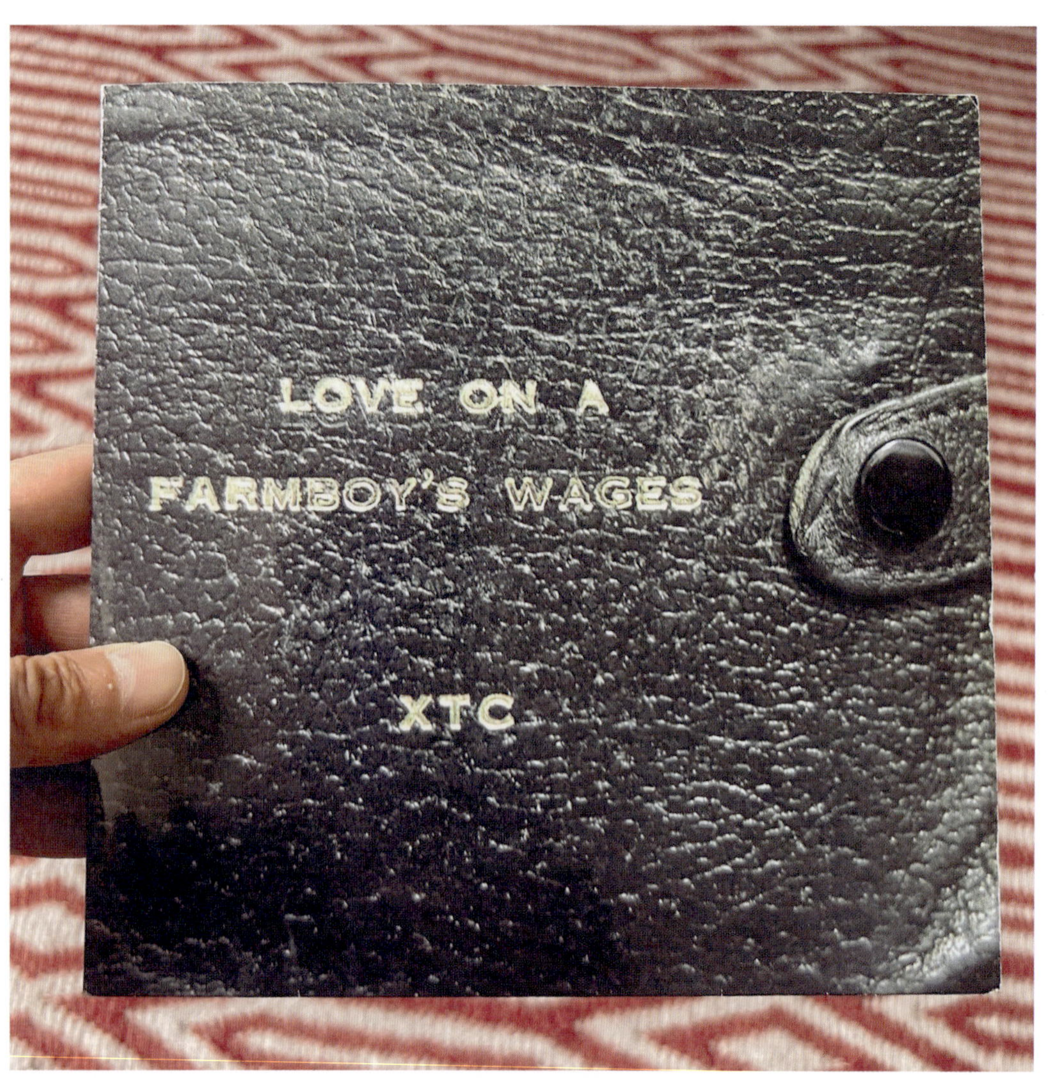

Simon Wallis.

Here are a couple of fantastic 7" single sleeve designs from the early 1980s
by XTC that I picked up in nice condition at my favourite second-hand record
shop. The first is a double single in a brilliantly conceived gatefold sleeve from
1983. It uses singer/songwriter/producer Andy Partridge's actual wallet – what
a superb design, it's such a lovely art object and a wonderful curiously pastoral
and timeless song. The rarity of double singles meant it was always so exciting
when they were released.

The next single is *No Thugs in Our House* from 1982. It's described on the cover as "a musical in three acts by XTC", cast of characters:

GRAHAM, a teenager
MOTHER, a busy housewife
FATHER, a conservative husband
POLICEMAN, a young constable

It's a great unsettling narratively driven song. The cover is a brilliant design opening up from the theatre stage that is die-cut to reveal a kitchen and an extreme right-wing teenager's bedroom above it. It includes inserts of characters from the song that could be used to act it out in this model cardboard theatre. So much attention to detail here, even the record label is splendidly done. XTC are one of the most important and influential bands of the 1980s and their music just gets better with time. I always think of them as the Philip Larkins of English pop. The careful crafting of their songs is matched by brilliant packaging in which Andy Partridge had the controlling creative hand: "I'd had a row with Virgin because they'd put Statue of Liberty out in a black and white sleeve with a picture of the lady herself, which I thought was so fucking rubbish, it radiated dullness. From then on I insisted on having some say in all future sleeves..I'm a big kid, I never lost my childlike appreciation of things. Too many people lock it out and throw their toys away and say, okay, I'm gonna grow up and be grumpy and miserable and not think about the magical side of things anymore..I didn't want to be the packhorse on someone else's money-making treadmill. I wanted to be a backroom boy record maker. No fame, just fine art."

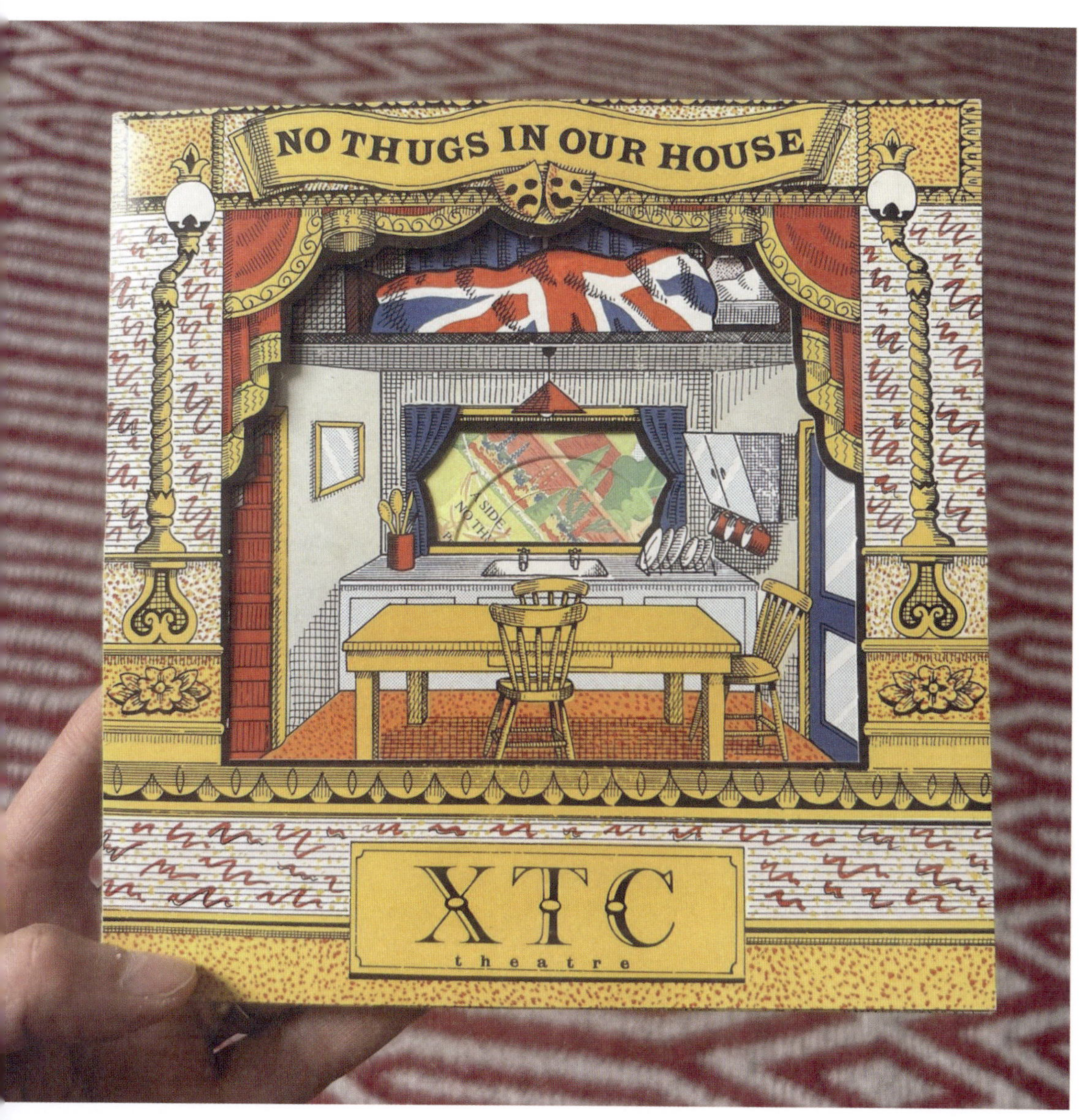

Simon Wallis.

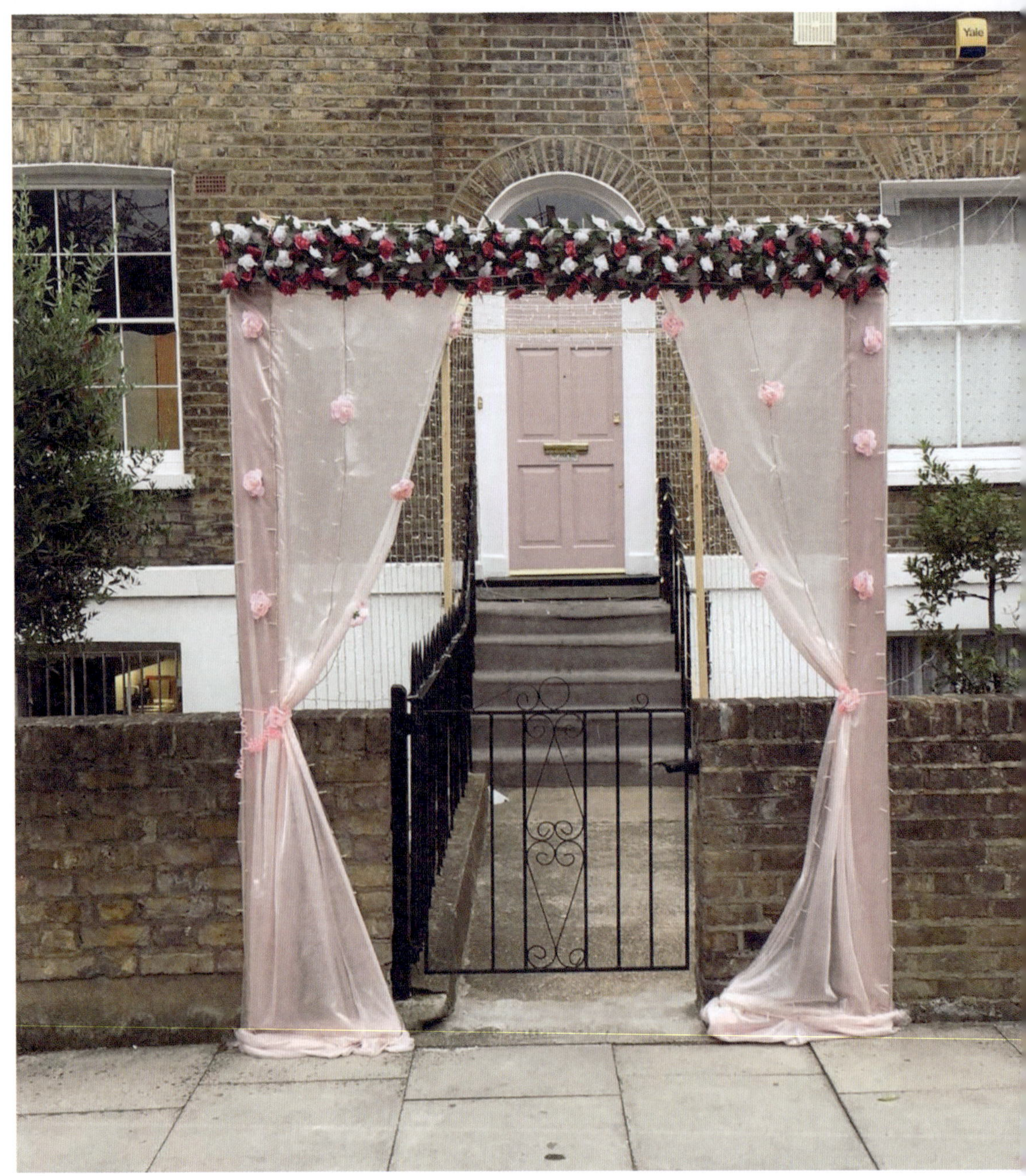

Calum Storrie: In De Beauvoir Town.

Wind Instruments

Wood-wind and brass instruments produce music when the player blows into them in some way. Air which is enclosed in a pipe or metal tube can be made to vibrate and give out a musical note. Try blowing across the top of a medicine bottle and you will hear some sort of musical tone. The pitch of the note depends on the volume of air in the bottle. If water is poured into the bottle so that there is less air to vibrate, the bottle plays a higher note. A long tube of vibrating air plays a low note, a short tube plays a high note. The air is vibrated in different ways in the various instruments, by blowing across a hole, through a mouthpiece, or by making the lips vibrate.

Some instruments have a number of holes in the tube of wood or metal. If all the holes are covered with the fingers the whole length of air in the tube will vibrate, but if some of the holes are uncovered, only a part of the air will vibrate. In brass instruments, valves and other devices are used to open up or close off extra lengths of tubing.

18

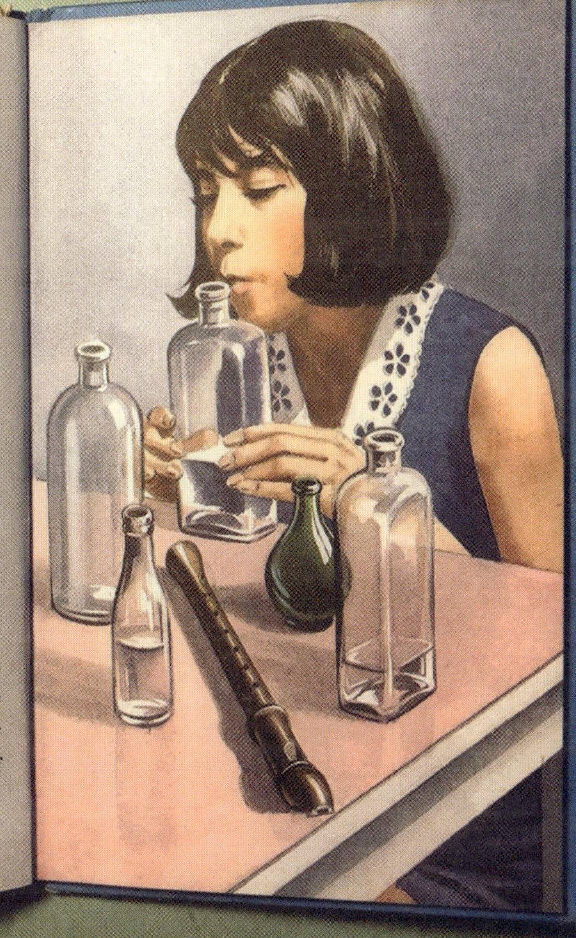

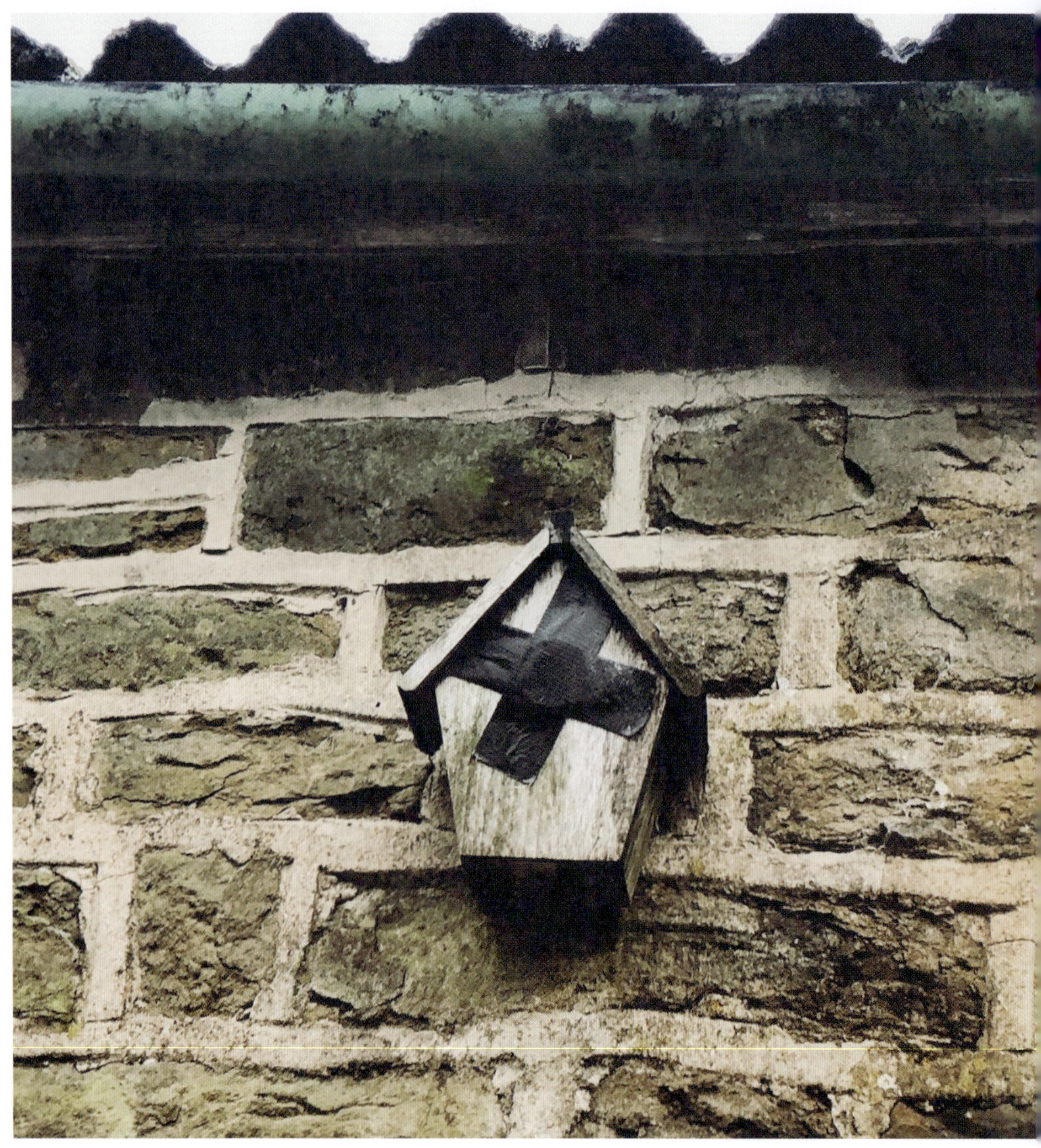

Jarvis Cocker: Even birds are getting evicted now.

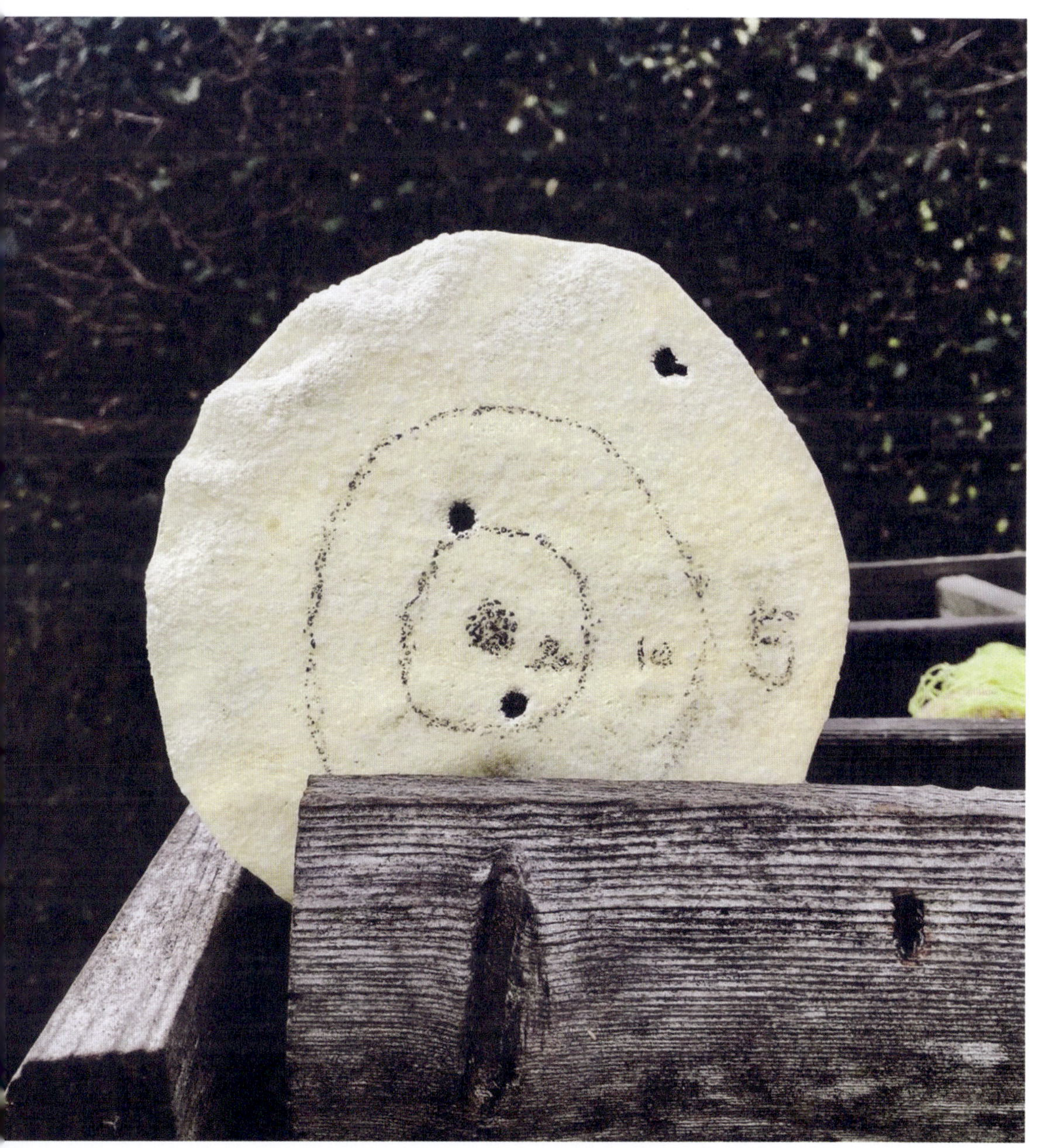

Jarvis Cocker: If you have any papadums left over from last night's take-away they make excellent targets for air rifle practice.

Head of Uncertainty and Scenarios

Department for Transport

Apply before 11:55 pm on Monday 7th November 2022

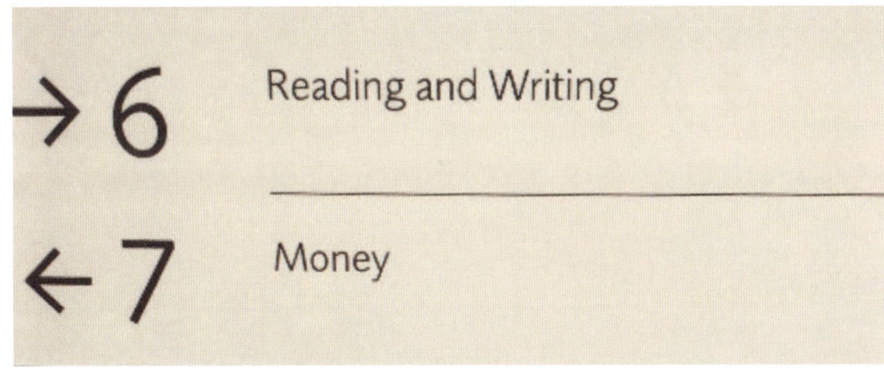

Hari Kunzru.

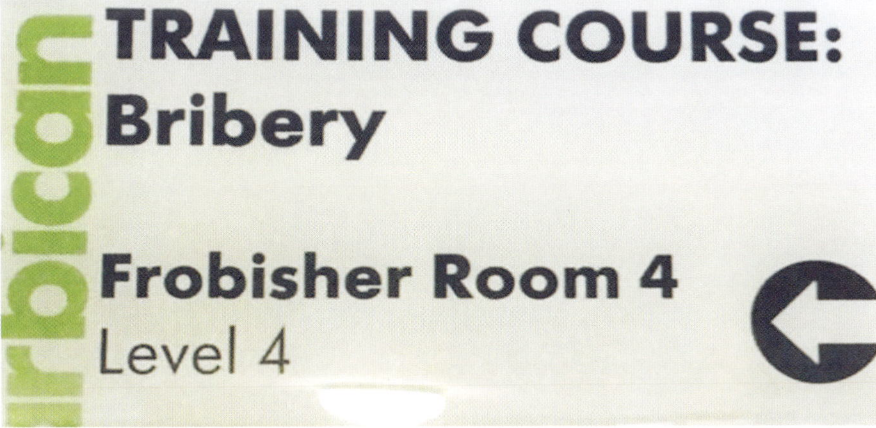

Will Ashon: Useful.

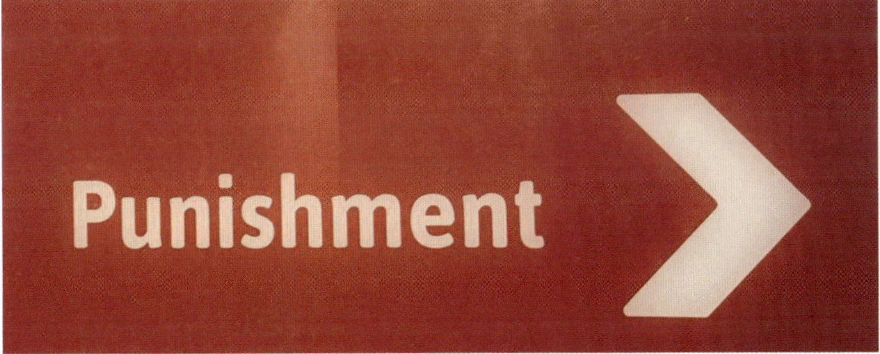

Carey Young.

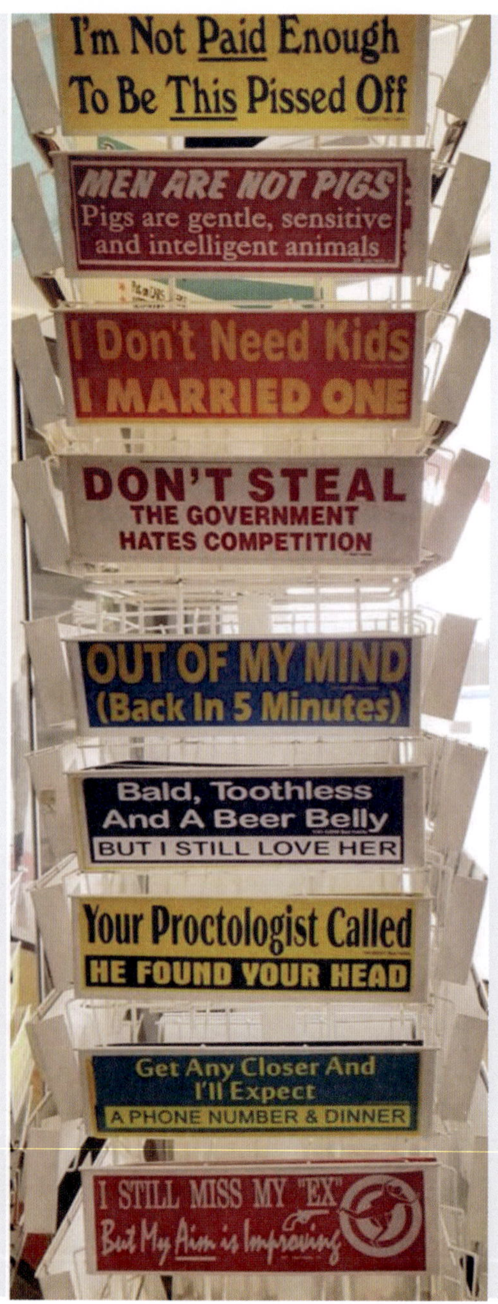

David Byrne: American wisdom.

TOP: Kamila Shamsie: Oh, the pathos. ABOVE: Ian Sansom: Shop sign.

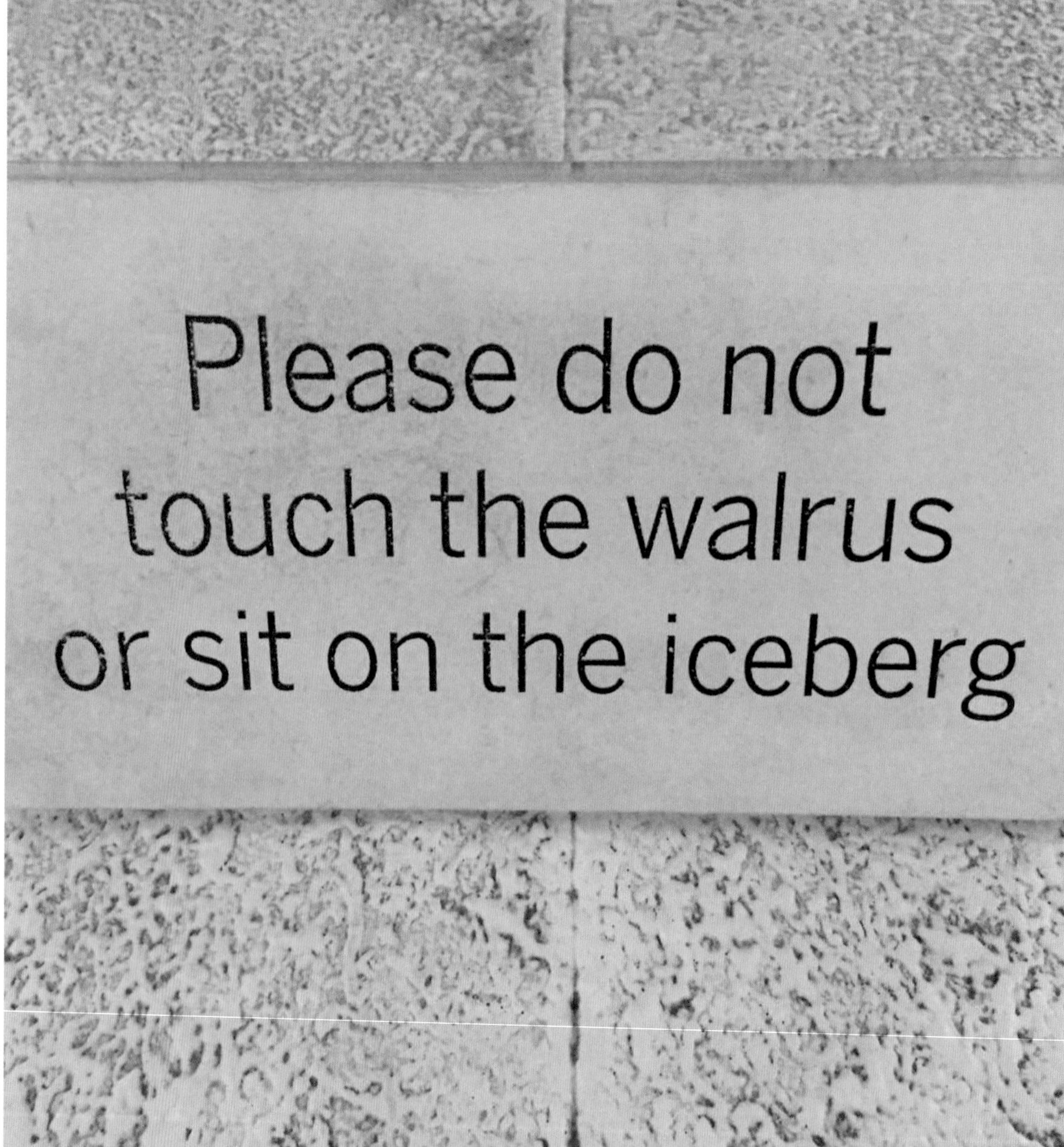

Nick Merriman: Generally good advice.

www.theredstoneshop.com
@redstonepressbooks